TRUTH, UNITY AND CONCORD

TRUTH, UNITY AND CONCORD

ANGLICAN FAITH IN AN ECUMENICAL SETTING

KENNETH SANSBURY

LONDON
A. R. MOWBRAY & CO LTD

TO

MY WIFE

TABLE OF CONTENTS

The authority and use of the Scriptures in the Anglican tradition. The effects of scientific discoveries and Biblical criticism. Interpreting the Biblical revelation in the thought-forms of today.

The problem of faith and history in the Gospels. Do they bring us reliable knowledge of the earthly Jesus or are they primarily evidence for the faith of the early Church? Three main answers: (a) Bultmann and the extreme form critics; (b) the school of 'critical orthodoxy'; (c) the post-Bultmann school. John Knox's *guidance in* The Church and the Reality of Christ.

The problem of the Old Testament in an age when the old methods of allegorizing are no longer possible. Three principles of interpretation: (a) acceptance and presupposition; (b) recapitulation and fulfilment; and (c) transformation and supersession. The use of the Old Testament in the Church's worship today.

The Reformers' appeal, in contrast to that of the Anabaptists, was to Scripture as received by the 'ancient Catholic Church.' The appeal of Hooker to Tradition and Reason over against the narrow Biblicism of the Puritans. The growth of the Old and New Testaments in the context of the life of the Old and New Israels respectively. The Bible rightly interpreted only from within the life of the Church. Yet the Church not 'over' the Scriptures but 'under' them.

The Creeds

appointed. The development of the three-fold ministry of bishop, priest and deacon. The 'pipe-line' theory of apostolic succession to be rejected, yet the same guidance of the Spirit to be recognized in the evolution of the historic ministry as in the formation of the New Testament Canon.

Renewal. Only if Christians have a fresh vision of Christ and love him above all else will the union of the Church be worth anything.
Mission. This rightly understood only within the context of God's eternal purpose to unite all things in Christ. The Christian involvement in the life and problems of the world. The formation of a Christian 'mind.' The call to commitment.

ACKNOWLEDGEMENTS

THE thanks of the author and the publishers are due to the following for permission to quote extracts:

A. & C. Black Ltd., *The Birth of the New Testament* by C. F. D. Moule; Basil Blackwell & Mott Ltd., *For Faith and Freedom* by L. Hodgson; Cambridge University Press, G. W. H. Lampe in *Soundings* ed. A. R. Vidler; Collins Publishers, *Le Milieu Divin* by Teilhard de Chardin; J. M. Dent & Sons Ltd., *Laws of Ecclesiastical Polity* by R. Hooker, Everyman's Library edition; Faber & Faber Ltd., *God was in Christ* and *The Theology of the Sacraments* by D. M. Baillie; Independent Press Ltd., *Technology, Community and Church* by H. Cunliffe-Jones, and *Christian Unity: Some of the Issues* by J. Huxtable; John Knox Press, *The Church as the Body of Christ* by Eduard Schweizer; Longmans, Green & Co. Ltd., *Early Christian Creeds* by J. N. D. Kelly, *Ministerial Priesthood* by R. C. Moberley, *Via Media* by J. H. Newman, and *The Gospel and the Catholic Church* by A. M. Ramsey; Hodder & Stoughton Ltd., *The Body of Christ* by R. A. Cole, and *Called to Serve* by E. M. B. Green; James Nisbet & Co. Ltd., *The Christian Sacraments* by Oliver Quick, and *Systematic Theology* by Paul Tillich; Penguin Books Ltd., *Pelican Commentary on the Gospel of St. Mark* by D. E. Nineham; The Society for Promoting Christian Knowledge, *Doctrine in the Church of England*, C. F. Evans *On the Authority of the Bible*, D. E. Nineham and J. N. D. Kelly in *The Church's Use of the Bible* ed. D. E. Nineham; Charles Scribner's Sons, *The Doctrine of the Atonement* by L. Hodgson; S.C.M. Press, *Worship and Mission* by J. G. Davies, *The Pioneer Ministry* by A. T. Hanson, *The Central Message of the New Testament* by J. Jeremias, *The Household of God* by L. Newbigin, *History Sacred and Profane* by A. Richardson, and *The Body*, *Honest to God* and *The Honest to God Debate* by J. A. T. Robinson; World Council of Churches, *The Relevance of Trinitarian Doctrine for To-day's Mission* by L. Newbigin.

Thanks are also due to the editor and publishers of the *Canadian Churchman* for permission to quote extracts from the issue dated June 1965; to the Church of England Newspaper Ltd. for permission to quote from the *Church of England Newspaper*, August 13, 1965; to the Church Missionary Society for permission to quote from the *C.M.S. News-Letter* No. 298; to the Society of the Sacred Mission for permission to quote from an article by G. Wilkins in the *S.S.M. Magazine*, September 1966; and to the Times Newspaper Ltd. for permission to quote from an editorial published in *The Times*, August 8th, 1964.

Should any acknowledgement have been omitted inadvertently, then this oversight will be rectified in subsequent editions if brought to the attention of either the author or the publishers.

PREFACE

THIS book has its ultimate origin in a lifelong concern and its immediate beginning in a particular occasion. The lifelong concern has been the exposition of the Anglican tradition of faith and order, the interpretation of one school of thought to another, and the setting of our inheritance in a world-wide and ecumenical context. Various factors have contributed to this direction of much of my ministry—a home in which a strong Evangelical influence and a strong sense of churchmanship were equally present, the opportunity of reading for the theological tripos at Cambridge under Sir Edwyn Hoskyns and of sharing in a simple 'parish-communion' type service in Peterhouse Chapel, membership of the Student Christian Movement and of the old Student Volunteer Missionary Union, and the privilege of doing my theological training at Westcott House under B. K. Cunningham. It was during my time at Cambridge that William Temple conducted a University mission and gave the addresses which he repeated at the other place five years later and which were then published as his Oxford addresses under the title *Christian Faith and Life*—one more example of the greater publicity that the older University always seems so adept at achieving. At any rate, they had a profound influence on me and helped me to see something of the wholeness of the Anglican tradition.

It was with this heritage that I taught theology at the Central Theological College, Tokyo, before the war, and sought to guide Lincoln in the post-war years when I was its Warden. When St. Augustine's College, Canterbury, opened as the Central College of the Anglican Communion and I became its Warden, I found myself inevitably involved in the process of interpreting 'Catholic' to 'Evangelical,' conservative to liberal, and vice versa, as we gathered into one family clergy of all races, continents and traditions of churchmanship and tried to help them understand each other and the place of the Anglican Communion in the larger circle of the whole Christian Church and of the world.

Later, as Bishop of Singapore and Malaya, I discovered that in a multi-racial and multi-lingual diocese to which all the different traditions of churchmanship were contributing, something of the same reconciling ministry was necessary. The bishop of that diocese has indeed to be a focal point of unity within his own communion and a leader in ecumenical co-operation: he has also the task of helping his people to see the implications of the Gospel for the social and political life of South East Asia.

So much for the lifelong concern. Now for the immediate occasion which set me to work on this book. In the middle of my time as Bishop of Singapore and Malaya there burst upon the world of religious thought the Bishop of Woolwich's *Honest to God*. There is no need to write of its impact here, for that is known to everybody. It is sufficient to say that a great many perspectives in the theological scene have changed and many things can never look quite the same again. Yet two or three months later there was a controversy on the opposite front. Canon J. D. Pearce-Higgins, on being collated Vice-Provost of Southwark Cathedral, made a formal protest against the legal requirement that he should publicly assent to the Thirty-Nine Articles of Religion before being admitted to his new office.

A considerable correspondence ensued in *The Times* and elsewhere, in the course of which Conservative Evangelical spokesmen stoutly defended the Articles as the Church of England's confession, to which it was inevitably bound. Just as the whole Church in early centuries had been guided to say a final 'no' to Arianism, Apollinarianism and the other heresies in the formulation of the Creeds, so the Church of England had been led to make a final pronouncement on the authority of scriptures, justification by faith, predestination and election, transubstantiation and the rest, in the sixteenth century. No loyal Anglican could do other than accept the clear guidance of the Spirit given in that Reformation age.

Towards its close I took part in the correspondence in *The Times* and tried to outline the kind of doctrinal outlook which in my view would receive widespread support among Anglicans.

The authentic Anglican temper, I suggested, is not one which believes that our doctrine and practice were finally determined in the sixteenth century, but one which, holding to our heritage as Catholic and Reformed and making its appeal to reason, is ready to reinterpret our understanding of the Gospel for each particular age. The Thirty-Nine Articles, as I believe, enshrine some truths of the Gospel rediscovered in the Reformation, but they carry the marks of current controversy and breathe too often the atmosphere of the age in which they were written. Who today, for instance, could hold the doctrine of the godly prince in anything like its sixteenth-century form?

As a result of my contribution to *The Times* I was asked by Messrs. A. R. Mowbray & Co. whether I would like to expand what I had written into a book. In what some readers may think was a rash moment I accepted, and this work is the result. It has grown from what was originally intended to be a paperback into a sizeable volume, and it has taken me three years to complete, for the life of a missionary bishop constantly travelling in the heat and humidity of a diocese just north of the equator does not provide much leisure time for scholarly pursuits.

The book, as will be seen, is based on the Lambeth Quadrilateral, which plays a greater part in ecumenical conversations than do the Thirty-Nine Articles. I have not attempted to write anything approaching a 'Bicknell' under this guise, but rather to consider under each head some of the issues that seem to me significant for theological thinking and for the Church's life in the world today. My hope is that what I have written may help to give guidance, particularly to clergy and thoughtful lay people who are bewildered by the present climate of thinking and find so many of the familiar landmarks disappearing. In saying that, I do not mean that I am sounding the call of 'back to the old ways.' The 'old-time religion' is good enough for us, if by it we mean the unchanging Gospel of God's redeeming love in Christ for all mankind. It is not good enough for anybody, if we mean that the thought-processes, the forms of expression and the type of church life it produced are adequate for our radically

B

different situation. My hope and prayer is that what I have written may help some at least who hold the Christian faith as the Anglican Communion has received it to see the way forward in this ecumenical and at the same time secularized age.

The task of finishing this work was not made easier by the fact that in the summer of 1966, when the book was three-quarters completed, I was called back to London to become the General Secretary of the British Council of Churches, with which post I also hold that of an Assistant Bishop in the Diocese of London. It was only after some delay that I was able to pick up the threads again and bring the work to a conclusion. I must make clear, of course, that the British Council of Churches has no responsibility, direct or indirect, for its contents. I hope, however, that those who belong to other member-Churches of the Council than mine, as well as Anglicans of other schools of thought, will feel, if they read this book, that it is not lacking in the ecumenical spirit, even where they are not able to accept its conclusions.

In conclusion, I must express my indebtedness to my wife who has read the whole book in typescript and done a great deal of the proof-reading. I wish also to express thanks to my son, the Rev. C. J. Sansbury, for his theological comments and criticisms; to Mr. A. J. Bryant, of Messrs. A. R. Mowbray & Co, who has shown exemplary patience in the delays over the book's completion; and to my two secretaries, Miss Dolly Ong, the Bishop's secretary in Singapore, who very kindly continued typing chapters after I had returned to England, and Miss Anne Borthwick, lately secretary to the General Secretary of the British Council of Churches, who with equal kindness typed the last three chapters for me in her spare time. Needless to say, I alone am responsible for the views expressed in the book.

✠ KENNETH SANSBURY, *Bishop*

London
Feast of the Epiphany, 1967

THE HOLY SCRIPTURES

The Holy Scriptures of the Old and New Testaments as 'containing all things necessary to salvation,' and as being the rule and ultimate standard of faith

INTRODUCTION

THERE can be no doubt that in its teaching over the past four hundred years the Anglican Communion has given a place of central and decisive importance to the Bible. It has recognized that here is the supreme authority in the sphere of Christian doctrine. Whatever reservations Anglicans may have had about others of the Thirty-Nine Articles, at least the declaration with which Article VI opens has claimed general allegiance. Holy Scripture, it declares, contains all things necessary to salvation: nothing which cannot be read in its pages or proved from them is to be made a necessary article of the Christian faith or taught as though without believing it men and women would be debarred from salvation. At the Ordination of Priests and the Consecration of Bishops a searching question is put to those who are to receive the Laying on of Hands, to ensure their acceptance of this principle in their preaching and teaching.

The Anglican family of Churches has not only accepted the supreme authority of Scripture as a basic principle, but in its forms of worship makes the fullest use of Biblical material. The Bible, it is clear, is not just an external book to be appealed to for doctrinal decisions, it is a book to be lived with as a source of spiritual life in which the great truths of the Christian faith may come alive in the congregation of the people of God and in the minds and consciences of individual believers. Thus the services of Mattins and Evensong include the daily recitation of the Psalter and the regular and orderly reading of the Old and New Testaments. The service of Holy Communion includes the Ministry of the Word in its lections for Epistle and Gospel, and the other services of the Prayer Books of our communion (with the unhappy exception of the 1662 Confirmation order) either include a lection to show the Biblical basis of the Sacrament or other rite, or else (e.g. the Marriage Service) make a specific reference to some Biblical passage.

3

The basis of the radical changes made in the structure of Anglican worship in the Reformation period was that the services, without completely breaking with the past, should be essentially Scriptural in doctrine, 'much agreeable to the mind and purpose of the old Fathers' and more profitable to the worshippers than the order which they replaced.[1] We may not agree that they always succeeded in their aim. We may be desperately aware how remote many of the forms of service are from people today. Yet we must recognize gratefully how much material patterned on the Bible the Reformers have bequeathed, which has nurtured the faith and life of many generations of Anglican worshippers, and in many cases continues to do so today.

It was natural then that when the Lambeth Conference of 1920 issued its *Appeal to all Christian People* it should include, as the first element in the basis of Unity which it proposed to other Churches, a reassertion of this fundamental conviction—the Scriptures as containing 'all things necessary to salvation' and as 'the rule and ultimate standard of faith.'[2] Similarly, the authority of Scripture has been one of the first principles accepted in the Church unity schemes in which different branches of the Anglican Communion have been involved. The Constitution of the Church of South India introduces the section on *The Faith of the Church* with a statement clearly accepting 'the Holy Scriptures of the Old and New Testaments as containing all things necessary to salvation and as the supreme and decisive standard of faith.'[3] The Ceylon Plan and the North India and Pakistan Scheme make closely parallel declarations.[4] And the Report of the Conversations between the Church of England and the Methodist Church begins its Theological Considerations by recalling that in the *Interim Statement* 'the agreement that "the Holy Scriptures are the inspired witness to the revelation of God, and constitute the

---

[1] The Preface to the B.C.P. *Concerning the Service of the Church*, the original Preface of 1549.
[2] Lambeth Conference, 1920 Report, p. 134.   [3] P. 4.
[4] S. F. Bayne, *Ceylon, North India and Pakistan*, pp. 23 and 120–121.

supreme rule of faith" was declared to be an important part of the common ground between our two Churches.'[1] Similar statements are to be found in all the other Church Union Schemes.

The Bible is indeed uniquely authoritative for all Christian Churches. But it is important to notice that the ground of the Bible's authority has significantly changed as a result of the scientific revolution in our thinking about the nature of the world and of the critical study of the Bible itself. Through most of the Christian era before modern times the Bible was regarded as authoritative because it was believed to contain the truths of the Christian religion in a verbally inspired and infallible form. Of course, even within that framework of doctrine the Bible could in practice be seen in varying perspectives. The early church profoundly reinterpreted the books of the Old Testament in the light of its faith that in Jesus Christ God had visited and redeemed his people. 'A theory of plenary inspiration was a very different thing in practice, when combined with the extreme allegorism of some of the Alexandrian Fathers, from what it was when combined with the literalism of some of their Antiochene contemporaries.'[2] The great Reformers' emphasis on the Word of God as the living proclamation of Christ in the Gospel which is received in the human heart by the inward testimony of the Holy Spirit is to be distinguished from the kind of Fundamentalism which identifies the Word of God completely with the words of Scripture, and interprets them in the manner of a lawyer construing a will.

Today, however, that traditional way of thinking about the authority of the Bible is no longer possible. The discoveries of the sciences have transformed our knowledge of the universe— the nature of its physical structure, the immensity of its size, the unimaginable length of time during which the evolutionary process has been in operation. The work of literary and historical criticism and the impact of related sciences—anthropology, archaeology and the comparative study of religion—have profoundly affected our approach to the Bible and helped us to

[1] P. 15.   [2] D. E. Nineham, *The Church's Use of the Bible*, p. 146.

understand its emergence in the setting of the ancient cultures of the Middle East. Myth, folk-lore, legend and saga have frankly to be recognized within its pages, as well as history, prophecy, poetry, drama, gospel record and letters.

When the new discoveries made their first impact in the nineteenth century, it was inevitable that they should create widespread dismay. How could the Word of God be thought of as speaking through the pages of a book written in the thought-forms of a long past age? How could the Bible be authoritative, if its history was not always reliable, still more, if its portrayal of God in, e.g., parts of the Old Testament could be condemned as sub-Christian? The 'impregnable rock of Holy Scripture' of which Gladstone wrote seemed to have dissolved into shifting sands, and the Christian believer appeared to be faced with harsh alternatives. If he wished to retain belief in the Divine authority of Scripture, he had, it seemed, to cling to the traditional position and close his mind to the new discoveries. Or else he had to accept the new discoveries and then find himself led to place the main emphasis on the human element in the Bible. The Bible, he was told, was authoritative because it represented the fine flowering of a nation with a genius for religion, because it told the story of religious evolution from animism to Jesus Christ, because it was a record of man's profound religious experience.[1]

There is no need here to recount the story of how Biblical scholars have come to recognize both the Divine authority of Scripture and the human elements within it. In England scholars such as S. R. Driver of Oxford, and the Cambridge trio—Westcott, Lightfoot and Hort—showed how sound Biblical scholarship could be combined with Christian faith. On the European Continent by common consent the turning point from the prevailing nineteenth century approach both to the Bible and to theology generally dates from the publication at the end of the First World War of Karl Barth's *Commentary on the Epistle to the*

---

[1] William Temple once said of a book about Old Testament religion written in this vein that it might have had as a sub-title 'What a lot of ancient Semites thought about God.'

Romans. Men were not nearly so sure about unbroken progress in society from lower to higher forms nor about man's religious achievements after the blood-baths of France and Flanders. The patent failure of Western civilization led to a new openness to the perspective of the Bible, in which the living God is revealed as taking the initiative, as addressing man in his creatureliness, his sin and his divine destiny, as acting in judgement and salvation. The authority of the Bible, men came to see afresh, lies in its divinely inspired witness to that unique revelation of God.

Thus, the Old Testament records the unfolding revelation and purpose of God, as he makes himself known in a series of 'disclosure situations'[1] in the changing vicissitudes of Israel's history, and yet points forward to a fulfilment which Christians believe lies beyond its pages. The New Testament embodies the apostolic proclamation that that revelation of God is summed up and that purpose fulfilled in the life, death and resurrection of Jesus Christ, in the recreation of the Israel of God by the power of the Spirit, and in the expanding life of the Church, as it breaks through the barriers of race, class and sex and becomes a truly catholic society. In these great and unrepeatable events, the New Testament asserts, God's saving purpose is revealed and its final consummation assured. 'He has made known to us in all wisdom and insight the mystery of his will, according to his purpose which he set forth in Christ as a plan for the fulness of time, to unite all things, things in heaven and things on earth' (Eph. 1. 9–10).

In our approach to the Bible, then, two things are necessary. The first is readiness to accept the results of scientific investigation, to follow where a sane and reverent critical study leads in its conclusions and to wrestle with the task of reinterpreting the Biblical revelation in the thought forms of today. 'The authority ascribed to the Bible' said the report *Doctrine in the Church of England*, 'must not be interpreted as prejudging the conclusions of historical, critical and scientific investigation in any field, not excluding that of the Biblical documents themselves.'[2] As D. E.

---

[1] The phrase is one used by A. Richardson. See *History Sacred and Profane*, pp. 223 ff.
[2] P. 32.

Nineham has written, 'The revelation was through words and actions, but there is no question of God's taking steps to ensure that every statement or action which was to be a vehicle of revelation should be precisely designed to express the divine mind—even the divine mind for a particular situation.'[1] We cannot follow the Conservative Evangelical line, which with all its valuable contributions to Biblical study can never accept in full the evidence about itself which the Bible reveals to critical examination, because of a preconceived theory of plenary inspiration. There can be no question of 'thus far and no farther.'[2]

But the critical study of the Bible must be 'sane and reverent.' No scholar can make a worth-while contribution to Shakespearian study if his sole concern is for the history of the folios and he has no ear for the music of Shakespeare's words and no appreciation of Shakespeare's insight into the human heart. The Christian student of the Bible needs to be open to the Word of God, humbly prepared to listen and willing to accept in and through the written words the revelation of a God whose thoughts are not always our thoughts and whose ways are not always our ways. 'The Church has not made up its gospel from its own experience, but has received it from witnesses, and the Holy Spirit assures us that their witness is true. The message stands in its own truth and grandeur and in this sense is self-authenticating, for no higher guarantee can be given it, no greater authority than that of the living Word of whom it speaks and who uses it as the vehicle of his saving action.'[3]

---

[1] *The Church's Use of the Bible*, p. 152.

[2] The most significant thing about J. I. Packer's '*Fundamentalism*' *and the Word of God* is that it argues deductively from what the Bible is supposed to be, not inductively from the evidence of what its structure and composition are. His later work *God Has Spoken* in the Christian Foundations series published by the Evangelical Fellowship of the Anglican Communion follows the same method.

[3] *Report of the Anglican–Methodist Conversations*, p. 15.

I. THE AUTHORITY OF THE GOSPELS

I

THE understanding of the Bible as authoritative because it
bears witness to the saving acts of God in Israel, in Christ and in
the Christian Church, because through the words and thought-
forms of a particular age it conveys the Word of God to us
in our contemporary situation, means that our interpretation
of the Scripture can never remain static. Each generation has
its own problems in distinguishing between the heavenly treasure
and the earthly vessel in which it comes to us. Each generation
has the task of expounding the Bible in terms that are relevant
to the people of its day. At the present time, as it seems to me,
there are three main areas in which we are called to examine
the authority of Scripture afresh.

The first concerns the *kind of authority the four Gospels bear in
relation to the central elements of the Gospel*—the birth, life, ministry,
death and resurrection of Jesus Christ, all that goes to make up
the second paragraph of both the Apostles' and Nicene Creeds.

In pre-critical days the Gospels were accepted as plain, straight-
forward accounts of what actually happened, books written
within the Church but also biographies of Jesus which could be
woven together to form a continuous narrative of the earthly
life of the Son of God. This is still a common method in sermons
and in devotional writing. The traditional way of basing the
Three Hours' Service on Good Friday on the Seven Words from
the Cross is the most conspicuous example. But many of us
preach all the time as though each incident in the Gospels had
been reported direct by an eye-witness. We go, too, for our
meditation to books such as Temple's *Readings in St. John's
Gospel* or J. R. H. Moorman's *The Path to Glory*, which with all
their spiritual insight often by-pass the critical questions that
underlie the text.

Yet if one 'assured result' of modern critical study of the
Gospels stands out above others, it is that the Gospels are not

that kind of document. For long it has been recognized that the Fourth Gospel contains a large interpretative element in its composition. The evangelist is concerned not just with 'what actually happened' but with its significance. He writes so that his readers may behold the 'glory as of the only Son from the Father' (1. 14), that they 'may believe that Jesus is the Christ, the Son of God, and that believing (they) may have life in his name' (20. 31). For this purpose he groups his narrative material according to the themes he is expounding. In the discourses and dialogues which he builds on to his narratives he blends traditional sayings of Jesus and his inspired reflections on the inner significance of the narrative in question, with the result that the Johannine Christ, John the Baptist and the evangelist use an indistinguishable style. There may, indeed, be a stronger historical tradition behind St. John's Gospel than has always been supposed and one independent of those available to the Synoptists,[1] but there can be no doubt that in this Gospel we have, not an exact photographic reproduction of the Jesus of Galilee and Judaea, but a portrait of the Word made flesh, a portrait painted from our side of the resurrection and exaltation of Christ, and of the gift of the Spirit, the other Counsellor, a portrait painted by a man of faith to enable others to share the faith by which he lived.

What form-criticism and subsequent study of the Gospels have shown is that, if St. John is not concerned to write biography as we understand that art today, neither are the Synoptists. They may retain more closely the authentic flavour of Jesus' earthly ministry, but their gospels also are works of 'explanation.'[2] The first converts were confronted with the preaching of the kerygma, the Gospel of God's decisive action for man's salvation in Jesus Christ. But, 'when one comes to think about it, it is obvious enough that, once someone had accepted the kerygma, he would need a filling out of it and (as it were) an "embodiment" of the Jesus who had been thus briefly proclaimed as Lord.'[3]

---

[1] Cf. C. H. Dodd, *Historical Tradition in the Fourth Gospel.*
[2] C. F. D. Moule, *The Birth of the New Testament,* p. 86.
[3] C. F. D. Moule, *op. cit.,* pp. 86–87.

The materials which were used by the evangelists for this 'embodiment' of Jesus, however, passed through a considerable process of development in the oral tradition stage. They were collected, as it were, backwards. The first preaching of the Gospel laid its main emphasis on the lordship of the Risen Christ. 'Let all the house of Israel know assuredly that God has made him both Lord and Christ, this Jesus whom you crucified' (Acts 2. 36). It was important, therefore, to collect the testimony of those to whom the Risen Christ had appeared (1 Cor. 15. 5–8).

This proclamation inevitably raised questions in the minds of the hearers, particularly Jewish hearers. 'If this Jesus of Nazareth is, as you say, the appointed Messiah, the promised King, how do you account for the fact that he was crucified, and so passed under the curse of the Law upon everyone who hangs on a tree? Surely you are talking blasphemy!' The Christian answer was the narrative of the Passion, recounted in such a way as to show that Jesus went to his Cross in fulfilment of Old Testament prophecy. He was the true Passover lamb by whom God had wrought a greater deliverance than that of the Israelites from Egypt, the One by whose blood-shedding God had established a new covenant with the true Israel, the Messiah who fulfilled the role of the Suffering Servant of 2 Isaiah and who gave his life a ransom for many.

Who then was this Jesus of Nazareth who thus died for our sins, and rose again for our justification? What authority was there in his teaching and his deeds to justify practices in the early Church for which Christians had to face criticism? What guidance had he given his disciples which could help Christians in their worship and witness and in the problems of discipline that arose in their congregations? Stories about Jesus and records of his sayings were collected to answer such questions. They were told to 'embody' the figure of Jesus the Lord, as the church remembered him and as it recalled his authority for their lives. In the process of telling a story for new situations, the form or shape of the story could sometimes be modified. Parables spoken

in one set of circumstances might well be given another interpretation in a fresh situation, miracles such as those of the Feeding
of the Multitudes appear to be described in terms of later liturgical
practice at the Eucharist, post-resurrection insights may sometimes have been read back into the days of the Lord's earthly
ministry.

Lastly came the question: 'How did God's act of salvation in
Jesus Christ all begin?' To that question Mark gave the answer,
'It began with the preaching of John the Baptist,' Matthew and
Luke, 'It began with the action of the Holy Spirit in the conception of Jesus in the womb of the Virgin Mary,' and John, 'It
began with the eternal Word of God taking flesh and dwelling
among us.'

We are here beginning to pass on to the next stage in the
transmission of the traditions about Jesus. For the evangelists
were not just collectors of stories; like St. John the Synoptists
are painting portraits of Jesus—Mark, one of Jesus the Son of God,
who comes to his glory by way of suffering; Matthew, one of
Jesus as the Davidic King, who fulfils and transcends the Old
Testament in his universal kingdom and who gives to the new
people of God the new law of the kingdom of heaven; Luke,
one of Jesus as Universal Saviour whose work is continued in
the expansion of the early church from Jerusalem to Rome,
and whose mission when properly understood should commend
itself to the Roman authorities. They may not have been able to
shape all their material for the purpose,[1] but there is no doubt of
the prominence they give to certain themes.

Getting back to the actual Jesus of Galilee and Judaea, then,
is not as easy as once was thought. The nineteenth-century
movement to reconstruct the life of Jesus by stripping off all
the supernatural elements and producing a simple prophet of
righteousness suited to the idealism of the age has ended in

---

[1] Cf. D. E. Nineham's Pelican Commentary, *St. Mark*, p. 29. 'In searching the Gospel
for a single and entirely coherent master-plan, . . . scholars are looking for something
that is not there.' C. F. D. Moule, *op. cit.*, pp. 89–90. 'It embraces a considerable breadth
of tradition, and no one absolutely consistent outlook can be extracted from it.'

failure. 'Albert Schweitzer, in his classic work, *The Quest of the Historical Jesus*, has erected its memorial, but at the same time has delivered its funeral oration.'[1] But the twentieth century has posed for us an even more urgent question. Do the Gospels bring us reliable knowledge of the earthly Jesus of Nazareth, do they provide us with adequate evidence for the historic statements of the Creed? Or are they primarily evidence for the faith of the early Church, which has read back its post-resurrection convictions into its records of Christ's earthly ministry?

2

Three main answers to this question may be distinguished. The first is *the sceptical approach of the extreme form-critics*, of whom R. Bultmann has been the powerful leader in Germany. However we may react to his total position, at least we must recognize that his purpose is basically an apologetic and evangelistic one. He is concerned to disentangle the Word of God as it confronts us in the Cross in judgement and redemption from the first century world view and 'cosmic myths' in which the significance of the 'Christ event' has been set forth in the New Testament and in traditional orthodoxy, for in his view these have become incredible to modern man. In the process of demythologization and reconstruction, Bultmann has been influenced by a number of factors which he has brought to the study of the New Testament. First, he was brought up in the 'history of religions' school and, in fact, edited the second edition of W. Bousset's *Kyrios Christos*. This school of thought 'tended to regard early Christianity as merely one of the cults of a dying-and-rising God which flourished in the Hellenistic world; its symbolic truth was connected only accidentally with the historical Jesus of Nazareth.'[2] Thus, Bultmann's form-critical work for all its brilliance was done under the influence of a theory which

[1] G. Bornkamm, *Jesus of Nazareth*, p. 13.
[2] A. Richardson, *op. cit.*, p. 139. Bishop S. C. Neill has recently emphasized that all the evidence points to a Gnostic borrowing from Christianity of the concept of salvation through death and resurrection, and not the other way round. Cf. *The Interpretation of the New Testament*, pp. 179–181.

emphasized the likenesses rather than the differences between the New Testament and the mystery-religions. This led him to reject in the former whatever could find some sort of parallel in the latter, regardless of chronological sequence.

Secondly, his apologetic purpose made him reinterpret the New Testament in exclusively existentialist terms, for this has been for him the one philosophy that can meet the needs of modern man. Existentialism stands at the opposite pole from the basic principle of so much modern thinking, namely that the sole avenue to truth is the way of scientific investigation and that what cannot be verified by scientific experiment has no meaning. Existentialism proclaims with great vehemence that we have another source of knowledge, knowledge of our existence, knowledge of our predicament in face of the complexities of a terrifying world. It goes on to assert that it is only as we face that predicament with resolution and courage that we pass from 'unauthentic existence' to 'authentic existence,' are set free from slavery to the blind forces at work in the world around us and enter on a life of personal responsibility. Some existentialists think in terms of the individual making his lonely decision, others lay stress on the meeting of persons in existential 'I—Thou' relationships.

There is much in this which Christians must find congenial. Time and again, preachers have emphasized that faith in the New Testament is not just intellectual assent to the statements contained in the Creeds, it is trust in, committal to the God of which they speak. When they have spoken of the Atonement and used the varying pictures given us in the New Testament, they have frequently made clear that none of them counts for us unless at the end we can say from experience—'The Son of God who loved me and gave himself for me.' As Bishop Gore used to say repeatedly, 'We must never separate what God has done for us from what God does in us.' The death and resurrection of Christ only become 'existential' for us, as we die with Christ and rise again to newness of life in him.

Yet Christianity has always held that what happens to us in the living encounter of faith is consequent upon what first happened in historical reality to Jesus Christ. By contrast Bultmann treats the Gospel evidence for the historical Jesus with a radical scepticism. Christ did of course die, but the story of the resurrection is a mythological way of affirming the 'ever-present reality' of the Cross as the place where the Word of God uniquely confronts men in judgement and salvation. That is central. To seek supporting evidence in historical records is to be like the Jews who sought after a sign; to respond in sheer faith to the Word of God declared in the Cross is to live 'by faith alone.'[1]

Bultmann has certainly posed a powerful challenge to historic Christianity, but it is doubtful if he has provided an enduring resting place for our understanding of the New Testament. For it is difficult to rest satisfied with an interpretation of the Gospels which leaves the Cross in such stark isolation.

Thus, it is significant that not a few of Bultmann's followers are tending to take one of two paths. Those who share his scepticism and his existentialism to the full ask why he does not get rid of the last remnant of 'mythology' he has retained—the concept of an act of God in Jesus Christ. Let him follow the demythologizing path to the end, they urge, and recognize that the whole theistic framework of the New Testament is merely a primitive way of describing the change from 'unauthentic' to 'authentic' existence. Others who hold firmly to the truth of the kerygma, the proclamation of the Gospel, are increasingly coming to see that, if the Cross is indeed the instrument of God's saving work, that is because it is the climax of a life that points inevitably forward to it and does not stand irrationally alone.

[1] It is interesting to note how often over-zealous upholders of the doctrine of justification by faith misinterpret its meaning through seeing it in isolation from the rest of the New Testament. *Sola fide* has been interpreted, not just as 'by faith apart from the works of the Law' (its proper meaning), but as 'by faith apart from sacraments' or as 'by faith apart from sanctification' or as 'by an individual's inner feelings of faith.' It has been left to Bultmann to add a further misinterpretation—'by faith apart from historical evidence.' For the unduly narrow basis of much Lutheran theology, cf. S. C. Neill, *op. cit.*, pp. 188–189.

C

So we see renewed attempts being made today to press back through the written and oral tradition of the Gospels as revealed by literary and form-criticism to the historical Jesus.[1]

3

At the opposite pole from Bultmann are those who represent what might well be called *the critical orthodoxy which has dominated British New Testament scholarship* over the past thirty years or so. C. H. Dodd, T. W. Manson, W. Manson, Vincent Taylor and Alan Richardson are among its distinguished exponents, and it would probably be true to say that most British students over the age of fifty and a great many under that age have accepted the interpretation of the Gospels which with minor differences they have presented to us. Such scholars accept *ex animo* the methods of literary and form-criticism, they would in no case claim that the Gospels are mere newspaper reporter's accounts of 'what actually happened' but would agree that they are written 'from faith to faith' by men who looked back on the events of Christ's earthly ministry from the other side of the Cross and Resurrection.

But they would claim that it is inherently absurd to imagine that the Christian Church came into being on the basis of a Word of God coming to men through the preaching of the Cross, unless, in fact, there was something about the Figure that hung there which distinguished his Cross from all other crosses. It is absurd too, they would say, to imagine that that Figure, who stands out so clearly from the pages of the Gospels, is just the creation of later faith or that his burning and dynamic words are so overlaid with later interpretation that they can now be regarded only as the products of the Christian community. The trouble with Bultmann and his entourage, says Alan

---

[1] For short accounts of Bultmann's teaching and subsequent developments, see *Kerygma and Myth*, vols. I and II; S. C. Neill, *op. cit.*, pp. 222–235; A. Richardson, *The Bible in the Age of Science*, chap. 5; and R. H. Fuller, *The New Testament in Current Study*, chaps. 1–3.

Richardson, is that they start with a 'dogma' derived not from a proper study of the Gospels, but from the presuppositions of nineteenth-century liberal theology, that 'any kerygmatic or Christological statements that appear in the Gospels—such as that Jesus thought of himself as the Messiah—must be deemed to be unhistorical, since they must be a reading back of the kerygma of the post-Easter Church into the life and times of Jesus.' The only truly scientific method is to test out various hypotheses and see which gives the most satisfactory account of the New Testament evidence. Alan Richardson believes that the hypothesis which most fully meets this requirement is 'that the theology of the New Testament as a whole is based primarily upon Jesus' own interpretation of his mission and person in the light of his understanding of the Old Testament' and he points out that this is the principle of interpretation used in his *Introduction to the Theology of the New Testament.*[1] With this position the other scholars mentioned above would generally agree. They would all hold also that the resurrection faith which underlies the whole New Testament cannot be dissolved into a primitive way of declaring the enduring significance of the Cross. At every point it bears witness to the conviction that something had happened which had transformed the disciples from despair to certitude. The God and Father of the Lord Jesus Christ had begotten them again to a living hope by the resurrection of Jesus Christ from the dead (1 Pet. 1. 1). Their faith was a response to a Divine action, not the source of a mythological story.

How all this works out in the practical exposition of a Gospel can be seen in G. B. Caird's Pelican Commentary, *Saint Luke.* Here full recognition is given to the positive contribution of form-criticism to our understanding of the Gospel, but the shortcomings of its more extreme exponents are trenchantly criticized (pp. 21 and 22).

[1] *History Sacred and Profane*, pp. 141–142. This is essentially the position of O. Cullmann, *The Christology of the New Testament* and of Fr. Hebert's work, *The Christ of Faith and the Jesus of History.*

4

Today, however, we must distinguish *a third group*, which is
profoundly influenced by Bultmann, but which does not share
his extreme scepticism. It includes writers such as G. Bornkamm
in Germany, John Knox in U.S.A.[1] and the colleagues and
disciples of R. H. Lightfoot in Britain. The approach of writers
of this school, which is likely to be increasingly influential among
younger students, is well illustrated in the other two Pelican
Commentaries on the Synoptic Gospels, D. E. Nineham's *Saint
Mark* and J. C. Fenton's *Saint Matthew*. A comparative study of
these two commentaries with that of G. B. Caird on *Saint Luke*
makes clear the different emphasis of the two ways of approach.

When such a comparison is made, it becomes clear that those
who belong to this third group are much less sure than those of
the second, that, e.g., the Marcan outline of Jesus' ministry with
Peter's confession at Caesarea Philippi as the watershed separating
the first half of the Gospel from the second is historical. They
are a good deal more ready to believe that the evangelists may
have read back their post-resurrection faith in Jesus as Messiah,
Saviour and Lord into their accounts of the earthly ministry; as
D. E. Nineham puts it, an ancient writer believing in Jesus as
Christ and Son of God might well feel that 'any account of his
earthly life which did not make that clear would be misleading
and would not convey the true meaning of the events it pro-
fessed to describe.'[2]

But, unlike Bultmann, they believe that the figure of the
historical Jesus is not irrecoverable. 'When we reconstruct the
units of tradition on which the Gospels are based,' says D. E.
Nineham, 'not only do we find that the units on which Mark is
based presuppose broadly the same Christ as the finished Gospel,
but we find that other units, preserved independently in other
places and used by the other Evangelists, also presuppose a
fundamentally similar figure.' He goes on to point out that 'our

[1] Cf. G. Bornkamm, *Jesus of Nazareth*, and J. Knox, *The Death of Christ* and *Jesus, Lord
and Christ*.
[2] *Op. cit.*, p. 25.

basic picture of Christ is thus carried back to a point only a quarter of a century or so after his death.' 'The Jesus of Mark . . . is beyond any doubt basically a figure of early first-century Palestine and not an invention of late first-century Rome.'[1]

The echoes of Bultmann, which have been somewhat muffled in Britain, are likely to reverberate round the schools of New Testament scholarship for a long while yet. Scholars will continue to discuss the relation between the Jesus of history and the Christ of faith, and will continue to come to more conservative or more radical conclusions, as the case may be.[2] Meanwhile, the Christian Church will continue to recite the second paragraphs of the Creeds and to celebrate the sacrament of Christ's redemption; those who are aware of the issues will not infrequently wonder whether the New Testament evidence is strong enough to support the assertions of the Creeds or to justify the sacramental practice.

In this situation I believe, *pace* A. T. Hanson, that John Knox gives us much help in his work, *The Church and the Reality of Christ*. When we estimate the place of any great figure in the history of the world, we turn first to the things which he said and did, to his energy and resolution and sense of dedication to his life's work. But we also take into account the influence he exercised, the way in which armies were inspired by his generalship, or nations moved by his statesmanship, or audiences captivated by his music, as the case may be. And then we try to assess the results in subsequent history—the consequences of a victorious military campaign, the redrawn map of political frontiers, the response in generation after generation to the compelling power of his music. All these factors are weighed in the estimate of a man's greatness.

---

[1] *Op. cit.*, p. 50.

[2] A strong reassertion of the 'orthodox critical' standpoint has recently appeared in *Vindications, Essays on the Historical Basis of Christianity*, edited by A. T. Hanson, who severely criticizes the form-critical presuppositions of D. E. Nineham and the existentialist approach of John Knox. A. T. Hanson's treatment of D. E. Nineham is itself severely criticized in a review by P. K. Walker in *Theology*, Nov. 1966, pp. 508–509.

So with the great central assertions of the kerygma. 'The Event of Christ' says John Knox, includes 'the personality, life and teaching of Jesus, the response of loyalty he awakened, his death, his Resurrection, the receiving of the Spirit, the faith with which the Spirit was received, the coming into being of the Church.'[1] He goes on to point out that these are not just items in a chronological series. They are parts of a whole, and that whole is in fact 'the coming into being of the Church,' the community 'with which the New Testament puts us directly into touch.'[2] It is as we enter that community by Baptism that we come to share the Church's memory of Jesus of Nazareth, acknowledge him as Lord, accept that he died for our sins and rose again for our justification and receive his Spirit. In that moment of existential self-committal, the whole kerygma ceases to be just a series of consecutive statements about the past and becomes a contemporary fact for our lives today.

When, therefore, we look back to the New Testament documents, and particularly to the Gospels, we shall not find faith dependent on whether this or that particular claim, e.g., to be Messiah was or was not an actual utterance of the historic Christ. For the Christ in whom we believe is larger than the sum total of the words and deeds of Jesus which a rigorous criticism can accept as genuine. He includes all those things inevitably (and we cannot dispense with an adequate historical basis), but he includes also all that the early Church under the overwhelming impact of his life, and still more, of his death and resurrection and of his continuing presence in the Spirit within the community of the Church, felt inevitably driven to assert of him. All this is evidence for what Christ was, and is, and what God has done, and continues to do, through him.

At the end of his Introduction to the Pelican Commentary, *Saint Mark*, D. E. Nineham includes two quotations, the latter now quite famous, from Leonard Hodgson's Gifford Lectures, *For Faith and Freedom*. Both are relevant and can fittingly sum up

[1] *Op. cit.*, p. 23. Cf. *Jesus, Lord and Christ*, p. 217.   [2] *Op. cit.*, p. 22.

this discussion. 'The developed doctrine (of the person of Christ) is not simply concerned with what he thought of himself while on earth, or what his disciples thought of him, but with what he was.' 'What must the truth (about Christ) be, and have been, if it appeared like that to men who thought and wrote as they did (in the books of the New Testament)?'[1]

In the last resort the Christian confesses Christ as the remembered and ever-present Saviour and Lord through the impact made on him by the compelling Figure that confronts him in the Gospels, through an act of faith that the witness of the apostolic Church to his person and significance in the books of the New Testament is true, and through the verification of that faith in his own experience of forgiveness and newness of life as a member of Christ's Body the Church today.

[1] Pp. 51 and 52, where the references are given to L. Hodgson's Gifford Lectures.

II. THE PLACE OF THE OLD TESTAMENT

I

THE second area of discussion in considering the authority of the Scriptures concerns *the place and significance of the Old Testament*. Bultmann, for instance, finds no place for the Old Testament in his reinterpretation of the kerygma. The Word of God that confronts us in judgement and salvation in the preaching of the Cross stands starkly alone. Of course, the history of the Old Testament period has deeply affected Western civilization and we can gain an 'understanding of existence' from our 'critical dialogue' with the Old Testament books. But the same is true of ancient Greece or Rome. 'The history of Israel is not for Christians the history of revelation.'[1]

There are not a few Christians who might not put their difficulties in the same way, but who would have a sneaking sympathy for Bultmann. They might not want to eliminate the whole Old Testament, but they certainly want to cut down drastically the amount read in Church. The debates in the Convocations of Canterbury and York a few years ago on the Revised Lectionary and the rejection of the proposal to seek statutory authority for it alone in place of all others revealed a sharp clash between those who want to retain the widest selection of Old Testament lections and those who believe that many of those chosen can only be misleading or even what one proctor called 'spiritual junk.'

Such a judgement on various parts of the Old Testament contrasts sharply with the statement of Article VII that 'both in the Old and New Testament everlasting life is offered to mankind by Christ.' That statement goes back in turn to St. Augustine's famous remark, 'In the Old Testament the New lies hidden, and in the New Testament the Old lies open.' St. Augustine's epigram arises from the way which had become

---

[1] Cf. A. Richardson, *The Bible in the Age of Science*, p. 113.

traditional in his day of understanding the relation of the Old Testament to the central truths of the Christian Gospel.

Thus, it was customary to ransack 'the Old Testament for passages which seem to predict the kind of spiritual reign which Christ has in fact established, or which seem to foreshadow his birth, passion and resurrection, or which represent the character of the Messiah as resembling our Lord's, or which anticipate the rejection of the Jews and the call of the Gentiles.' Not merely proof-texts but whole passages in which they were set were thus interpreted as direct prophecies.

There still remained large sections of the Old Testament which could not be so understood. These, too, had to be given a Christian interpretation and the method used was that of allegory, carried often to fantastic lengths; 'the only limits are those set by one's mental dexterity, the fecundity of one's imagination—and what the pious reader will stand.'[1]

As we shall see, there is indeed a correspondence between Old and New Testaments, a relationship of promise and fulfilment, a recapitulation of the history of the old Israel in the new. That is the basic truth which patristic writers were asserting. Within strict limits there may also be a place for allegory. But with their unhistorical approach it was difficult for them to see the process of organic growth and development at work. For them the two Testaments were on a level and, although of course it never happened in the experience of anyone, they seem to have imagined that a person reading the Old Testament aright would in fact find himself faced with the Gospel, even without going on to read the New Testament. The truth is of course different. *Pace* Article VII, the Old Testament does not offer men salvation in Christ, it reveals an unmet need and looks forward in prophecy and vision to a fulfilment of hopes of God's coming Kingdom which are never more than partially and fitfully realized within the Old Testament itself. Everlasting life is offered to men by Christ in the New Testament alone, and the Old Testament can be seen as pointing forward to that climax,

[1] J. N. D. Kelly in D. E. Nineham (ed.), *The Church's Use of the Bible*, p. 47.

only when it is interpreted from our side of the Cross and the Resurrection.

This is, in fact, how the apostolic writers approached the matter. On the one hand, they were confronted with the Figure of Jesus Christ, who had lived and died and risen again for their salvation. They knew in their experience that through him they had been translated from darkness to light, they were no longer slaves but sons who could cry 'Abba, Father,' and with St. Thomas they acknowledged Jesus as 'My Lord and My God.' On the other hand, they were Jews who had inherited the Old Testament as Scripture and who were heirs of the whole revelatory history of Israel from the first promise to Abraham that in his seed would all the families of the earth be blessed. Between the person of Christ and the Scriptures of the old covenant there was an interchange of interpretation, and the apostolic kerygma was the result. Thus, the categories and thought-forms, the imagery and the picture-language of the Old Testament were used, by Jesus himself and still more by the apostolic Church, to explain the significance of his person and mission. At the same time, the fact of Jesus and his particular history involved looking at the Old Testament in a fresh way. The Old Testament came to have a very different appearance when seen as leading up to Jesus of Nazareth, Messiah, Saviour and Lord, from what it had, and has, in the traditional teaching of Jewish orthodoxy.[1]

2

We may distinguish three principles in the Church's approach to the Old Testament, which were at work in the apostolic age and which are always valid.

The first may be called, for want of a better term, *acceptance and presupposition*. By that I mean that the New Testament stands directly in the succession of the distinctive revelation of

---

[1] If A. T. Hanson is right in his book, *Jesus Christ in the Old Testament*, in arguing that the Church of New Testament days believed that Jesus Christ was present and active in the Old Testament story, then the difference between Jewish and Christian interpretation of the Old Testament is all the greater.

God given in the history of old Israel and in the prophetic interpretation of that history. It depends on what has been made
known before and builds on it, without necessarily having to
fight old battles over again. Consider some of the distinctive
elements of that Old Testament revelation. In contrast to the
tribal gods of the peoples around who sank or swam with the
fortunes of their peoples, the Old Testament proclaims the living
God who of his own free will enters into covenant relationship
with Israel, but who is in no way committed to them by any
natural ties. Yahweh is the Creator of heaven and earth, and
psalms such as 19. 1–6 and 105 celebrate the wonders of his
creative handiwork, but he is very different from the Canaanite
baals with their roots in the natural processes of seed-time and
harvest. The sphere of action in which Yahweh most clearly
reveals himself is not nature, but history, and it is significant
that the festivals of new moon and spring time and ingathering
are transformed in Israel's religious life into commemorations of
God's gracious actions in her early history.[1] Yahweh is the
Saviour and King of his people, who rules and guides them
according to his purpose. But he is also a God of righteousness
and holiness, a God whose wrath strikes in judgement when his
people are faithless, who did not hesitate to allow Israel to dis-
appear in exile or Jerusalem to be destroyed, when first the
northern kingdom and then the southern proved faithless. Yet
in the darkest hour prophet and apocalyptist hold out the promise
of a Day when God will act again for the salvation of his people,
when a King will reign in righteousness and the earth shall be
full of the knowledge of the Lord, as the waters cover the sea
(Is. 32. 1; 11. 9).

As the Wisdom writers make clear, God is also immanent in
the world by his word and by his wisdom. When God performed
his creative work, wisdom was beside him 'like a master work-
man.' She is 'a breath of the power of God, and a pure emanation
of the glory of the Almighty' and 'because of her pureness she

[1] A. Richardson, *History Sacred and Profane*, pp. 219–220.

pervades and penetrates all things (Prov. 8. 22–32; Wisd. 7. 24–25).

Correlative with the revelation of God is the picture of the people of God, brought into being by his mighty act of deliverance, often beset by the rise and fall of empires and weakened by its sins, and yet with the assurance that it is still a key part of God's saving purpose for all mankind, which one day will be fulfilled. In this community the individual finds his true place in God's scheme of things. He is made in the image of God, yet fallen. He knows the reality and power of sin, he is given the promise of forgiveness and he looks forward to the day of God's final eschatological victory over all the powers of darkness and evil.

Just because Christians have traditionally taken all this for granted as caught up in and included in the faith of the Gospel, it is worth emphasizing how much of it has direct relevance in non-Christian cultures today.[1] Shinto in Japan, the lower forms of Hinduism in India, the widespread practices of animism in South-East Asia and on the African Continent give the battle between Yahwism and the Canaanite baal-worship a contemporary significance. The prophetic insistence that God abhors the offering of the prescribed cult-worship, when it is regarded as a substitute for justice and honest dealing among men, is relevant to people in many lands who see no connection between the national religion and its rites and the political, economic and social life of the country. Without the Old Testament we should have few clues to help us discern the principles of God's action at work in the world of nations today. Above all, at a time when serious thinkers try to find an escape from materialism in the monism of Hindu thought or the high-minded agnosticism of Theravada Buddhism, or alternatively commit themselves to dialectical materialism or to secular humanism, the deepest affirmations of God's transcendence (in the Old Testament generally) and of his immanence (in the Wisdom Literature in

---

[1] Cf. G. E. Phillips, *The Old Testament in the World Church.*

particular)[1] need to be grasped and proclaimed afresh. The New Testament does not affirm all these things with the same emphasis as the Old, just because it takes them for granted. A Christianity, therefore, which ignores the Old Testament will seriously distort the New, and in all likelihood will end up with a sentimentalized and reduced version of the latter into the bargain.

3

The second principle may be defined as *recapitulation and fulfilment*. If the Event of Christ includes his life, teaching and work, all, that is, which went before his death and resurrection, as well as all that follows after in the gift of his Spirit and the bringing into being of his Church, its significance is made all the greater when it is set in the context of the long history of Israel back to the call of Abraham, and behind that to the creative purpose of God in bringing this whole universe into being. The Event of Christ is thus placed in organic relationship to what took place 'in the beginning,' just as the New Testament looks forward to its culmination in the 'regeneration of all things' at the last day. The God who 'has spoken to us by a Son, whom he appointed the heir of all things, through whom also he created the world' is the same God who 'in many and various ways spoke of old to our fathers by the prophets' (Heb. 1. 1).

One of the evidences for seeing the power of the same God at work in the histories of the two Testaments is the fact that in so many ways the New Testament events recapitulate the Old. There are what Phythian-Adams called 'homologies,' i.e. 'the parallel which is drawn between the divine operation in the First Redemption and in the second.'[2] Just as New Testament scholars have made clear that behind all the apostolic writings there stands the kerygma which interprets the Event of Christ in

---

[1] The impact of the Bishop of Woolwich's *Honest to God* suggests that this is an under-emphasized note in Western, and particularly Protestant, theology which nevertheless 'rings bells' for many brought up in the scientific disciplines of our time.

[2] W. J. Phythian-Adams, *The Way of At-one-ment*, p. 11. Cf. A. G. Hebert, *The Authority of the Old Testament*, pp. 218–219.

terms of God's decisive act of salvation, so Old Testament
scholars have pressed beyond the source-analysis which occupied
so much attention in former generations and shown us that the
authors of the various strata of the Pentateuch and the editors
of Samuel-Kings and of Chronicles are rewriting the history of
Israel in terms relevant to their own environment and age,
yet are basing their work ultimately on the kerygma which
underlies the whole Old Testament.[1] A brief summary of this
kerygma is given in the recital made by people of later days,
when they brought the first fruits of their crops to the sanctuary:

A wandering Aramaean was my father; and he went down into Egypt and
sojourned there, few in number; and there he became a nation, great, mighty
and populous. And the Egyptians treated us harshly, and afflicted us, and laid
upon us hard bondage. Then we cried to the Lord, the God of our fathers,
and the Lord heard our voice, and saw our affliction, our trial and our oppression; and the Lord brought us out of Egypt with a mighty hand and an outstretched arm, with great terror, with signs and wonders; and he brought us
into this place and gave us this land flowing with milk and honey (Deut.
26. 5–9).[2]

Many problems still remain to be solved in regard to the
actual course of historical events. Did all, or only some, Israelites
come out of Egypt through what was regarded as a marvellous
Divine deliverance? What extraneous elements have become
attached to the story of the wanderings in the wilderness? Does
not archaeology make impossible the linking up of the fall of
Jericho and the destruction of Ai with the migration of the tribes
which had crossed the Red Sea under Moses? As with the interpretation of the Gospels, so with the Pentateuch there are radically
different schools of interpretation, with G. von Rad and his
associates adopting the same form-critical and kerygmatic
approach as Bultmann and W. Eichrodt giving greater historical
value to the tradition.

Yet, whatever the final decision in regard to the historicity
of this or that element in the tradition of Israel, there can be no

[1] Cf. A. Richardson, op. cit., pp. 220–221.
[2] Cf. G. Von Rad, Genesis, S.C.M. Commentary, pp. 13–16.

doubt of the historical fact that this is how the tradition came to be rehearsed in later generations. God had chosen them in his inscrutable purpose of love, he had marvellously delivered them and brought them into a covenant relationship with himself, he had supplied them with the manna and water from the stony rock when they were hungry and thirsty, he had guided them with the pillar of cloud by day and the pillar of fire by night, he had enabled them to overcome their enemies, had led them into the promised land and had made the dwelling-place of his presence among them in the inmost sanctuary of the Temple.

Even within the Old Testament itself the fact of 'homology' exists. Jeremiah and the prophets of the Exile look forward to a new exodus, not this time from Egypt, but from all the countries whither he had driven them (Jer. 14. 14 f.), to a new covenant, not to be written this time on tablets of stone, but in the hearts of God's people (Jer. 31. 31–34), to a return of the presence of God to a restored sanctuary, set in the midst of a people recreated by the outpouring of the Spirit of God upon them (Ezek. 43. 2, 4–7 and Ezek. 37).[1]

Such prophecies were never completely fulfilled in Old Testament times. 'All these, though well attested by their faith, did not receive what was promised' (Heb. 11. 39). By contrast, the New Testament claims, the redemption history of Israel is recapitulated in the redemptive work of God in Christ. The great moments of the Old Testament kerygma find their parallel in the New Testament in the Incarnation, Cross and Resurrection of Christ, in the new covenant in his blood with the new Israel to whom the terms used to describe the old Israel can freely be applied (1 Pet. 2. 5 and 9–10), in the gift of the Spirit and the sacraments of baptism and the Eucharist, and in the Church's earthly pilgrimage in the face of many enemies to the heavenly city, the New Jerusalem, which needs no temple, 'for its temple is the Lord God the Almighty and the Lamb' (Rev. 21. 22). Similarly, all the passages in the Old Testament which could be regarded as having a Messianic reference are reinterpreted of

---

[1] A. G. Hebert, op. cit., p. 145.

Jesus Christ, while the prophecies which looked forward to the coming Kingdom of God were regarded as finding at least the beginning of their fulfilment in the Kingdom which Jesus proclaimed and inaugurated. The Epistle to the Hebrews is a long argument designed to show to Jewish Christians in danger of falling back into observance of the Jewish sacrificial system that by the all-sufficient sacrifice of himself in perfect obedience to the Father Jesus Christ, our great high priest, really bridged the gap between sinful man and a holy God, of which the Levitical sacrifices, and supremely the ritual of the Day of Atonement, were an outward but ineffective symbol.

The Old Testament, then, points forward to, illumines and finds its completion in the revelation of the New Testament. The two together make up the story of the people of God. They are, both together, our story and, if Christians can find illumination of their history in the Old Testament, they can also learn from its warnings. God's judgements on old Israel can be repeated in the history of the new people of God, if they are faithless (1 Cor. 10. 1–13). Over us also hangs the possibility of final rejection, 'If God did not spare the natural branches, neither will he spare you' (Rom. 11. 21).

It must be admitted that sometimes Old Testament texts are used woodenly in the New Testament,[1] but generally the apostolic writers are concerned to keep to the main lines of typological parallel between the two Testaments. Unfortunately, many patristic writers and some modern ones have not exercised the same restraint. To judge from some expositions, all New Testament writers were walking Cruden's Concordances: they could not mention a word without every Old Testament use of it being in the back of their minds. We shall certainly miss much of the meaning of Scripture if we do not recognize the place of typology in it, but we shall be wise to restrict our use of it to the same main lines as we find in the Bible.

---

[1] Matthew's correction of Mark in the light of Zechariah's prophecy of 'the ass, and a colt the foal of an ass' is a notable example (Mk. 11. 1–10; Mt. 21. 1–9; Zech. 9. 9).

What of the allegorical or mystical use of the Old Testament? St. Paul admittedly uses this method in an *ad hominem* argument addressed to Judaizers who were familiar with its Rabbinic use (Gal. 4. 21–31). But he uses it to illustrate a truth of the Gospel established on other grounds. This is the acid test. If allegory is used to establish what a passage *really* means (unless, as probably in the case of the book of Jonah, it is so intended by the author), then any passage can be made to mean anything. Thus, Philo was able to read Platonic and Neo-Platonic philosophy into the Pentateuch. The liturgical and devotional use of the *Song of Songs* in the manner of St. Bernard is legitimate, because the imagery of the bridegroom and the bride is used of Yahweh and Israel in the Old Testament, and of Christ and the Church in the New. The parallel use of passages in the Wisdom literature which personify Wisdom as 'mystically true' of the place of the Blessed Virgin Mary in the economy of grace, and as supplying Scriptural support for e.g. the dogma of the Corporal Assumption is not legitimate, for the New Testament contains no plain evidence to support such doctrine, however much it may inspire us to honour our Lord's Mother for her utter dedication and obedience to the will of God.

Mystical interpretation should be kept in strict bounds for a further reason. In our contemporary age men are trained in disciplines which above all impose respect for the evidence. Fanciful allegorizing can suggest to modern man at best something fanciful and unreal, at worst it can look like semantic cheating.[1]

4

The third principle at work is that of *transformation and supersession*. The Old Testament contains a variety of prophecies and hopes of God's coming reign. Some looked forward to a

[1] E. J. Tinsley in a chapter 'Parable, Allegory and Mysticism' in A. T. Hanson (ed.), *Vindications*, argues that there is a greater use of genuine allegory in the Scriptures than most scholars allow and he distinguishes it from the 'naive' allegory referred to above. He points to A. Camus, *The Plague*, and W. Golding, *Lord of the Flies*, as works which make a strong impact on modern man through using the method of genuine allegory.

D

Divine ordering of the course of history which would make the
Jews 'top nation' and Jerusalem a centre showing forth the glory
of God and the perfection of his reign so gloriously that nations
would come to its light and kings to the brightness of its rising
(Is. 60. 3). The Psalms of Solomon, which are contemporary
with the New Testament, show that this hope of national
deliverance from the power of Rome remained powerful, and
the Zealots were advocates of direct action. Others shared the
apocalyptic hope of a divine breaking-in from without, which
would end the present world-order and establish God's kingdom
in a new heaven and a new earth. Schweitzer believed that Jesus
shared this second hope and went to his Cross to force God's
hand.[1] Subsequent New Testament scholarship has not substan-
tiated this view any more than it has upheld Harnack's description
of Jesus' message as essentially one of the fatherhood of God and
of his kingdom within men's hearts. The Kingdom of God as
proclaimed and inaugurated by Jesus Christ has affinities with
Jewish hopes, yet radically transforms them.

Similarly with the mission of Jesus as Messiah. There are
obvious links both with prophetic hopes of a King who would
reign in righteousness and with apocalyptic hopes of a son of
Man who would come on the clouds of heaven. But Jesus was
no passive figure carrying out to the letter a clearly defined
programme laid down for the Messiah in the Old Testament.
Had he been that, the Jews would not have crucified him.
What we find in the Gospels and in the kerygma is the proclamation of One who takes the Old Testament imagery and transforms
it. A Messianic King who came to his glory by fulfilling the role
of the Suffering Servant—this was something radically new and a
stumbling block of the first order to the old Israel.

The Gospels, too, point to One who both in teaching and,
when need arose, in action showed himself Master over the Law.
To the Scribes the Pentateuch was like the Ark of the Covenant,
God's infallible word for his people. Their task was to expound
it and elaborate its provisions by an extended system of casuistry

[1] Cf. *The Quest of the Historical Jesus, passim.*

to the constantly changing circumstances of people's lives. But Jesus spoke 'as one who had authority and not as their Scribes' (Mt. 7. 29). He could act as 'Lord even of the Sabbath' (Mk. 2. 28). At the heart of the teaching material which the first Gospel brings together in the Sermon on the Mount is the constantly reiterated 'It was said . . . but I say to you.' The whole series of traditional moral and ceremonial laws which derived ultimately from Moses had become in its fully developed form after the Exile a unified code imposing far-spreading obligations on all faithful Jews. Jesus fulfils, and supersedes it all. Love of God and, springing from that, love of one's neighbour—this is the basic requirement of Christ. Unlike some expositions of the 'New Morality,' that does not involve for his followers any less obligation than the Law imposed, but infinitely more. Jesus presses his hearers back behind the observance of law *imposed as law* to the inner springs of life—behind the act of murder to the angers and resentments which are its cause, behind the act of adultery to the lustful desires which have been nurtured, behind current Jewish practice of divorce to the Divine purpose in creation of an enduring union of one man with one woman, behind permission for revenge and encouragement of neighbourly conduct within certain limits to the spirit of unlimited forgiveness and all-embracing neighbourliness.

We are here out of the realm of law altogether and confronted with far more searching demands that only bring upon us added condemnation. But we are out of the realm of law also in the Gospel of God's free acceptance of us in forgiveness and renewal at the Cross of Christ. Justification by Divine grace received through faith and not by the works of the Law is at the heart of the kerygma and St. Paul defends it on the ground that it is a resassertion of the relationship of grace and faith established between God and Abraham (Rom. 4). The Law was a temporary measure, but its day is now over. The character and conduct of a Christian is not something by which he earns salvation, it is the fruit of a new relationship freely granted by God in Christ. Thus, in the one place where St. Paul refers to the Decalogue he goes on to say, as Jesus had done, 'The commandments . . . are summed up in this sentence, "You shall love your neighbour as yourself." Love does no wrong to a neighbour; therefore love is the fulfilling of the law' (Rom. 13. 9–10). No doubt in working out the implications of the sovereign demands of Love the apostolic Church drew on Old Testament ethical teaching interpreted in a Christian sense, just as it borrowed from Stoic and other pagan writers, but 'what is striking is the degree to which the distinctiveness of the "in the Lord" permeates and sets its stamp upon the Christian ethical instruction. It is against membership in the Christian community that conduct is tested.'[1]

It is no wonder that converts from a dissolute background should be tempted to interpret the liberty of the Gospel as licence or that conservative Jewish-Christians should have been shocked by such dangerous 'liberalism.' It is possible to see the influence of the latter on such a passage as Matthew 5. 18 and 19, which is so strangely at variance with the main emphasis of the Sermon on the Mount; and of course the Epistle to the Galatians reveals clearly the lengths to which such Jewish-Christians could go in resisting the lifting of the requirements of the Law from converts, Jewish or Gentile. That parts of the Old Testament should be superseded was quite beyond their spiritual grasp.

5

What does all this involve for *the use of the Old Testament, particularly in the services of the Church today?* Obviously the passages which fall into the first two categories above have a rightful place, and a lectionary will be designed to help worshippers grasp the essential elements of the Old Testament revelation through the 'salvation history' of the old Israel. Yet there are problems to be faced. For the way in which a crucially important element of the kerygma is told may itself be a stumbling block. No one can doubt, for instance, the basic

---

[1] Cf. C. F. D. Moule, *The Birth of the New Testament*, p. 135. The whole context is important.

importance of the deliverance from Egypt in the faith of the Old Testament and in its typological significance for the New. It foreshadows God's mightier victory over the powers of evil in the Cross and the Resurrection of Christ and so provides appropriate lections for Easter-tide. Yet the story of the plagues of Egypt and of the drowning of the Egyptian horsemen as told in Exodus implies that each disaster for Israel's enemy was the direct and immediate will of God. The Hebrew mind could not distinguish between purpose and consequence, nor was it able to separate the ultimate will and purpose of God from his providential over-ruling of a given situation, in order to bring good out of evil and make even the wrath of man to praise him. It was this difficulty which led to such strong protests in Canterbury Convocation against the provision of Exodus 14 as the only choice for the first lesson at Evensong on Easter Day every year. Certainly passages need to be chosen with extraordinary care for our literal-minded congregations today, and not a few should be read only on condition that they are prefaced by some explanatory comments.

What of the parts of the Old Testament that fall into the third category? Some fall so far below the Christian standard that in my judgement we should recognize frankly that they have been superseded. I entirely agree with C. F. D. Moule[1] that the ordinary Christian ought not to be asked to recite the imprecatory psalms, for instance, for I believe that he is not capable of the mystical or poetical heights to which a Fr. Hebert or a C. S. Lewis can attain. This is not to lapse into sentimentality or minimize the Biblical emphasis on Divine judgement. But there are better ways of stressing that note than by expecting worshippers to recite such verses as Psalm 109 vs. 15–19, which breathe the very spirit Christ called his followers to transcend (Mt. 5. 43–48).

There are other passages in this group, however, which can help people just because they meet them where they are with their

---

[1] 'Understandest thou what thou singest?' Art. in *Theology*, vol. LXI, 1958, pp. 405–408.

inadequate hopes and partial understandings. The book of Job, for example, is quite inadequate as an 'answer' to the problem of innocent suffering, but it raises the problem at a level where many people wrestle with it. The measures of an Ezra may be harsh and repellent, but they speak of one necessary element in the Church's life—withdrawal from the world, however far short they may fall in their failures to stress the other side—involvement in the world, 'holy worldliness.' Like the Law, they may serve as the 'paidagogus', the slave who brings the children to school and whose task is then done (Gal. 3. 25-26). Provided they are placed in the right context for the hearer (and that condition is essential), they too may serve as the means by which bewildered men and women may be brought through doubt and perplexity to the feet of Christ.

III. SCRIPTURE, TRADITION AND REASON

I

THE third matter for discussion is the relationship of *Scripture, Tradition and Reason*. This may seem a hoary and well-worn subject, but it is very much a live issue at the present time. The Majority Report of the Anglican-Methodist Conversations contains a whole chapter on the subject (ch. 2), in the course of which it quotes approvingly a sentence from the *Interim Statement* to the effect that 'there is room for diversity of interpretation and for differing estimates of the light which history, tradition and learning may throw upon the meaning of God's Word' (p. 17). By contrast, the Dissentient Report commits itself to a sharp—in my view far too sharp—distinction between Scripture and Tradition. 'Tradition' it says 'represents the worldliness of the Church, Scripture points it to its supernatural origin and basis' (p. 58). Conservative Evangelicals in the Church of England have generally favoured the latter point of view.[1]

At the same time the relation of Scripture and Tradition and the extent to which the critical study of the Bible may be pursued with approval in the Roman Catholic Church were subjects of sharp discussion and division at the first session of the Vatican Council. Robert Kaiser in the chapter of his book *Inside the Council* entitled 'The Winds of Change,' recounts the background tussles over the years between the Biblical scholars associated with the Pontifical Biblical Institute who knew that the old 'fundamentalist' approach to the Scriptures was no longer possible and the Curialist conservatives who were concerned that traditionalist ways should prevail. These struggles came to a head in the critical debate on the *schema* on Revelation in the first session. This *schema* maintained the Counter-Reformation distinction between Scripture and Tradition as the two sources of revelation, and upheld a view of the Bible which depreciated modern Biblical scholarship.

[1] Cf. J. I. Packer (ed.), *The Church of England and the Methodist Church, passim.*

'Its adoption,' said Cardinal Bea, 'would close the door to intellectual Europe and the outstretched hands of friendship in the Old
and the New World.' As for the chapter on the two sources of
revelation, sixteen Fathers spoke against it, 'pointing out the
impossibility of separating Scripture and tradition and the need for
the interpretation of the two.'[1] In the end Pope John withdrew
the entire *schema*, so that it might be rewritten by a Commission
representing not just the post-Tridentine traditionalists, but the
Biblical theologians who believe that much light has been shed
on the Scriptures through the Spirit's working in scholars outside as well as within the Rome obedience. The *schema* finally
adopted at the third session gives full opportunity for the new
influences to make themselves felt over the next generation.
Scripture, Tradition and Reason are a lively subject for discussion
in the Roman Catholic Church today.

It is also worth noting that 'Tradition and the Traditions' was
one of the subjects discussed at the Faith and Order Conference
in Montreal in 1963. Moreover, it is clear that, as the Church of
England takes up the task of revising the Book of Common
Prayer, much will depend on the underlying assumptions which
church members have in regard to the relation of the three
elements. An approach based on the majority view of the
Anglican-Methodist Report will produce different results from
one based on the dissentient standpoint.

We begin our consideration of this subject with *the period of
the Reformation*. There is no doubt that the English Reformers
and those of the Continent were at one in asserting the supreme
and sole authority of Scripture in 'all things necessary to salvation,'
i.e. in essential doctrines. We have already made reference
to Article VI and to the questions addressed to those about to be
ordained to the sacred ministry or consecrated to the episcopate.
Similarly, Article VIII asserts that the three Creeds (Nicene,
Athanasius's and the Apostles') 'ought thoroughly to be received
and believed; for they may be proved by most certain warrants
of Holy Scripture.' The Church has authority in the ordering

[1] *Op. cit.*, pp. 159 and 172.

of worship and in settling controversies of faith, but this authority is subject to 'God's word written,' the Church itself being 'a witness and keeper of Holy Writ,' not a body with power to make other doctrines matters of essential faith (Art. XX). General Councils have authority, only in so far as their conclusions are 'taken out of Holy Scripture' (Art. XXI).

These Articles were directed at the Council of Trent currently sitting, and owe some of their wording to that fact. In particular they were aimed at Trent's declaration on Scripture and Tradition, first made in 1546. After affirming that the truth and discipline of the Gospel of Christ 'are contained in written books and unwritten traditions' which have come down from apostolic times, that declaration continued, 'this Synod receives and venerates, with equal pious affection and reverence, all the books both of the New and the Old Testaments . . . together with the said Traditions, as well those pertaining to faith as those pertaining to morals. . . .'[1]

The issue was clear-cut, yet, as C. F. Evans has pointed out, the actual position of the Roman Catholic Church has been both better and worse than the declaration of Trent, which has been the orthodoxy of Roman Catholic seminaries for four centuries. On the one hand, 'it is surprisingly difficult to discover what precisely these traditions are.' The theologians are 'remarkably fugitive, even coy, about the matter' and usually come up with some such tradition as the Christian observance of Sunday as a day of worship. On the other hand, 'the practical uselessness of the decree of Trent is indicated by the more recent dogmas pronounced by the Church of Rome, in which the attempt to find their basis in such unwritten traditions handed down in unbroken succession is frankly abandoned, and the place of traditions is taken by tradition, understood now as that which is believed by the present consensus of the faithful.' The Roman Catholic Church has been in grave danger of becoming 'what Abbé Loisy was excommunicated for saying it was . . . the greatest mystery religion of all time, which lives not by any

[1] H. Bettenson, *Documents of the Christian Church*, p. 365.

faithfulness to a Jesus of history but by the worship of the Son of God and by sacraments which produce saints.'[1] Nothing can be more important for the Roman Catholic Church's witness to the Gospel or for the ultimate unity of Christendom than that the strong revival of Biblical and patristic studies which has made itself so powerfully felt in the sessions of the Vatican Council should effectively checkmate the dangerous tendencies to cut the links with Christian history.

The Churches which passed through the Reformation were emphatic about the supreme authority of the Scriptures, because for their leaders so much of the teaching and practice of the medieval and the contemporary Roman Catholic Church contradicted the plain witness of the Bible. The Gospel was good news of a Divine act of deliverance through Christ from the guilt and power of sin, to be received in faith, but for ordinary Christians it had been transformed into an elaborate system of law, by which with the help of God and the performance of correct rites men could achieve salvation. The uniqueness and perfection of Christ's saving work was undermined by current teaching that the Mass was a propitiatory sacrifice for the living and the dead, in which in some sense Christ was immolated afresh. The fullness of God's forgiveness was denied by the teaching that while a sinner could be released in a moment from the guilt of his sins through the grace of God, yet he still had to suffer the punishment due for them—hence the doctrine of Purgatory as a place of penal suffering. The sale of Indulgences and the endowing of private Masses to shorten the time one would have to endure oneself or one's loved ones would have to endure before admission to Heaven had come suspiciously close to suggesting that salvation was something obtainable for money down. Legends and superstitions about the Saints, real or mythical, abounded and had come to overlay the elementary facts of the Gospel.

Yet it must also be emphasized that in the great central affirmations of the Christian faith the Reformers were at one with

---

[1] Cf. *On the Authority of the Bible*, p. 75.

the Roman Catholic and the Orthodox Churches. There was no repudiation of the doctrines of the Incarnation and the Trinity, no denial of man's fallenness nor of God's provision of a way of salvation (however much their exposition might differ), no rejection of the doctrine of Church and sacraments (however much their teaching and practice might vary), no refusal to look beyond this life to the ultimate realities of heaven and hell. Reformers such as Luther, Calvin or Cranmer were profound students of the Fathers and of the Church of the first centuries. Thus (to take one example) 'Calvin set himself to study the exposition of the Fathers in order to let the understanding of the ancient Catholic Church guide him in developing and ordering the positive content of the Christian faith unhindered by the "speculative notions" and "sophistical dialectics" with which theology had been corrupted in medieval scholasticism.'[1]

The Reformers' appeal to Scripture was, in fact, the appeal to Scripture as received by the 'ancient Catholic Church.' It was an appeal to the first ages of the Church over against medieval assertions and superstitions. It was an appeal which contrasted with that of the Anabaptist groups and which contrasts sharply with that of the many Protestant sects which still continue to mushroom, all of which have this in common, that they believe that 'Christianity is the religion of a book, a collection of infallible oracles capable of use apart from the Church.'[2] The one basic difference between them is that each sect believes that its founder alone had the key to the true interpretation of this infallible book.

2

We now turn to *the Anglican position*. Certainly the Church of England, along with its emphasis on the supremacy of Scripture, has always set the Bible in the context of the life of the Church of the first centuries. One of the Homilies speaks of the first Six Councils as 'received of all men.' When Jewel published

[1] T. F. Torrance, *A Calvin Treasury*, Intro., p. vii.
[2] *Anglican-Methodist Conversations Report*, p. 15.

in 1562 his famous *Apologia pro Ecclesia Anglicana* against the attacks of Rome, his appeal was to the Scriptures and the first six centuries. Those responsible for the drawing up of the Articles in their final form were also responsible for the *Reformatio Legum Ecclesiasticarum*, published in the same year 1571, though the latter never received authorization. In that document the commissioners stated, 'We embrace and hold with great reverence the four General Councils of Nicaea, Constantinople, Ephesus and Chalcedon.' One cannot but regret that this statement, positive and of abiding value, was not included in Article XXI. The negative opening sentence of that Article is understandable against the background of Trent, but quite indefensible on any Scriptural grounds as a general principle, and now obsolete. Convocation did, however, pass a Canon in the same year directing the clergy in their preaching to 'see that they never teach ought in a sermon, to be religiously held and believed by the people except what is agreeable to the doctrine of the Old and New Testaments and what the Catholic Fathers and ancient bishops have collected from the same doctrine.'

If the Church of England had to fight a battle against Rome on the one side and the Anabaptists on the other, as the Reformers had to do on the Continent of Europe, it soon had to fight a battle with those at home who regarded it as inadequately Reformed. The Articles were attacked for not asserting decisively enough the distinctive tenets of Calvinism, and the view was put forth with increasing emphasis that the authority of Scripture extended, not just to doctrines 'required of necessity for salvation,' but to the forms of worship, the use of traditional customs, and the pattern of the ministry.[1] There was a hard struggle to retain the use of the cope in cathedrals and even the surplice

---

[1] History repeated itself at the National Assembly of Evangelicals in October 1966, when a resolution was proposed, affirming the supreme authority and sufficiency of the Bible in all matters of Church doctrine and Church government. There was an Anglican amendment to delete the words 'and Church government' on the historic sixteenth-century ground that Scripture does not lay down a blueprint for the ministry, and that the threefold historic ministry is 'not repugnant' to the teaching of the New Testament. The amendment was defeated, and the original resolution carried by a large majority—perhaps a pointer to the composition of the Assembly.

'that rag of Popery' in parish churches, let alone the requirements of the Ornaments Rubric. There was a battle royal over the retention of liturgical worship, ceremonies such as bowing at the name of Jesus, the Sign of the Cross in Baptism and the wedding-ring in marriage. Above all, there was a clamour that the historic threefold ministry of bishop, priest and deacon should be replaced by the complete Presbyterian system, as practised in Geneva.

In fairness to the Puritans who made these demands it must be said that their main concern was for a truly spiritual ministry in a Church which was showing clear signs of the trials through which it had passed and in which most of the bishops were still very prelatical and many of the parish clergy illiterate and worldly. Though standards rose through Elizabeth's reign, far too many had been ordained without any proper testing of vocation or training.[1] Yet at a deeper level there was a fundamental difference in temper. The characteristically Puritan cast of mind wanted to break the links with the past and start afresh on a new basis, determined entirely by its own understanding of the pure Word of God. The characteristically Anglican spirit was anxious to correct abuses, and to recognize the supreme authority of Scripture in essential doctrines, but in face of Puritan attacks increasingly determined to retain customs and traditions of the past, provided they were 'not repugnant' to the Word of God. In these matters the Church had authority (Art. XX), and the Church of England exercised that authority in a way that showed her continuity with the Church of ancient times.

The great expounder of the Anglican position as distinct from that of the Puritans was Richard Hooker in his *Laws of Ecclesiastical Polity*. Hooker had no doubt that the Word of God is to be found supremely in the Scriptures, but this Word is not to be thought of in isolation. There is a divine Law by which God upholds all things, and this Law man can grasp and obey in some measure by that faculty of Reason, 'the director of man's

[1] S. C. Neill, *Anglicanism*, pp. 126–128.

will by discovering in action what is good' (1, VII, 4). God's supreme Word in Scripture is to be set, then, in a wider context than that of the Scriptures alone. Furthermore, the authority of Scripture must be seen as extending only to 'things unto salvation necessary.' 'The testimonies of God are true ... perfect ... all-sufficient *unto that end for which they were given*' (2, VIII, 5, my italics). If Rome has erred by not accepting that all-sufficiency, the Puritans have grown to a dangerous extremity, 'as if Scripture did not only contain all things in that kind necessary, but all things simply.' And Hooker adds a solemn warning, 'We must ... take great heed, lest in attributing unto Scripture more than it can have, the incredibility of that do cause even those things which indeed it hath most abundantly to be less reverently esteemed' (2, VIII, 7). It is on that basis that Hooker builds his defence of the continuance of those practices and institutions in the Church of England which the Puritans wanted removed, either because they had no direct Scriptural warrant or because they approximated too closely to Rome.

Hooker thus established on a broad philosophical and Scriptural foundation the characteristic Anglican appeal to Scripture as interpreted, not in terms of a narrow Biblicism but in the context of the historic Church, not in terms of a book miraculously fallen from heaven, but in the context of God's wider revelation in the order of nature and in the moral law. Scripture, Tradition and Reason all have a place in the Anglican understanding of Authority,[1] and there can be no doubt that this threefold appeal, together with the practice of regular liturgical worship through the Book of Common Prayer, helped the Anglican Church to ride the storm of nineteenth-century Biblical criticism better than some other Christian bodies.

---

[1] The historical position of the Church of England is well summed up in Canons A3 and A5, 'The doctrine contained in *The Book of Common Prayer and Administration of the Sacraments and other Rites and Ceremonies of the Church according to the Use of the Church of England* is agreeable to the Word of God. The form of God's Worship contained in the said Book ... is not repugnant to the Word of God ...' (A3). 'The doctrine of the Church of England is grounded in the Holy Scriptures and in such teachings of the ancient Fathers and Councils of the Church as are agreeable to the said Scriptures ...' (A5).

3

We must now try to evaluate *the situation today* in the light of the modern study of the Bible and, as we do so, we shall find all three factors at work. First, we must recognize that modern scholarship has made clearer than ever before the close links between the Bible and the people of God. In the era of the old Israel there were first the 'mighty acts' in which God was seen to be at work delivering his people from Egypt, entering into covenant relationship with them and giving them the beginnings of a moral code. As the generations passed, worshippers at the shrines recited a credal form of thanksgiving in which they declared God's mighty works of old.[1] Prophets, called by God from among them, interpreted the meaning of their history and spoke the word of judgement and salvation. Lawgivers elaborated the moral and ceremonial codes to fit changing circumstances. Psalmists composed the hymns that formed part of the worship of the Second Temple. Wisdom writers reflected on the workings of Divine Wisdom in the world at large and in the kind of character God required of his servants. Apocalyptists joined their visions to those of the prophets, as they also looked forward to the coming Day of the Lord.

But only after centuries of Israel's history were the documents which enshrined God's word to his people through the centuries collected and given the sort of authority that belongs to the word 'Scripture' so that subsequent generations might enter in a vital way into the heritage of the people of God. The Pentateuch received its final shape in the fourth century B.C., the Prophets later still, and the Writings not until the Christian era. Indeed, the different attitudes adopted in different Churches to the Apocrypha bear witness to the fact that even now there has been no final reconciliation of the Hebrew and the Greek Canons.

The position is no different in regard to the New Testament. There was first the coming of Christ, his life, death and resurrection, and in response the new redeemed community of the

---

[1] See p. 28 above.

Church which knew the power of his Spirit. It was from this community that the apostles and the missionaries proclaimed the kerygma—the good news that in Christ the Old Testament prophecies were fulfilled, and that through him God had wrought the salvation of the world and brought into being a new people of God, in which Jew and Gentile alike shared a common inheritance in Christ. It is with this new community in its developing life and witness as the instrument of God's universal purpose that the entire New Testament is concerned. 'The analysis of the Scriptures' writes C. F. Evans, 'has made us aware of the continuing life of the Church in the first century as the very motive out of which it has pleased God to give us his word. We are made aware that the Scriptures contain patterns of preaching, forms of catechetical instruction, embryo creeds, which have already taken shape and been formulated before the writers in whose writings they now appear put pen to paper. There is evidence that the liturgical worship of the Church has already had something to do with moulding what we are reading.'[1] It is significant, too, that C. F. D. Moule's *The Birth of the New Testament* should have as its chapter headings the titles 'The Church at Worship,' 'The Church Explains Itself,' 'The Church Under Attack,' 'Building the Superstructure and Consolidating,' 'Variety and Uniformity in the Church.' And to this can be added the testimony of John Knox: 'New Testament scholarship has for a generation been saying in effect: "What we have in the New Testament is a record and reflection of the life and thought of the early Church . . . What confronts us immediately and directly in the New Testament documents is simply and only the primitive community—what it remembered, what it knew, what it thought, what it felt." '[2] We may want to qualify that statement and add that under the guidance of the Spirit what the early Church 'remembered' was the truth about Jesus and what it knew, thought and felt was a Divinely inspired grasp of and response to the God-given Gospel, yet the fact remains that what God gave was given in the context of the

---

[1] *Op. cit.*, p. 77.   [2] *The Church and the Reality of Christ*, p. 9.

developing life of the Church. The New Testament is in fact the Church's tradition at the fountain-head, the stream as it begins to flow.

That brings me to the second main point. Neither the Old Testament nor the New are static documents, nor is it possible to harmonize everything within them. Certainly there is an over-arching unity, but within that unity considerable varieties of interpretation of the Word and Acts of the living God. In the Old Testament the prophetic understanding of Israel's history is not the same as the priestly, the rigorism of Nehemiah and Ezra contrasts with the universalism of Ruth and Jonah, prophetic visions of the coming kingdom of God differ from those of apocalyptists. The different parts of the Old Testament refract something of the glory of God, but sometimes the light is partial and sometimes dimmed as it passes through the minds of men who belong very much to their times and who see the truth of God from different standpoints.

With the unveiling of the glory of God in the face of Jesus Christ a new era in Divine revelation began. Within the life and fellowship of the Church Christians discovered under the Spirit's guidance more and more of the unsearchable riches of Christ. The concept of the Kingdom of God, so prominent in the Synoptic Gospels, passed into the concept of eternal life in the Fourth Gospel. The categories in which Christians sought to describe their Saviour and Lord were again and again found to be inadequate, and we can trace the progression from Rabbi through Messiah and Son of God to the Cosmic Agent of Creation in Colossians and the Logos of St. John. The redeeming character of his death and resurrection was expounded through a variety of metaphors, some used by one author and some by another. The Spirit, first thought of as a Divine influence, came to be recognized as an intensely personal presence, through which men and women were incorporated into Christ. The significance of the Church of Christ grew, as experience of the new life in the Spirit deepened. The expectation of Christ's coming in glory on the clouds of heaven within the lifetime of the

E

first generation gave place to the Fourth Gospel's emphasis on Christ already come again in the coming of the Spirit, on the Lucan expectation of a long era of missionary expansion and on the vision of the Epistle to the Ephesians of a Divinely worked-out cosmic and universal purpose.

As the Church began to face the problems of the second generation, so it began to adapt and order its life. Baptism was extended to the children of believers. The Eucharist was separated from the Agape. Apostolic emissaries such as Timothy and Titus settled for a period in certain churches. A standard of conduct for the settled ministry began to be worked out. So the books which had apostolic authorship or at least apostolic sponsorship and which preserved the orthodox teaching began to be collected to safeguard the purity of the Gospel, as the Church faced the attacks of Gnosticism, and finally after doubts and divisions of opinion the Canon of the New Testament was completed and closed, though not finally till the fourth century.

It is a mistake, however, to make an absolutely sharp distinction between canonical and uncanonical books. The great majority of them, of course, have an unquestioned supremacy, they are 'the cradle wherein Christ is laid,' to quote Luther's famous comment. Yet Luther could be critical of elements in the Epistle of James and in Revelation, and Calvin doubted the authenticity of 2 Peter, James and Jude. 2 Peter, which is just as pseudonymous as the Gospel of Peter, 'got in by mistake.'[1] It is clear that the stream of tradition flowed on, with books that hovered on the edge and finally got into the Canon shading off into those that hovered on the edge and finally were excluded. 'The Bible is now as it were open at both ends. Emerging from a mist of legend at one end, departing in a haze of apostolic pseudo-nymity at the other, the canon of Scripture can hardly be taken by us with that deadly seriousness with which our forefathers have taken it.'[2]

[1] J. N. Sanders, *Peake's Commentary*, New Edition, para. 594d, p. 680.
[2] C. F. Evans, *op. cit.*, p. 77.

4

What does all this involve for our understanding of *the relation between the Bible and tradition*? Essentially, I believe, that there is a two-way traffic between them. The Bible is rightly interpreted only when it is approached from within the life of the Church, when the evidence of the sub-apostolic age, in particular, is used to help us see which of the developing elements of faith and practice passed into the life of the Church, and in what form, and which ran out into the sand. It is failure to approach the Scriptures in this way which has led the Seventh Day Adventists, for instance, to cling to the Sabbath and the Mormons to practise baptism for the dead. By contrast, the Creeds not only provide us with a convenient summary of the teaching of the Bible, but also enable us 'to understand the scriptural teaching without going through the long and painful search which was a necessary preliminary to the Church's foundations.' The Evangelicals who said this in their Report to the Archbishop of Canterbury, *The Fulness of Christ*, went on to say that to do justice to this 'catholic emphasis,' Article VIII, 'requires supplementing by a positive statement of the value and use of the Creeds, such as that of the Church of South India which accepts them not merely as consonant with the biblical faith but "as witnessing to and safeguarding that faith." '[1] This is the way of approach to the Scriptures which has received remarkable confirmation from the modern study of the Bible.

But the traffic is two-way. As Archbishop Laud expressed it, 'the key that lets me in to the Scripture is the tradition of the Church; but when men are in, they hear Christ himself immediately speaking in Scripture to the faithful, and his sheep not only hear but know his voice.'[2] Whatever 'rough edges' there may be on the boundaries of both Old and New Testament Canons, the great central books bring us into touch with the 'mighty acts' of God and with the response of faith, life and witness that they produced in the Old Israel and in the apostolic

[1] *Op. cit.*, p. 80.   [2] *Conference with Fisher*. XVI. Works, Vol. 2, p. 115.

generation of the New. They do not give us 'a collection of inerrant propositions and irreformable demands and prohibitions, guaranteed by their direct divine origin as timelessly valid and universally binding'—a view of the Bible which, as D. E. Nineham points out, 'anyone who takes part in the meetings of the synods of the various Churches as they attempt to lay down "the biblical norms" of orthodoxy and Christian behaviour must be aware (is still) very much alive.'[1] Rather, they bring us into touch with the living God himself, as he condescends to make himself known through human agents of a particular age and as he reaches down to our level in the humility of the incarnate life of Christ through which he reconciled the world to himself. It is as we immerse ourselves in the Scriptures, using all the resources of modern scholarship, seeing the books of the Bible in their historical perspective, and at the same time tasting and seeing that the Lord is gracious, that we come to know God and not just truths about him.

It is from that living contact, renewed in every generation in fresh study of the Scriptures, in the life of worship and in the fellowship of the Christian Church, that we test the Church's developing tradition. Of it we ask at each stage, not 'is there a text in Scripture explicitly affirming this?' but 'taking Scripture as a whole, is this a development which expresses the truth of God as revealed in the Bible in proper balance, or is it a development which perverts that revelation?' The justification of Infant Baptism does not depend on whether there were or were not children included in the household of the Philippian jailer, but on whether, taking the entire New Testament picture of Christ as the Second Adam, the Head of a new humanity, this is a legitimate development. Prayers for the faithful departed do not stand or fall by whether Onesiphorus was already dead when the prayer of 2 Timothy 1. 18 was penned, but on the general teaching of the New Testament about the state of the redeemed between death and the final consummation of all things, as that has to be understood in a day when in contrast to the expectation

---

[1] *The Church's Use of the Bible*, pp. 147 and 148.

of the Parousia in the first generation, two millenia of Christian history have now almost passed. The threefold ministry of bishop, priest and deacon does not depend on whether it can be historically proved that bishops succeeded the apostles in every case by an unbroken sequence of ordinations, but on whether or not we are led to see in the universal acceptance of the threefold ministry the same guidance of the Spirit as we see at work in the delimitation of the Canon of the New Testament, because in fact the pattern of the bishop as chief shepherd under Christ of his flock best reflects the intensely personal relationships of the New Testament.

As the Lambeth Conference 1958 Committee on 'The Holy Bible: Its Authority and Message' said:

'The Anglican Communion appeals to the whole of that primitive tradition of which the Sacraments, the Creeds, the Canon of the Bible, and the historic episcopate are all parts. The New Testament is thus not to be seen in isolation: the Church preceded it in time, and it was within the Church, with its Sacraments, Creeds and Apostolic Ministry, that the New Testament was canonized. The Church is the witness and keeper of Holy Writ, charged to interpret it and expound it by the aid of the Spirit of truth which is in the Church. But on the other hand the Church is not "over" the Holy Scriptures, but "under" them, in the sense that the process of canonization was not one whereby the Church conferred authority on the books, but one whereby the Church acknowledged them to possess authority. And why? The books were recognized as giving the witness of the Apostles to the life, teaching, death, and resurrection of the Lord and the interpretation by the Apostles of those events. To that apostolic authority the Church must ever bow.' Thus, 'in the formation of the Canon of the New Testament, the books which composed it were added to the Canon of the Old Testament, as it came to be accepted as authoritative in the Church.'[1]

To that extended quotation may be added some words of the Report of the Montreal Conference on Faith and Order in 1963, which were endorsed in the Nottingham Conference Section I Report the following year. 'We exist as Christians by the Tradition of the Gospel . . . *testified in Scripture*, transmitted in and by the Church through the power of the Holy Spirit. . . .

[1] Lambeth Conference 1958 Report, 2, 4 and 5.

By the Tradition is meant the Gospel itself, transmitted from generation to generation in and by the Church, *Christ himself present in the life of the Church.*'[1]

[1] *Unity Begins at Home*, pp. 59–61. The final words of the quotation were placed in italics by the Nottingham Conference section concerned.

THE CREEDS

The Apostles' Creed, as the Baptismal Symbol; and the Nicene Creed, as the sufficient statement of the Christian Faith

INTRODUCTION

On August 8th, 1964, *The Times* gave pride of place among its leading articles to one with the title 'Honest or Not.' The article was ostensibly a comment on the annual conference just concluded of the Modern Churchmen's Union, which had taken as its subject, 'Symbols for the Sixties,' but it was concerned with all attempts to restate the historic Christian faith, from the liberalism of a generation ago with its questioning of the Virgin Birth and the Empty Tomb to the far more radical reconstruction of the Bishop of Woolwich's *Honest to God*, which is 'presented in terms so far removed from supernatural religion as it has been believed that it would be more correctly styled a form of pantheistic humanism.' 'There must appear something fundamentally false,' said *The Times*, 'about (a man who cannot accept the entire Creed *ex animo*) who will recite the Nicene Creed at the head of his congregation.'

The article naturally won strong support from conservative churchmen, but its basic position was equally strongly questioned by those who, like Miss Violet Wilkinson, Lecturer in the Teaching of Religion at Oxford, believe that it is important to 'distinguish between truth and the words in which truth has been traditionally expressed.'[1] Thus, the Bishop of Birmingham, then President of the M.C.U., challenged 'the primary assumption' of the article 'that Christianity was once and fully delivered in unalterable formularies. It is assumed to be of no account that with time some of these formularies become difficult to understand, and some impossible to accept.' The Bishop then proceeded to throw down the gauntlet. 'When a clergyman recites a form of words more than 16 centuries old he commits himself to an acceptance of its general intention. He is not supposed to be committing himself to a literal affirmation of each individual statement, such as would be expected in a personal affidavit.' But he made clear that few, if any, members of the M.C.U.

[1] Quoted from a letter to *The Times* in July, 1963, in *The Honest to God Debate*, p. 23.

go beyond the permissible limits of loyal membership of the Church of England, as proposed by the Doctrinal Commission.[1] The alternatives, it is clear, are not just credal fundamentalism on the one hand and the radical theology of what might be called the Robinson-Van Buren-Wren-Lewis axis on the other.

This then is the contemporary context in which the Lambeth Quadrilateral statement about the Creeds must be considered. First, however, it is important to remind ourselves briefly of their great weight of authority. Both the Apostles' and Nicene Creeds have their origin in the instruction given to candidates for Baptism. They are to 'be regarded as a by-product of the Church's fully developed catechetical system.'[2] The beginnings of such creeds are to be found in the New Testament itself, which contains a number of examples of miniature creeds,[3] and it was from such beginnings that the Old Roman Creed grew, and still later the Apostles' Creed in the Western Church. Since the eighth century it has formed part of the Baptismal rites of the Latin West, but from the time of its final redaction it has fulfilled a wider function and formed part of the divine office. Words used by St. Augustine at an earlier period applied with even greater force when the form of the Creed was finally determined. 'Say the creed daily' he told his people. 'When you rise, when you compose yourself to sleep, repeat your creed, render it to the Lord, remind yourself of it, be not irked to say it over.'[4]

At the Reformation the authority of the Apostles' Creed was recognized by Luther, Calvin and Zwingli, and was rejected only by Anabaptists. In the Church of England it received unusual prominence through its recitation twice daily in Mattins and Evensong, and the suspicion with which it was once regarded in Orthodox circles as a purely Western *symbolum fidei* has long since gone. 'Its prestige has been enhanced and extended by its acknowledgement by several ecumenical gatherings as a uniquely authoritative statement of Christian belief.' Not only was reference to the Apostles' as well as the Nicene Creed included in

---

[1] *The Times*, August 12th, 1964.   [2] J. N. D. Kelly, *Early Christian Creeds*, p. 51.
[3] *Op. cit.*, pp. 13–23.   [4] *Serm.* 58, 11. See J. N. D. Kelly, *op. cit.*, p. 370.

the Lambeth Quadrilateral, but at the first World Conference on Faith and Order at Lausanne in 1927 'churches from the East as well as the West recited it in unison at the opening session and joined in acclaiming it as a fitting expression of the Christian message.'[1]

The same catechetical and baptismal background exists in the case of credal formularies in the East. But in the face of heresies they came to be promulgated by General Councils as tests of orthodoxy also. As C. H. Turner once put it, 'the old creeds were creeds for catechumens, the new creed was a creed for bishops.'[2] What we call the Nicene Creed today is basically an Eastern baptismal confession, but into it have been inserted the crucial Christological clauses designed to preserve the faith of Nicaea and to it new clauses relating to the Holy Spirit have been added. At the Council of Chalcedon (A.D. 451) this creed was quoted as 'the faith of the 150 fathers' who had assembled at the Council of Constantinople.

Partly through its intrinsic merits and partly because of its connection with the great patriarchal see of the East, this Creed quickly became not only the regular baptismal creed of the Eastern churches, but, more important, the Creed of Eucharistic worship, 'the continuous doxology of the faithful, Sunday by Sunday,'[3] This practice dates from the sixth century in the East, and it then gradually spread through the churches of Western Europe until finally it was included in the Roman liturgy in 1014. The so-called Nicene Creed is the ecumenical creed *par excellence*, accepted and used in East and West alike, though the East can rightly blame the West for adding the *filioque* clause on its own authority. The churches of the Reformation accepted this, as well as the Apostles' Creed, so that here indeed we have a declaration of the orthodox Christian faith, as the Church down the centuries has been led to accept it and to use it, not only as a doctrinal test, but as a great act of praise and thanksgiving. The

[1] *Op. cit.*, p. 368.
[2] *History and Use of Creeds and Anathemas*, quoted *op. cit.*, p. 205.
[3] Turner, *op. cit.*, quoted Bicknell, *Thirty-Nine Articles*, revised ed., p. 160.

Church of South India has accepted the two Creeds.[1] and the churches now seeking unity in Ceylon, North India and Pakistan, and elsewhere, stand in the same great tradition.[2]

The Apostles' and Nicene Creeds, then, come to us with the consensus of East and West, of Catholic and Reformed, of old-established churches and those entering on a new-found unity in many parts of the world. Yet it is significant that the Church of South India, at least, felt it necessary to add a qualifying clause[3] and, as the Bishop of Birmingham's letter implied, the Doctrinal Commission of the Church of England had already envisaged an adherence to the central truths of the Gospel without a strict acceptance of every clause in the Creeds in its literal sense.[4] The language and thought-forms which express the truth in one age need modification or revision if the same essential truth is to be expressed in the light of the fuller knowledge and different mental climate of a later age. We must face the question how far the truths expressed in the Creeds need restatement today.

[1] *Constitution of the Church of South India*, p. 5.

[2] Cf. Statements in Ceylon Scheme and in North India, and Pakistan plan of Union (S. F. Bayne, *Ceylon, N. India, Pakistan*, pp. 23–24 and p. 121). It is interesting to note that the Church Union Scheme in Australia, in which Congregationalist, Methodist and Presbyterian representatives have participated adds to the two Creeds the Chalcedonian Decree of A.D. 451.

[3] *Op. cit.*, Appendix I, 'The Basis of Union,' p. 72, note 1.

[4] Cf. Note, *On the Application to the Creed of the Conception of Symbolic Truth*, p. 37. Cf. Archbishop Temple's comments in his Chairman's Introduction, p. 12.

I. BELIEF IN GOD

I

THE first issue that arises as a result of recent controversy concerns our belief in God. Can we in any sense that does not do violence to the ordinary meaning of words continue to say 'I believe in one God the Father Almighty, Maker of heaven and earth, And of all things visible and invisible'? On the one hand, some have welcomed the Bishop of Woolwich's *Honest to God* and similar writings with relief and thankfulness. To them the freshly-minted 'image of God' in terms of depth, as the Ground of our Being, has made faith in God again possible in a scientific world. On the other hand, there have been cries of alarm and despondency. Have we not here an example of a Bishop who is undermining the very citadel of Christian faith?

Since the publication of *Honest to God* we have been made aware that John Robinson does not stand alone and that a new school of thought has sprung up which shares many of his presuppositions and conclusions and which proclaims what in America is called a 'death of God' theology. Its creed has been summed up as 'There is no God, and Jesus is his Son.' Whether the exponents of this type of thinking expressly reject everything approaching the traditional belief in God or whether they merely remain agnostic, they are all agreed that the centre of faith for the modern man who would be a Christian (or at least, the 'way in') must be the Jesus of Galilee and Judaea who set forth in word and deed the ultimacy of love and called men to 'opt for an agapeistic way of life.'[1] It is a puzzling, and in many ways, ironical feature of this theology that it should make this direct appeal to the Jesus of history without apparently ever seriously facing the important issues raised by Bultmann.

[1] In addition to *Honest to God* (esp. chap. 4), cf. W. and L. Pelz, *God is no More*; Paul van Buren, *The Secular Meaning of the Gospel*; W. Hamilton, *The New Essence of Christianity*; and T. W. Ogletree, *The Death of God Controversy*.

The Bishop of Woolwich would not, I think, go as far as some exponents of this type of thinking. His conclusions are certainly drawn more tentatively than is the case with some more confident works across the Atlantic—or indeed nearer home. But his writings are the best known, at least in the British scene, and we will treat them as representative of a type of thinking with which the Church must reckon today. If in the end this chapter parts company with his conclusions, then *ex hypothesi* it rejects those of more radical writers.

Perhaps the first thing to be said is that Bishop Robinson has done us all a service by making us examine afresh the foundations of the Christian creed. We can all get so absorbed in matters that, however important, are secondary such as the exact terms on which Anglican-Methodist union can come about or the shape new churches should take to express our recovered ideals of Eucharistic worship, that we forget how far the very idea of God has been crowded out of the minds of those who have been trained in science or philosophy to trust only what can be verified by observable experiment.

Secondly, it is good to have been reminded afresh both by Bishop Robinson and by some of his reviewers that Christian theology has never claimed to be able to describe God as he is in himself. The faith of the whole Old Testament stems from the tradition of the Exodus, as it was recited by the worshippers at the shrines and recorded in the documents that make up the Pentateuch. Yet in that very cradle of the Old Testament revelation two moments are of great significance. The first is in the narrative of Moses at the Burning Bush (Ex. 3. 13–15). When Moses asks for God's name, i.e. that which admits to knowledge of him in his inner being, he receives the reply 'I am (will be) who I am (will be),' God is not to be known in himself, but in his work in creation and in his ordering of history, particularly as that is unfolded in his dealings with his people. The second is in the story of Exodus 33. 17–end. Moses asks to see God's glory, but this is denied him—'man shall not see me and live.' Then in anthropomorphic terms the passing of God's glory is described, but Moses is only permitted to see 'the after-glow which he leaves behind him, but which may suggest what the full brilliancy of his presence must be' (S. R. Driver). It is true that elsewhere Moses is spoken of as seeing God's glory, along with the chosen leaders of the Hebrews (Ex. 24. 9–11), but this is an exceptional privilege never granted to the general body of Israel. God made himself known in speaking his word to his messengers or in his action in nature and history, but men could never know more than he chose to reveal of himself. The tremendous speech from the whirlwind in Job 38 and 39 is designed to impress upon Job the utter inability of finite man by searching to find out God or comprehend his ways.

Similarly, in the New Testament, St. Paul, when caught up into the seventh heaven, heard 'things that cannot be told, which man may not utter' (2 Cor. 12. 4), while St. John affirms that 'No man has ever seen God' (1. 18); only as God has chosen to unveil his glory have we been granted a vision of what God is like (1. 18 and 14. 9). If God has revealed himself in word and action, it yet remains true that in his inner nature and being he is, in Luther's phrase, *Deus absconditus*, the hidden God.

When the Christian Church moved out into the world of Greek philosophy, it came into contact with a system which knew nothing of an Incarnation. Acutely aware of the finite limits of the human reason, Greek philosophers, as they reached out after God if haply they might find him, felt impelled to describe the nature of deity in negatives. All they could positively assert was that God was not this and not that, he could not be described in any terms that could suggest human limitations in his being. It is arguable that some Greek influences, not least those of Neo-Platonism and the pseudo-Dionysius, and some derived forms of mysticism that flourished in the Middle Ages perverted the Christian tradition, because they were basically inimical to the claim that God has revealed himself in a particular history. Yet it remains true that the doctrine of the Trinity, for instance, as stated in the Athanasian Creed, is not a 'revealed truth' handed down on a platter from on high. It is the Church's groping attempt under the guidance of the Spirit to safeguard the revelation of God as transcendent, incarnate and indwelling, which had been given through the decisive events of the Old and New Testaments and by which alone the Church lives. 'We speak of Three Persons' said St. Augustine, 'not that that might be spoken, but lest nothing should be said' (*De Trin.* v. 9).

Then again, the Bishop of Woolwich has done a service to many by bringing home to them in a vivid way what is implied in St. Augustine's statement, namely that 'all credal statements, all doctrines, are explications, definitions in the intellectual field, of the commitment contained in the words "I believe in." They describe not truths in themselves out of the context of any personal response, but a relationship-in-trust to the various aspects of the truth as it is in Jesus.' Happily, in the chapter from which this quotation is taken in *The Honest to God Debate*, Bishop Robinson safeguards himself more clearly than he did in the earlier work from a completely subjective understanding of truth. 'To stress this existential, experiential element behind all the Christian's affirmations' he writes, 'is not in the least to say that they are purely subjective, in the sense that they represent merely his way of looking at things, his resolve to think or live in a certain manner. . . . They are expressions of trust in a Reality which is trust-worthy; and the clauses of the Creed, the doctrine and forms of the Church *describe this Reality, not just the individual's inner state*.'[1]

In a review from a very different theological quarter Dr. D. M. Mackay, Professor of Communication at Keele University, writing in *The Christian Graduate*,[2] makes the same point 'that the answer to contemporary linguistic challengers, sceptical of the meaningfulness of Christian affirmations, is to be sought in terms of the knowable events and relationships of ordinary Christian experience.' It may be difficult to make the term 'God' meaningful in isolation, yet 'concepts such as "rebelling against God," "being forgiven by God" and the like have a direct

---

[1] *Op. cit.*, p. 244. The italics are Bishop Robinson's.
[2] Vol. XVI, No. 3, Sept. 1963.

semantic link with day-to-day Christian experience, of a most practical kind.' Professor Mackay is emphatic that this is not to say 'that statements about God are really statements about human experience,' only to state that we must be 'ready to leave hyphens about some of our terms.'

Again, Bishop Robinson has done us all a service by insisting against all our temptations to departmentalize life and confine God to the sphere labelled 'religion,' that he is at the heart of life, involved in all the rough and tumble of everyday existence, operative in all the departments that we label secular. The Bishop finds himself constantly returning to a passage in which Jeremiah addresses Jehoiakim, son of Josiah. To do justice and righteousness, to judge the cause of the poor and needy—'is not this to know me? says the Lord.'[1] And our Lord says the same in the great picture he paints of the Last Judgement and the separation of the sheep and the goats. The test is not whether one is 'sound' in doctrine or 'correct' ecclesiastically, but whether one has shown compassion to those whom Jesus is ready to call his brethren.[2]

If a proper involvement in the life of the world is urgently necessary in the churches of the West, it is even more so in the area where I have recently been working, South-East Asia. There one finds only too often a pietistic tradition of Christian faith and life that sees little or no relation between the Gospel and the social and political life of the various countries. As a shrewd Scottish missionary with many years' experience in both China and South-East Asia put it once in conversation, 'We should be bringing our faith into all sides of the developing life of this part of the world. Instead of that, too many of us are content with building a series of Christian ghettos.'

The Bishop of Woolwich, then, has caused a vast breath of fresh air to blow through our inherited systems and traditional ways, and at not a few points we can only confess ourselves guilty. We have too often talked as though we had God in our pockets and had access to his every thought. We have not always

---

[1] Jer. 22. 15 f. Cf. *Honest to God*, p. 60.   [2] Cf. Mt. 25. 31–end.

F

recognized that the revelation of him in Scripture is given through pictures, symbol and imagery and have been apt to objectify such language as though it were describing God's nature and being in purely rational terms. We have been content too frequently to keep our ecclesiastical systems going and let the world with its agonies and its ecstasies, its hopes and its fears, pass by unheeded.

2

Yet having said all that I must go on to state my conviction that Bishop Robinson's Tillich-style attempted reconstruction provides no more permanent resting place for our faith in God than does Bultmann's concentration on the word of God confronting us existentially in the Cross alone offer a satisfactory reinterpretation of the New Testament. Either there must be a recovery of theism, purged of course of the crudities and inadequacies to which we can so obstinately or ignorantly cling, or else the movement must go the other way into acceptance of secular humanism. I do not believe the treasure of the Christian revelation which the Bishop is so keen to preserve can be contained in a vessel which for all his disavowals seems to come dangerously close to a refined form of pantheism.

My reasons for saying this are two. First, is the kind of *understanding of transcendence* which he urges really tenable? The Bishop of Woolwich, following Tillich, repudiates naturalism on the ground 'that our being has depths which naturalism, whether evolutionary, mechanistic, dialectical or humanistic, cannot or will not recognize. . . . There are depths of revelation, intimations of eternity, judgements of the holy and the sacred, awareness of the unconditional, the numinous and the ecstatic, which cannot be explained in purely naturalistic categories without being reduced to something else.' That is finely said. But the Bishop follows Tillich also in repudiating any idea that such recognition of transcendence commits us to belief in 'a "superworld" of divine objects. It does mean that, within itself, the finite world points beyond itself. In other words, it is self-transcendent.'[1] This, says Bishop Robinson, is 'Tillich's great contribution to theology—the reinterpretation of transcendence in a way which preserves its reality while detaching it from the projection of supranaturalism.'[2]

Transcendence is one of those blessed words which can obscure as much as clarify thought, and one cannot use it without taking as a warning Professor Hodgson's confession about it.[3] Yet frankly is not this attempted Tillich-Robinson reconstruction an example of wanting to eat one's cake and have it? How can the finite world 'point beyond itself,' if the 'ultimate' level of reality to which it points is in fact exclusively within itself? Does our own human experience support such a conception? Through memory and the ability to correlate and reflect on our experiences and to plan for the future we can in a measure rise above or pierce below the ebb and flow of temporal events. Yet we know well that that power of transcendence is only 'in a measure.' We are dependent all the time on the right chemical functioning of our brain-cells and the proper ordering of our whole physical organisms; a severe cerebral haemorrhage or senile decay will reduce or destroy that power. Again, we know that we can never escape completely the influences of our heredity and environment; we all bear upon us the stamp of our cultural heritage, our community tradition, our family life. We have to accept the truth that in this finite existence the experience of complete transcendence is not possible for us, precisely because we are still involved in finitude.

The fact is that, if the word 'transcendence' is to be used in any absolute sense, it postulates the existence of that which transcends independently of that which is transcended. That does not mean banishing God to some boundary situation 'out there.' In rejecting that Tillich is rightly reacting against Barth

[1] *Honest to God*, pp. 55–56, quoting Tillich, *Systematic Theology*, vol. II, p. 8.
[2] *Op. cit.*, p. 56.
[3] 'The word "transcend" . . . is one that I often find myself tempted to use when I don't quite know what I mean, and want a word to act as a cloak for confusion of thought.' *The Doctrine of the Atonement*, p. 147, f. 7.

with his massive over-emphasis (in his main theological work[1])
on the infinite gulf between an utterly holy God and utterly
sinful man, while failing to recognize the great tradition concerning the immanence of God in classical Christian theology. But
it does mean recognizing that 'the transcendent in the midst'
means more than acknowledging a dimension of depth in all life.
For if the transcendent is only such a dimension, then it partakes
of the transient character of this whole universe and, if by some
cosmic catastrophe this universe disintegrated into nothingness
tomorrow, it would disintegrate also. When Bishop Robinson
speaks of depths in our being—'depths of revelation, intimations
of eternity, judgements of the holy and the sacred, awareness of
the unconditional, the numinous and the ecstatic,' he is making
an apologetic appeal of great cogency to some people[2] which
can open the way for them to faith in the God who is 'God from
everlasting, and world without end' (Ps. 90. 2). But to use words
such as revelation, eternity, the unconditional, the numinous
otherwise, suggests stealing the theist's linguistic clothes while
he is bathing, it looks like trying to carry all the overtones of
ultimacy and eternity into a dimension of life which, however
significant and important, is in the last resort neither ultimate nor
eternal.

3

My other difficulty arises from the obscuring of *the category
of the personal* in both Tillich and Bishop Robinson, and indeed
in all who follow this type of thinking.

These writers are rightly concerned to destroy crude and
unworthy conceptions of God as an Old-Man-with-a-beard-in-
the-Sky, a Nobodaddy 'up' or 'out there.' But they are concerned also to deny what such concepts were trying to express.

---

[1] But see *The Humanity of God.*

[2] But not all. Cf. John Huxtable's remark, 'I heard one clergyman declare that a
number of his parishioners took barbiturates reinforced with alcohol when they had
looked at the depths of their being . . . "the depths of our life" or what appears to be
those depths do not always bring us any reassuring conviction about ultimate reality'
J. C. Neil-Smith (ed.), *Praying for Daylight*, p. 75.

God, they say, is not one object among other objects, not *a* Being set alongside other beings. 'When Tillich speaks of God in "depth,"' says John Robinson, 'he is not speaking of another Being *at all*. He is speaking of "the infinite and inexhaustible depth and ground of all being," of our ultimate concern, of what we take seriously without reservation.... The word "God" denotes the ultimate depth of all our being, the creative ground and meaning of all our existence.'[1] With such a reinterpretation of the word 'God' the whole concept of Divine personality requires transposition to another key. 'To say that "God is personal" is to say that "reality at its very deepest level is personal," that personality is of *ultimate* significance in the constitution of the universe, that in personal relationships we touch the final meaning of existence as nowhere else.... To believe in God as love ... is not the feat of persuading oneself of the existence of a super-Being beyond this world endowed with personal qualities. (It) is ... the well-nigh incredible trust, that to give ourselves to the uttermost in love is not to be confounded but to be "accepted," that Love is the ground of our being, to which ultimate we "come home."'[2] In similar vein John Macquarrie defines 'God' as 'the religious word for Being, understood as gracious.'[3]

Now there is much here which is only restating in modern terms the classical doctrine of Divine immanence, that 'in him we live and move and have our being.' Yet I cannot help agreeing with John Huxtable that Bishop Robinson and others of his school have 'often painted issues too sharply ... posed some false alternatives and ... more than once tipped the baby out with the bathwater.'[4] Once again it seems to me they want all the overtones of theism without its embarrassments for many in the modern world.

To put the issue as bluntly as possible, we must face the fact much more clearly than these writers do that *there is no such thing*

---

[1] *Honest to God*, pp. 46 and 47.   [2] *Op. cit.*, pp. 48 and 49.
[3] *The Honest to God Debate*, p. 188, quoted by J. Robinson, p. 260.
[4] *Op. cit.*, p. 68.

as Love, no such thing as Grace or graciousness. Love is a quality of persons, which presupposes self-consciousness and an affective relationship of a particular kind with the beloved. Grace is the outgoing expression of that affective relationship towards the one who is loved. Neither exists on its own. Wipe out the whole human race, and so far as this world is concerned you have wiped out love, whether you spell it with a small 'l' or a capital 'L', *unless* in, through, above, beneath this Universe there is a God of such a kind that, whatever else you say about him, you acknowledge as an integral part of his nature and being, that which corresponds to, while no doubt also far surpassing, what in us is self-consciousness and the power of entering into affective relationships with others. When Bishop Robinson quotes Feuerbach to the effect that to deny God, the subject, is by no means to deny the attributes of divinity, such as love, wisdom and justice and confesses that this is very near to the position he is taking, he is, in my view, committing himself to a strictly non-sense statement.[1] Either love, wisdom and justice are attributes of a God who is sufficiently personal to be able to love, be wise and act justly or they are human attributes which we seek to impose on an indifferent world. They do not float in the air, nor can they be built into the structure of any ultimate reality that is conceived of as without 'self-consciousness.'

There can be no doubt which of the alternatives is true to the Biblical revelation of God and to the main stream of Christian theology, liturgy and devotion all down the centuries. For it is through the unfolding record of the Old and New Testaments that we learn of God's attributes. We find ourselves challenged by the righteousness of God as we hear the prophets of Israel denouncing in God's name the social wrongs, the oppression and the corruption of the people of their day, calling upon them to do justly, to love mercy and to walk humbly with their God, and holding out to them the alternatives of judgement and salvation, of life and death. We are led to see the utterly paradoxical wisdom of God in the 'foolishness' of Calvary, where Christ is revealed as

[1] *Honest to God*, p. 50.

'the power of God and the wisdom of God' (1 Cor. 1. 20–25).
We meet his love supremely in the utter self-giving of Christ
to the death of the Cross for us men and for our salvation. It is
only because the author of the Johannine writings has *first* written
'God so loved the world that he gave his only Son' (Jn. 3. 16)
and 'In this is love, not that we loved God but that he loved us
and sent his Son' (1 Jn. 4. 10) that he can then go on to draw the
conclusion 'God is love' (1 Jn. 4. 16). Only in the same way
can we make the same confession.

So also it is only if God is our Father in a sense which bears
some analogous relationship to what we know in human experience of fatherhood, as well as the Ground of our Being or
any similar abstraction, that we can properly be 'accepted' and
'come home' and receive the adoption of sons. Similarly, prayer
in any sense which is other than neo-Platonist or Buddhist,
prayer which is authentically Christian, is built on the postulate
of a God whom we can properly address as *Thou*, the God and
Father of our Lord Jesus Christ, with whom we can enter into
communion, the God who is always more ready to hear than
we to pray, and wont to give more than either we desire or
deserve. And it is surely significant, in the light of Bishop
Robinson's statement that all doctrines and patterns of worship
both express the element of trust in a Reality which is trust-
worthy *and* describe this Reality, that eighteen pages later he
frankly says that he does not pray to the ground of his being, but
to God as Father.[1]

God, we must affirm, if we are to be true to the Bible and
classical Christianity, is both transcendent over the Universe,
so that if it ended tomorrow he would still be 'there' and also
immanent in it at the centre of all the processes of nature and
the life of the world and the relationship of men and women;
'closer is he than breathing and nearer than hands and feet.'
He cannot be reduced to the scale of one Person among other
persons, yet if he transcends our understanding of personality
there is that in him which relates to us as person to person, as

[1] Cf. *The Honest to God Debate*, pp. 244 and 262.

One who addresses us and whom we can address, who loves us with a love of which Calvary is the only measure and who calls us into the relationship of sons and daughters in his divine family.

Only if we hold fast to *that* affirmation, I submit, can we sincerely continue to say 'I believe in God the Father Almighty, Maker of heaven and earth, And of all things visible and invisible.'

II. THE GOSPEL OF RECONCILIATION

THE second paragraph of the Apostles' and Nicene Creeds concerns the person and work of 'Jesus Christ, his only Son our Lord.' The Apostles' Creed keeps to 'factual' statements, though some of its phrases (e.g. 'And sitteth on the right hand of God the Father Almighty') portray in picture-language truths for which no other phraseology is available. The Nicene Creed contains a similar recital of the basic facts of the kerygma, but into this recital, as we have seen, have been inserted the Christological phrases designed to rule out the Arian interpretation of the person of Christ. Further, the facts themselves are given their kerygmatic interpretation. The Incarnation was 'for us men and for our salvation.' Jesus 'was crucified also for us under Pontius Pilate.' His resurrection was 'according to the Scriptures.' The Creeds stand in lineal descent from St. Paul's summary of the kerygma as he had received it and passed it on (1 Cor. 15. 1–7).

Here, then, we come to the heart of the Gospel, to the pronouncement on which the whole New Testament and the Christian Church is built. In the person and work of Jesus of Nazareth, the Son of God, incarnate, crucified and risen, it proclaims, Almighty God, the Ultimate Reality and the Ground of our being, has acted decisively on the plane of history to remedy a broken and twisted relationship between his creation, with man as its earthly crown, on the one hand and himself, whose very nature is holy and righteous love, on the other. On so central a theme with all its many-sidedness, a whole volume (or indeed a series of volumes) could be written. I have neither the competence nor the opportunity to carry out such a task, but must content myself with writing of some particular aspects of the theme which seem to me matters of discussion and controversy at the present time. These can be grouped under two main heads.

I

First, we must face the fact of evil with all the disorder it brings into the life of the world and the heart of man. This was not a popular theme in the optimistic days of the nineteenth century. The spread of education, the advance of liberal ideas, the growth of tolerance and the establishment in ever wider circles of the institutions of democracy—these, it was believed, would in time cure the world's ills. It was the age of Liberal Protestant idealism, the era when from a very different angle Swinburne could sing, 'Glory to man in the highest, For man is the master of things.'

Along with the optimistic strain, it is true, there went others— the wistful agnosticism of many of the Victorian thinkers and that underlying sense of disquiet which the Greeks of old associated with nemesis. Kipling's Recessional, despite its phrases that echoed a ruling race's sense of superiority, nevertheless gave expression to the unease of those who believed that so unabashed a display of imperial pomp and splendour was tempting Providence. Yet it was not till after the first World War, and indeed till the decade of the thirties when the aftermath of the Depression merged into the events that foreshadowed World War II, that the Biblical doctrines of the sinfulness of man, of his inability to save himself and of God's provision in Christ of a way of deliverance and atonement began again to strike home to many. In Fascism and Nazism, in the fanatical militarism of Japanese State Shinto, and in the steam-roller ruthlessness of the Soviet Communism of those days, St. Paul's mysterious language about 'wrestling against principalities and powers' took on a new and dreadful meaning. Evil was indeed abroad in the world.

On the Continent of Europe Karl Barth and Emil Brunner 'spoke to men's condition.' In the United States Reinhold Niebuhr in his many works such as *Moral Man and Immoral Society* and *The Nature and Destiny of Man*, relentlessly laid bare the ambiguities of the forces at work in nations, societies and individuals. For people of my generation he made clear that love was not a principle that could be 'applied' direct to nations (as

the vociferous members of the Peace Pledge Union thought):
justice was the highest principle that could regulate the affairs of
any corporate society. As so often, theological thinking in Britain
dragged behind, but it was significant that, writing in 1937,
Archbishop William Temple in his Chairman's Introduction
to the Doctrine Report should have recorded 'a certain transition
of interest' in the minds of the members of the Commission.
Having begun their work in the nineteen-twenties, they had
taken up the tasks which World War I had compelled theologians
to lay aside, the implications of a theology of the Incarnation.
Archbishop Temple then wrote prophetically 'If the security of
the nineteenth century, already shattered in Europe, finally
crumbles away in our country, we shall be pressed more and more
towards a theology of Redemption. In this we shall be coming
closer to the New Testament. We have been learning again how
impotent man is to save himself, how deep and pervasive is
that corruption which theologians call Original Sin. Man needs
above all else to be saved from himself. This must be the work
of Divine Grace. . . . We may call the thinkers and teachers of
the Church of England to renewed devotion of their labour
to the themes of Redemption, Justification and Conversion.'[1]

The particular embodiment of the forces of evil is different
today from that of a generation ago. But they are still active.
There is a demonic element in the white racism of Southern
Africa, and in the black racism apparent in some other parts of
the Continent. Lands which echo with slogans about the 'newly
emerging forces' are sometimes those which are marked most
clearly by corruption, inefficiency and crude imperialist ambition.
The prospect of a nuclear arms race between an increasing number
of nations means an ever-increasing threat to the peace of the
world and, even if that be avoided, the tragic diversion of
resources sorely needed for the raising of the standard of living of
the poorer countries. Communism and the 'free world' still

---

[1] *Doctrine in the Church of England*, pp. 16–17. Perhaps Archbishop Temple's words help
to explain in part the renewed strength of Conservative Evangelicalism, which lays its
main stress precisely on these things.

confront each other, despite some easing of tensions between the Soviet Union and the West, and in the capitalist countries only too often management and labour view the other as 'the enemy' or 'the other side.' The lazy conservatism of too many old-established firms on the one hand and the widespread 'slack-during-normal-working-hours-and-increase-the-amount-of-overtime' outlook on the other go far to explain Britain's present industrial troubles.

The reality of evil is brought home to us in other ways also. Psychology has made clear how small is the area of our personalities controlled by our reason. If in the world at large all kinds of political, economic and social pressures restrict our freedom, it is also true that the forces operating in our sub-conscious as a result of heredity or early environment powerfully influence our conscious thinking and our decisions. Only too often, indeed, in popular thinking the recognition of this fact has resulted in a further ill—the undermining of a sense of individual responsibility. People can too easily excuse themselves on the ground that they suffer from impulses too strong for their control, like the small son of a friend who, when rebuked for being naughty, replied, 'Oh, but this is one of my bad days.' Yet for the Christian believer the very inter-locking of the generations and the inter-action of personality on personality which psychology has made clear is a powerful vindication of the traditional doctrine of Original Sin, that 'fault and corruption of the Nature of every man, that naturally is ingendered of the offspring of *Adam*' (Art. IX). There is indeed a solidarity of mankind in evil, in what the existentialists call 'unauthentic existence.' Men may not call this 'sin,' for sin is a concept that makes sense only against a background of faith in God, and in so many that faith has faded away. Yet Donald Baillie is, I believe, right in suggesting that modern man 'has a kind of *moralistic substitute* for the sense of sin, and that this . . . is the chief cause of that perennial *malaise* which surely underlies the superficial complacency of the modern mind. . . . A man is secretly sick of his unworthy past, but he does not know what to do with it, and therefore cannot face it. The sense of it becomes a repressed complex, festering uneasily under the surface. . . .'[1]

Certainly many modern novels and plays lay bare the reality of evil and guilt in the relationship of persons in modern society and in the heart of the individual. Camus' *The Plague* describes under the symbol of an outbreak of bubonic plague in an Algerian city the slow deterioration and demoralization of character in France under the Nazi occupation. Graham Greene's works constantly revolve round the themes of sin and guilt. John Braine in *Room at the Top* brutally exposes the corruption of character in a man who has sold himself for power, and in a subtler way Lord Snow explores the corroding effect of the same lust, whether in a Senior Combination Room at Cambridge or the corridors of Whitehall. What is the 'dustbin drama' except a morbid attempt to lay bare the element of corruption in the fabric of society? Hot-gospellers may think they have done their duty when they have put up on hoardings texts such as 'The wicked shall be turned into hell,' texts which in that unmediated form leave the average reader cold or resentful, but often in our time it has been those outside the Church who have really made us face in all its terrifying intensity the power of evil to destroy a society and to debase its members.

2

Does that, however, justify *the extreme pessimism of St. Augustine and the Reformers about the corruption of human nature*, the strong language of the middle section of Article IX and of Article XIII, and the passionate emphasis of Barth (at least in his earlier days) on the effacing, and not merely the defacing, of the image of God in man? I do not think so, and that for three reasons.

First, I do not believe it is consonant with the tradition that we have in the Gospels of the words and attitudes of Jesus. True, he had no illusions about the evil in man's nature (Mt. 7. 11; Lk. 11. 13), he knew what proceeded out of the heart of

---

[1] *God was in Christ*, pp. 162–163.

men (Mk. 7. 20–23) and, where a man's deepest need was forgiveness, Jesus gave him that gift first and only afterwards the
healing of the body (Mk. 2. 1–12, and parallels). Yet it is surely
significant that, in the first reference quoted above, our Lord can
still argue from the generosity of human parents toward their
children to the 'how much more' of the heavenly Father's
generosity to all who ask for his good gifts. So far from man's
reason being utterly corrupted, Jesus repeatedly answers a question
with a counter-question, he confronts people with the facts and
leaves them to draw the conclusions for themselves. If the blindness of the Scribes and Pharisees earned his stern condemnation,
the response of Gentiles deeply impressed him. He did not find
such great faith in Israel as he found in the centurion at Capernaum (Mt. 8. 5–13; Lk. 7. 1–10), his hesitation about stepping
outside the limits of his immediate mission to Israel was overcome by the faith and persistence of the Syrophoenician woman
(Mk. 7. 24–30; Mt. 15. 21–28). Tyre and Sidon had a greater
potentiality of response to his mission than Chorazin or Bethsaida,
Sodom would have responded better than Capernaum (Mt.
11. 21–24; Lk. 10. 12–15). Many from the east and west would
share in the Messianic kingdom (Mt. 8. 11); and among them
would be those who had never known the Son of Man but who
had served him, as they ministered to the hungry and the sick
and the needy, whom he was pleased to call his brethren (Mt.
25. 31–46).

Secondly, there can be little doubt that, intellectual and spiritual
giant though he was, St. Augustine was led to paint the world
and man's nature in darker colours than the Scriptures warrant
by particular factors in his own situation. His own dissipated
early life produced a violent and equally unbalanced insistence
on man's total corruption and helplessness. Even newborn babes
were guilty before God and under his condemnation.[1] His
conflict with the shallow, atomized view of human nature taught
by Pelagius, according to which each individual started life

---

[1] St. Augustine's teaching was based in part on his misinterpretation of the phrase
'children of wrath' in Eph. 2. 3.

with a clean slate, led him to re-emphasize his beliefs even more strongly. And, as Charles Raven reminded us shortly before his death, the fall of Rome and the overrunning of his own diocese by the Visigoths drove St. Augustine to a theology of despair. 'Read his last treatises in which he abandons the world as a mass of corruption, "massa perditionis" and regards the whole propagation of the human species as lust and abomination, thus turning his back on all the splendour of his previous vision.'[1]

The Very Rev. Dr. W. R. Matthews has recognized 'a saving inconsistency in Augustine's teaching . . . a mystical element which derives from his personal religious experience.' Could anyone who could say to God 'Thou art deeper in me than I am in myself' deny the same reality to others, and is that really reconcilable with a view of man as totally corrupt?[2] Moreover, recent study has shown that the great Reformers such as Luther and Calvin were not always so consistent and fixed as the systems established by their followers would suggest.[3] But there can be no doubt of the profound influence of St. Augustine upon them, and of St. Paul as read through Augustinian spectacles. They were in revolt against a too external concern in the medieval Church with 'sins' and against the shallow optimism of much Renaissance thinking about man.

Whatever the precise position of the great Reformers, there can be no doubt that the systematizers who followed them were led astray by their interpretation of 'the inspired writings as systems of theology' rather than 'as expressions of a revealing experience of God.'[4] As a result statements in St. Paul which in the first place were attempts to express one or other aspect of the saving truth of the Gospel became hardened in the Confessional documents into quasi-legal statements. This is true equally of the Thirty-Nine Articles. 'They deal with his (St. Paul's) inspired religious utterances as if they were legal pronouncements, and draw conclusions from them as a lawyer might do

[1] *Praying for Daylight*, p. 52. [2] *The Thirty-Nine Articles*, pp. 20–21.
[3] Cf. J. M. Shaw, *Christian Doctrine*, pp. 130–131, n.1.
[4] W. R. Matthews, *op. cit.*, p. 22.

from the words of an Act of Parliament. They obscure the teaching of the New Testament by getting it out of proportion.'[1] Here, then, is the second objection. The Augustinian-Reformation tradition, while rightly teaching the solidarity of mankind in sin, yet for reasons that owed more to historical circumstances than to a balanced understanding of the Bible pressed their teaching to a one-sided extreme.

Thirdly, the vastly changed world in which we live and the immensely enlarged horizons opened to us by the study of other religions and philosophies makes it impossible for us to be so harshly condemnatory of everything done apart from a conscious faith in Christ. We are bound to give weight to other elements in New Testament teaching. The Epistle to the Colossians speaks to us of a cosmic Christ, in whom all things were created and in whom all things hold together (1. 15 and 16). His presence and power, it follows, are at work where he is not known. The prologue to St. John's Gospel, like the rest of the Gospel, is written on more than one level. The coming of the Word made flesh in Jesus of Nazareth is all of a piece with the unceasing activity of the Logos, who is ever coming into the world as the true light that enlightens every man (1. 9). If the appalling catastrophe of World War I drove Karl Barth in his Swiss parsonage to despair about man, it had a quite different effect on Père Teilhard de Chardin serving as a humble stretcher-bearer on the battlefields. 'Even amid scenes of death and devastation he was carried away by a sense of fulfilment. . . . Life takes on a new savour in the heroic devotion to a grand ideal. Père Teilhard felt that the reality he had found at the front would be with him for ever "in the great work of creation and of sanctifying humanity."'[2]

Dr. Matthews points out that Articles IX, XIII and XVIII taken together rule out any idea 'that men like Socrates, Buddha or others of deep wisdom and heroic virtue who could never have heard the gospel of Christ might possibly escape

---

[1] *Op. cit.*, p. 23.   [2] *Le Milieu Divin*, pp. 22–23.

damnation.'[1] The present vicar of Great St. Mary's, Cambridge, H. W. Montefiore, a member of a distinguished Jewish family, protested at his institution to the parish against Article XIII on the ground that he could not reconcile it with the sincerity and devotion of many of his fellow-Jews. And G. W. H. Lampe has criticized it similarly on the ground that it does not square with life. 'This Article takes no account of the observable fact that the grace of God—the grace of the Logos who is incarnate in Christ—operates in those who may be at present unconscious of its source, and hence it implies that the good works done by the pious Jew, Muslim or sincere humanist owe nothing to God and are simply not pleasant to him.'[2]

The English temperament is, according to an accusation frequently levelled against us, incurably Pelagian, and it must be admitted that many of our compatriots do, in fact, believe, if they believe at all, in a religion of good works. Against all shallow optimism about the nature of man, we must be grateful to the Reformers for calling us to the truly Biblical doctrine that mankind is involved corporately in the *damnosa hereditas* of evil and that each of us does, in fact, through wilfulness or weakness yield to temptation, so that 'all have sinned and fall short of the glory of God' (Rom. 3. 23). We are right, too, to recognize how subtly selfishness and pride can insinuate themselves into even our finest achievements. Yet the Articles need radical revision if they are to present a balanced picture of the nature of man, as the whole New Testament evidence portrays it.[3] His condition is not wholly dark or utterly corrupt.

Again, phrases which point to the doctrine of Original Guilt need removing altogether, for while it must be recognized that infants are born into a race that is alienated from God, it is immoral to attribute guilt to those who have not yet reached the age of personal responsibility. St. Augustine was misled not only by his misunderstanding of Ephesians 2. 3, but also by his

[1] *Op. cit.*, p. 15.   [2] *The Articles of the Church of England*, p. 105.
[3] J. M. Shaw gives an excellent example of such a modified statement in the Declaration Act of 1892 issued by the Free Church of Scotland, *op. cit.*, p. 132.

G

interpretation of Romans 5. 12, in a way that the Vulgate permits, but the original Greek disallows. Children, whether baptized or unbaptized, can safely be entrusted to the care of a God whose nature is basically Love.

The same charity must be extended to those who have aimed at the highest they know, even though they have never heard of Christ. No doubt their search will never have been wholly free from error, and the Christian Church has an inescapable responsibility to make Christ known to them as the true and living Way and as the Saviour. Yet, as Kenneth Cragg and others have taught us,[1] that approach is not to be made in the spirit of harsh condemnation of everything that is dearest to them, because it does not spring 'of faith in Jesus Christ'; rather, the approach must be in the spirit of deep sympathetic understanding of what the Logos may have, in fact, shown them of truth, in preparation for the fullness of Truth in Christ our Lord. Those, too, who have died without the knowledge of Christ—the countless millions who form by far the largest part of the human race—cannot just be condemned to eternal damnation because of their ignorance. We can safely leave them in the hands of a faithful Creator, a God most fully revealed to us, we believe, in the assertion that (as Dr. Matthews emphasizes) is significantly absent from any of the Articles, namely that he is our Father in Heaven, One whose nature is essentially Love. Granted, the New Testament proclaims unequivocally that 'there is no other name under heaven given among men by which we must be saved' (Acts 4. 12), but who are we to deny the power of God to give the knowledge of Christ on the other side of death to those who have never had a chance to receive it here?

3

When the moral disorder and the pervasive power of evil in the world and in the lives of men are seen, not just in themselves, but in relation to a God whose essential nature is holy and

---

[1] Cf. e.g. *The Call of the Minaret* and the Christian Presence series.

righteous love they are properly designated sin. In particular, sin describes the element of conscious acquiescence in the power of evil, of open rebellion against God and disobedience to his Will. 'The nearest analogy to it is a profound breach of love and trust in human relationships, resulting in love being met with hate, ... a loveless self-centredness ... which, being a denial of our own true being and of its source, leads inevitably to spiritual death.'[1]

So we come to consider *the meaning of the Gospel of reconciliation*. Here several things need to be taken into account. The first is the existential interpretation which John Knox has strongly emphasized in his book *The Death of Christ*. The experience of deliverance from sin, of bondage to the powers of sin and death, and of tasting of the power of the age to come *plus* the experience of forgiveness, of guilt removed and of restoration to life in the family of God, he asserts, were realities known in the life of the early Church before ever there were worked-out explanations of the Atonement. The Church started from the known fact of her reconciliation through Christ to the Father, and then proceeded to try and explain this fact to herself and to others that they might share in the same joyful experience also.

In doing so, the Church had to put the Gospel into story-form. One story was of 'God's sending his own Son into the world to meet our enemies of Sin and death, of his struggle with them, of his victory over them.' 'In this story Christ appears as the Conqueror of Sin, Law and Death.' The other story was of 'the sinless Son of God, who suffered death upon the Cross for our transgressions and in our stead.' 'In this story Christ appears as the justifier, the reconciler, the "means of expiation" or in some similar role.' Strictly speaking, these two stories are contradictory, they 'cannot be mixed with anything like a logically coherent result.' But each bears witness in its own way to 'existential man and his redemption.' The truth which the Church found in its experience of the liberating power of the

---

[1] G. W. H. Lampe, 'The Atonement: Satisfaction or Sentimentality?' *Theology*, August, 1964, p. 341.

Gospel could not be, and cannot be, expressed in all its concrete meaning except in such stories, in 'the images of Christ the victor over the demons and of Christ the Lamb of God,' but it is important to understand that such stories do not explain 'in a causal or instrumental sense, the deliverance which God through Christ makes to us,' nor is the Church committed to the acceptance of the truth of these images. They do not describe objectively how God has ransomed and reconciled and made atonement for us in Christ, they are picture-language whose value lies in its power to bring us into the richness of the experience of deliverance and pardon which the Church of New Testament days found in Christ. 'Why this particular event (i.e. the event of Christ) had this particular result is a matter altogether beyond our knowing.'[1]

Existentialism, as we have already seen, has rendered a notable service in making clear to us that no purely rational, objective statements about ultimate realities can be, or in fact are, made. Always there is included the element of subjective judgement. But, as we have also seen, existentialism errs when it boils all philosophical or theological statements down to simple statements of a person's outlook or perspective on life. As the Bishop of Woolwich has stressed, they are also 'statements about the reality in which my life is grounded.'[2] Indeed, it is an essential part of a Christian's existential experience that in the deepest places of his being he knows he is being acted upon by, and responding to, a Power that is other than himself. He cannot make his creed 'It is in my life as if I were believing in a God who is a Father Almighty,' he must inevitably take the further step to 'I believe in God.'

So with the doctrine of the Atonement. No doubt the first experience of deliverance and of exhilarating joy came to the early Christians as the risen Christ made himself known to them and thereby banished all the despair and emptiness with which

---

[1] Op. cit., pp. 153–157. Page numbers refer to the American edition. An English edition has been published by Collins.
[2] The Honest to God Debate, p. 253.

the first Good Friday had left them. But that alone would not have made a Gospel. It was because this experience was set in the context of the Old Testament revelation, because they saw at once that in the event of Christ what was foreshadowed in prophetic utterance and sacrificial rite in the old dispensation had been fulfilled, because they knew in their transformed lives that in Christ God had indeed dealt with the problem of sin in all its complexity, that the experience had the particular 'feeling-tone' that it had. It is significant that John Knox speaks of 'the story of God's sending his own Son into the world' coming into being *almost as a part of the event itself.*[1] It is interesting, too, to note that Martin H. Cressay, in an eirenic article designed to help towards a sympathetic understanding of Conservative Evangelicalism, makes the point that its supporters stress the penal substitutionary doctrine of the Atonement, precisely because they hold 'that here we are given, as they believe on a scriptural basis, a clear account of God's action in Christ in its *objective* content.' It is the proclamation of a work done independently of sinful men which 'evokes a response from the human heart.'[2]

We may feel that the conservative 'quest for "objectivity" ' is a quest for something never fully granted to us here on earth, we must recognize that the Church has not accepted any one theory of the Atonement as its official doctrine and that all, besides having a speculative element about them, owe much to the sociological and psychological factors of the era in which they were developed. Yet the fact remains that the Gospel can remain a Gospel only if it points, not just to the Christian experience of liberation and forgiveness, but through these to their source in the action of God in Christ. Only if God has really come to our rescue, has dealt radically with the power of evil and has acted to put right the broken relationship between man and himself have we the good news which sinful man needs, if his heart is not to remain restless, his conscience troubled and

[1] *Op. cit.*, p. 154. My italics.
[2] 'What Makes Them Think Like That?' *Theology*, Dec. 1964. Italics mine.

his sense of alienation a continuing fact of his life. No doctrine of the Atonement which does not give that assurance can in my view be true to the historic witness of the Scripture and the continuing experience of the Church.

4

The second aspect of the Gospel of reconciliation which needs consideration is the hoary one—*is the Atonement primarily an act of God directed towards the redemption of man, or is it primarily an act of Man (in the person of the sinless Son of God) directed towards God?* On the one hand, there can be no doubt of the converting power of an 'objective' view of the Atonement as shown in the revived strength of Conservative Evangelicalism. On the other hand, we have had recently in *Soundings* a powerful plea from one who belongs to the Evangelical school of thought, though not to its conservative wing, for a frank acceptance of the full implications, as he sees them, of the doctrine of justification by the free grace of God to which man responds in faith alone. The Reformers, says G. W. H. Lampe, 'were aware that man cannot justify himself before God, and that all that is required of him is to accept the sonship that is freely given to him as a sinner. ... They did not, however, carry their doctrine of justification far enough. It was still set within a framework of merit and satisfaction: not the merits of men, including the saints, nor any satisfaction made to God by man, but the merits of Christ and the satisfaction offered by him to the Father.'[1] To attempt to retain an 'objective' view of the Atonement is to misunderstand the paradoxical way in which the Christian Gospel goes right against the presuppositions of all legalistic religion. It is to be blind to the truth that 'God's acceptance of man is not conditional upon anything that man may do. It is unrelated to justice, and it takes no account of merit or demerit.'[2]

Certainly, all sound interpretations of the Gospel of reconciliation start from the initiative of God's love. 'God so loved the

---

[1] *Op. cit.*, p. 185.   [2] *Op. cit.*, p. 177.

world that he gave his only Son.' 'God shows his love for us in that while we were yet sinners Christ died for us.' 'God was in Christ reconciling the world to himself.' 'In this is love, not that we loved God, but that he loved us and sent his Son.'[1] The Old Testament may contain pictures of mediators such as Moses standing in the breach before God, to turn away his wrath from destroying his people (Ps. 106. 23) or Phinehas interposing, so that the plague sent by God was stayed (v. 30), but the New Testament has outgrown all such conceptions. There is no question now of propitiating an angry God, so as to make him loving—the word translated 'propitiation' has been conclusively shown not to have that meaning in biblical Greek[2]—nor does the New Testament ever speak, as Article II does, of reconciling the Father to us. It is always God who takes the initiative in bringing back a fallen humanity to himself, and as Christians reconciled to God in Christ we have no need to pray as the Litany bids us, 'be not angry with us for ever.'

Nevertheless, as the Doctrine Report puts it, 'God's eternal and unchanging love . . . is more than benevolence. It is a holy love, and therefore always actively affirms itself both in condemning sin and also in striving to restore and to remake the sinner. Thus on the one hand, God's love upholds the moral order of the universe, which is manifested both in the consequences attendant upon sin, including alienation from God and moral degradation, and in the conviction of man's conscience that loss or unhappiness is due to him as a penalty for wrongdoing. The traditional phrase, "the wrath of God," should be interpreted in the light of these considerations. On the other hand, God's love, by its own characteristic activity of redeeming sinners, completes and transcends the moral order thus manifested.'[3] We may indeed agree that the traditional picture of the outraged father driving his daughter and her illegitimate baby out into the snow is no true picture of God's attitude towards us.

---

[1] Jn. 3. 16; Rom. 5. 8; 2 Cor. 5. 19; 1 Jn. 4. 9.
[2] See C. H. Dodd, *The Bible and the Greeks, passim.*
[3] *Doctrine in the Church of England,* p. 91.

But neither is the attitude of the parent in the police court who says 'I can't understand how my boy has got into the dock here. I have never denied him anything.' The father of the prodigal son waited and yearned for his son to come home, but it was only when the young man came to himself that the reunion was possible. Had he stayed content with the wastrels and harlots in the far country, still more if he had suggested bringing them home, reconciliation with the father would have been out of the question. For the deepest love which a parent can show to his children is that which desires what is morally and spiritually best for them. Love transcends law, but it does not violate it, and no parent who has the truest well-being of his family at heart will allow the home to become a moral shambles. That is why the glorious good news of the superabundant grace of God active for our salvation is always dependent in the New Testament on what Christ has done for us in his dying and rising again.

If the parable of the prodigal son had not been told to illustrate one, or at most two, aspects of the Gospel but were really to be in allegorical form an *evangelium in evangelio*, then it would describe the father's sending the elder brother into the far country after him. It would speak of the elder brother's search, his going from one degraded place to another, his entering into the shame and horror of the prodigal's condition, his acceptance of the enmity and violence of his brother's companions in misery and, last but not least, his rejection by his brother. It would go on to tell of his acceptance of and triumph over all these things, and it would then relate how the elder son picked up his younger brother and half-carried, half-supported him on the long journey home, and there spoke to their father the words of contrition and sorrow which the prodigal son was too ashamed to stammer out himself. It would then describe the father's welcome, not in any sense because there had been a change in the father from anger and vengefulness to love, but because the conditions were now different. The father's love had hitherto expressed itself in two ways. On the one hand, it had been revealed as 'wrath,' as hostility to the son's whole way of life. On the other, it had initiated the whole act of rescue. Now through the action of the elder brother his love could have free play without moral compromise.

Of course, no one allegory or parable can ever adequately represent the many-sided truth of the Gospel. In particular, the story of the prodigal son thus told cannot adequately represent the truth that God in Christ has effected the great work of reconciliation 'while we were yet sinners.' Incarnate in our human nature and as our representative Christ by his perfect and complete self-surrender of himself in utter obedience bridged the gap that separated us from God, before ever he brought us across the bridge. But the New Testament always stresses that it is for Christ's sake that God has forgiven us (Eph. 4. 32) and that we are 'justified by his grace as a gift, through the redemption which is in Christ Jesus, whom God put forward as an expiation by his blood' (Rom. 3. 25). St. Paul specifically emphasizes that this was 'to prove at the present time that God himself is righteous and that he justifies him who has faith in Jesus' (Rom. 3. 25 and 26). The classic passage which tells of God reconciling us to himself in Christ concludes with the declaration 'For our sake he made him to be sin who knew no sin, so that in him we might become the righteousness of God' (2 Cor. 5. 18-21). This kind of language speaks, not just to some crude sense that evil must be punished no matter who bears the punishment, but to a deep insight of the conscience that love, if it is to be true to itself at the highest level, can never be indifferent to moral categories. And if this be true of man at his highest, then how much more of the God revealed to us in the Scriptures as holy and righteous love.

Both the 'objective' and the 'subjective' doctrines of the Atonement, then, contain deep insights into the meaning of Scripture and the needs of the human heart. Different ages and different individuals may be led to emphasize one rather than the other. But the Church as a whole must retain both, while always refining away the crudities that may attach to any particular exposition. That God has reached down to our human level in

Christ and supremely at the Cross has 'taken the pain which is the child of sin and made it the parent not of further evil, but of good . . . raw material for increasing the world's output of goodness'[1]—this is near the heart of the Gospel, this is 'the essence of forgiveness,' this is the only ground that Christians can stand on when, in face of all the calamities, disasters and sufferings of a dark world they still dare to say 'God is love'. That God had at the same time provided for fallen man a way back to himself through Christ 'who through the eternal Spirit offered himself without blemish to God' (Heb. 9. 14)—this is also an essential part of the Gospel, this is the good news for the guilty conscience, this is the ground of hope for the new life in Christ.

5

The third aspect of the Atonement I want to say something about is its universality. The Calvinist formularies which emerged from the Reformation period taught the doctrine of double pre-destination—the elect predestined by Divine decree for eternal life and the rest foreordained by the Divine will for damnation. 'All are not created in equal condition'; wrote Calvin, 'rather, eternal life is foreordained for some, eternal damnation for others.'[2] Calvin taught this doctrine because for him God not only foresees human events but 'did also dispose and determine them by his decision' so that 'all things take place by his determination and bidding.'[3] In this the great Reformer is following in the footsteps of St. Augustine who also distinguished between those who belong to the number of the predestined and those who do not, and indeed is following one aspect of Hebrew thinking which we have already noted in the Bible—namely, its inability to distinguish between purpose and consequence. If something happened, it could only be because God willed it to happen. On this basis all events that take place in the world's history are read back into the Divine purpose. The area of human

---

[1] L. Hodgson, *The Doctrine of the Atonement*, p. 62.
[2] Institutes III, XXI, 5.   [3] Institutes III, XXIII, 6.

freewill and responsibility is drastically limited in such thinking, and the task of evangelism takes on a particular character. Thus Neo-Calvinists today argue the case for world-wide evangelism, not on the ground that God desires all men to be saved and to come to the knowledge of the truth (1 Tim. 2. 4), but on the ground that, as we do not know who are the elect and who are not, we must preach the Gospel to every creature, so that the elect may hear and respond in faith.

Article XVII on Predestination and Election supports such reasoning for, while it sounds moderate in that it does not expressly state that God has predestined some to curse and damnation, yet, as the Dean of St. Paul's has written, we cannot help asking whether this restraint is 'any more than verbal. . . . Not to be elected to life is equivalent to being elected to death.'[1] The phrase in the Burial Service 'shortly to accomplish the number of thine elect, and to hasten thy Kingdom' fits into the same theological tradition, and it is significant that several revisions in the Anglican Communion (e.g. the American, Canadian and Indian, and the proposed new Burial Service of the Church of England) have by revision of the wording or the omission of the prayer dropped a phrase so redolent of the Calvinist element in our tradition in the sixteenth century.

The student of Scripture, surveying its contents as a whole, can in my view only be led to the conclusion that the central theme underlying the Bible from beginning to end is God's universal purpose of unity for the whole cosmos and for all humanity within it. The opening narratives of Genesis set the scene for what follows by revealing through poetry and folk-tale the universal realities of creation, sin and judgement. With the call of Abraham the particular channel of God's working to restore the broken situation between mankind and himself is narrowed down to one people, but nothing is clearer in the prophetic denunciations of their evil ways and in the prophetic visions of the coming reign of God than that the Hebrew people were called not only to be loyal to God alone but also by their

---

[1] *The Thirty-Nine Articles*, pp. 12 and 13.

faithfulness to be the instruments of the world's salvation. If Nehemiah and Ezra could stress the exclusiveness of God's chosen people, the stories of Ruth and Jonah set forth a larger vision; the latter is a direct challenge to missionary service.

When we pass to the Gospels, we find indeed that Jesus was 'sent only to the lost sheep of the house of Israel' (Mt. 15. 24). The *first* purpose of his coming was to offer himself as Messiah to God's chosen people and to make effective at long last the promise given to Abraham (Gen. 12. 1–3). So he went up to Jerusalem and on Palm Sunday by a dramatic action made his great challenge and appeal to the national leaders of his nation. In the great eschatological moment of their history, however, they refused their great chance and crucified the Lord of glory. Yet God can always bring good out of evil, and in accordance with his determinate counsel and foreknowledge the Cross and Resurrection became the very means of the world's salvation. The old Israel was replaced by the new Israel, and the Church became the catholic society in which all human beings regardless of race, nationality, class or sex become one in Christ.

Whether the Epistle to the Ephesians is a genuine work of St. Paul resulting from the opportunity for reflection provided by his house-arrest in Rome or a product of the Pauline school summing up the significance of his tireless missionary labours, there can be no doubt of the context in which his life-work is set. God has made known the mystery of his eternal will and purpose 'to unite all things in Christ, things in heaven and things on earth' (1. 9 and 10); Christ has broken down the dividing wall of hostility between Jew and Gentile, so that in him both have access to the Father (2. 14–18); St. Paul has been commissioned to make all men see the plan of the mystery of God's unchanging purpose which embraces not only all humanity, but also 'the principalities and powers in the heavenly places' (3. 8–10).

Predestination, I believe, must always be interpreted in the context of this eternal and universal purpose of God. It is not a statement of God's decree to accept some and reject others, but a witness to the truth of all Christian experience that God's grace was at work in our environment, our upbringing and our souls before ever we responded to him. It is the glorious confession that by God's grace his universal purpose has been fulfilled in our lives 'as a kind of first fruits of his creatures' (Jas. 1. 18), the testimony that in us has been fulfilled already the Divine purpose that Christ might be 'the first-born among many brethren' (Rom. 8. 29), the head of a new humanity that 'reigns in life' through the gift of his salvation (5. 17–21). When we understand predestination in that context, we may indeed be thankful for the saving sentence with which Article XVII ends!

Does the Bible then teach universalism, that everyone will in fact be saved in the end? The answer, I believe, is 'no.' The Bible teaches clearly that God's eternal purpose is a universal one, and that remains the Christian hope. Nothing can be more significant in that connection than the way in which St. Paul concludes his long wrestling in Romans (chaps. 9–11) with the faithlessness and rejection of his own people, the Jews. Having wrestled with every conceivable argument based first on God's almighty power and then on man's responsibility for his own life to explain what he believes is a temporary phenomenon, his vision rises to a great conclusion in which faith and hope are blended—'the full number of the Gentiles come in and all Israel . . . saved' (11. 25 and 26)—and he is led to burst out into a great doxology (vs. 33–36).

Yet the fact remains that men are confronted with a choice between God and the forces of darkness, good and evil, for Christ and against Christ, which is no mere piece of play-acting, but has eternal consequences. Our Lord time and again confronts men with a call to decision and bids them enter by the narrow gate that leads to life (Mt. 7. 13 and 14). In such parables as the Unjust Steward and the Rich Man and Lazarus, he warns against the missing of opportunities which are here today and gone for ever tomorrow. And he does not hesitate to speak of the reality of Hell (e.g. Mt. 10. 28; Lk. 12. 5).

We are here face to face with the ultimate mystery of God's eternal purpose and the reality of human choice and free-will.

We may hope and pray indeed that that eternal purpose will be fulfilled in every life, just as St. Paul sought to understand the fulfilment of that purpose in the situation of Jews and Gentiles in his day. But we cannot assert positively the universalist doctrine that all mankind will inevitably be saved, for otherwise God would not be God. There are elements of revelation here which we must be content in our human finitude to leave unreconciled.

Yet if we must hold firmly to the reality of human choice, we must hold on equally to the eternal purpose of God to unite all things in Christ. The preacher of the Gospel is not giving himself to his task in the hope that on occasions at least he may be lucky enough to have some of the elect in his congregation to respond to his message. He is proclaiming a message that is of concern to all. 'The Gospel,' says F. D. Maurice, 'is the full discovery of him who is the living Centre of the Universe, the assertion that all men are related to him; the destruction of every wall of partition between Man and Man; the admission of all who desire it into fellowship with the Father of the whole family in Heaven and Earth.'[1] In the words of the Catechism, the Son of God 'redeemed me and all mankind' and in those of the Revised Catechism 'God, who through Christ has created and redeemed all things, will also, through Christ at his coming again, make all things perfect and complete in his eternal Kingdom.'

There, I suggest, we have the authentic Anglican temper, based firmly on the totality of Scripture and not on particular statements pressed well beyond anything said in Scripture to their logical extreme.

[1] *The Prayer Book and the Lord's Prayer*, p. 109, quoted A. R. Vidler, *The Theology of F. D. Maurice*, pp. 56–57.

III. THE HOLY SPIRIT AND THE CHURCH

I

THE Apostles' Creed, as we have seen, grew out of the old Roman Creed, and its third paragraph is a slightly enlarged version of the corresponding paragraph in the earlier document. The phrases 'Catholic,' 'The Communion of Saints,' and 'The life everlasting' have been added. In the Baptismal Services and the Order for the Visitation of the Sick in the 1662 Prayer Book, where the Creed appears in an interrogative form, the phrase 'resurrection of the flesh' is used instead of the more familiar 'resurrection of the body.' This is a more accurate translation of the Latin phrase *resurrectionem carnis*, but though early it is not Scriptural, and too often has carried with it the idea of the resuscitation of the material elements of the physical body. The phrase we use at Mattins and Evensong is more compatible with St. Paul's language about the resurrection of the dead. 'What is sown is perishable, what is raised is imperishable. . . . It is sown a physical body, it is raised a spiritual body' (I Cor. 15. 42 and 44).

The Creed of Nicaea contained simply the phrase 'And in the Holy Spirit.' In the form in which we use the Creed today this third paragraph has been considerably expanded. Phrases about the Holy Spirit have been added to rule out the teaching that he was just a creature, 'one of the ministering angels and superior to the angels only in degree.' Such teaching, which was put out by certain Arians and advocated by Macedonius, the Bishop of Constantinople, c. A.D. 360, was expressly condemned by the Council of Constantinople in A.D. 381. 'Christians were convinced that his working within their own souls proved him to be not less than divine.'[1]

The phrase 'who proceedeth from the Father and the Son' is, as everyone knows, one of the causes of controversy between

[1] E. J. Bicknell, *A Theological Introduction to the Thirty-Nine Articles*, pp. 121–122.

the Eastern Orthodox Churches and the Church of the West. The creed we call the Nicene Creed, the Creed of Constantinople, had just the words 'who proceedeth from the Father' and was designed to emphasize that the Holy Spirit derives his being from the being of God. It was one of the safeguards against Macedonianism. But the New Testament makes clear that there is an essential and vital link between the redemptive work of Christ in his life, death and resurrection, and the ever-renewed making present of the fruits of that redemptive work through the Holy Spirit in the life of the Church in every generation. The work of the Risen and Exalted Christ and the work of the Holy Spirit are indissolubly linked. It was to safeguard this truth, as well as to oppose heresy, that the Church in the West began to use the phrase 'from the Father and the Son,' and from this usage the additional clause found its way into the Creed in the West. The Eastern Churches can rightly claim that the additional clause lacks full Catholic authority, though they do not deny the truth the clause was intended to express.

In these days when the whole concept of God is under re-examination, such differences may well seem utterly unreal. Can we any longer put ourselves into the kind of mental framework that could imagine it could make meaningful statements about such abstractions? No doubt, we shall want to be a good deal more cautious than many of our forefathers, yet we shall miss the point of their struggles if we fail to recognize that the fathers of the Councils were not just trying to theologize for its own sake, but were doing their best with the tools at their disposal to safeguard the essential Christian experience, as they had entered into it on the basis of the New Testament revelation. On that basis we can hope that in due course East and West will agree on words that should satisfy both sides—'Who proceedeth from the Father through the Son.'

One point of detail remains. The Reformers omitted the word

'holy' from the adjectives descriptive of the Church, not on doctrinal grounds, but simply because they believed it lacked the support of the best manuscripts.[1] We now know that in this they were mistaken, and current Anglican revisions of the Prayer Book restore the epithet. The Niceno-Constantinopolitan Creed proclaims the four traditional characteristics of the Church as part of its essential structure—it is one, holy, catholic and apostolic.

The third paragraphs of the two Creeds thus run closely parallel. They are to be interpreted, not as a series of unrelated clauses, strung together like beads on a string, but as organically related to each other. We profess our faith in the Holy Spirit, who is God himself, the Lord, the Life-giver, One to be worshipped and glorified together with the Father and the Son in the unity of the Godhead, the inspiring Power and Guide of the one, holy, catholic and apostolic Church, which is the communion of saints, the blessed company of all faithful people.[2] By this one Spirit we have been baptized into the one Body, the Church (I Cor. 12. 13), and by our membership we already know through faith what it is to be risen with Christ and to enter into the essential quality of eternal life which is to know God and Jesus Christ whom he has sent (Jn. 17. 3). By our membership too we share together the great hope that what we have received in part here and now is only the foretaste, the first instalment of what we shall receive in the regeneration of all things in the Last Day.

It is only in this context of the Spirit's animating power in the life of the Church with all that that means in present experience and future hope that we can understand rightly the nature and calling of the Church.

---

[1] E. J. Bicknell, *op. cit.*, p. 161.

[2] The Latin phrase *Communio Sanctorum* can be interpreted either in a masculine or neuter sense. If the latter sense is given, the phrase means 'participation in holy things' i.e. the Sacraments, but the word *Sanctorum* is better construed as a masculine genitive plural.

H

Despite its place in the Creed, however, the doctrine of the Church was for too long overshadowed by the individualism that stemmed from the Renaissance. Its rediscovery in Christian thinking and fresh expression in the patterns of liturgical worship has been a notable development of the past half-century. It is now widely recognized in Protestant as well as in Catholic circles that the Church is no mere appendage to the Gospel, a useful association of those who have already made their individual response of faith to Christ, but an integral part of the Gospel itself. Various factors have contributed to this rediscovery. The first has been the movement known as biblical theology. Whereas Liberal Protestantism could dissolve the essential New Testament Gospel into a message of the fatherhood of God and the brotherhood of man and Evangelical pietism could think almost exclusively in terms of God's dealings with the individual, biblical scholars have made clear how central to Old and New Testaments alike is the theme of the People of God. 'The New Testament' it has been said 'knows nothing of a solitary Christian' and, if that judgement is amply supported by a study of the Epistles, form-criticism, despite unwarrantable scepticism about their historical value, has made it abundantly clear that the Gospels are inseparably bound up, not only with the Jesus of Galilee and Judaea, but with the faith, life and pastoral problems of the Church of the first century.[1]

Secondly, there has been the influence of the Ecumenical Movement. One of the surest evidences of the working of the Holy Spirit in the life of the Church is the way in which in a particular age Christians in different lands and traditions are gripped by a particular conviction about God's call to them in their generation. If the great missionary expansion of the Roman Catholic Church in the sixteenth and seventeenth centuries and the similar expansion of churches, both Catholic and Protestant, in the nineteenth century, was at its deepest level a response to the call of the Spirit, the recognition of the scandal

[1] See Section A, chap. I above.

of Christian divisions and the insistent call to unity are evidence of the Spirit's guidance in the twentieth century. Indeed, the two movements are integrally related. Divisions which could be tolerated through long familiarity in the 'Christian' countries of the West became a scandal in the 'missionary' lands of Africa and the East, and a denial of the Gospel before the non-Christian world. It is not without significance that the first major scheme of reunion between episcopal and non-episcopal churches should have been carried through in South India and that much of the urge toward Christian unity in the West comes as a back-thrust from the Church in what used to be called the mission-field.

Thirdly, there are the unceasing pressures of modern society away from the *laissez-faire* individualism of the nineteenth century towards the collectivism of the twentieth. The sheer size and cost of the machinery required for our technological age makes the big industrial unit a necessity. The super-market undercuts the private trader. Radio, TV, and the disc jockey spread a pop culture round the world. 'The basic economic fact of our time is not independence, but inter-dependence. . . . It is the age, for good or for ill, of planning, of welfare service and corporate ownership, and, internationally, of the super-state.'[1] The Bishop of Woolwich, who wrote the book from which this quotation comes, did so out of the conviction that 'in the Pauline concept of the body there is something of profound implication and relevance both for the understanding of this problem . . . and for its Christian solution.'[2] The Holy Spirit guides us, as wise householders, to take out of our treasure things new and old, according as they are needed in the changing climates of each age.

The New Testament doctrine of the Church can be summarized under three main definitions, each of which embraces a paradox. Both sides of each paradox must be held in tension if we are to be loyal to the full Biblical revelation, and it is largely because of failure here that the varied emphases of 'Catholic,' 'Protestant,' 'pietistic' and 'pentecostalist' traditions have arisen.

[1] J. A. T. Robinson, *The Body*, p. 7.   [2] *Op. cit.*, p. 8.

2

First, then, *the Church is the people of God, his Israel, at once continuous with the old Israel and inheriting the promises, the call and the judgements delivered by God to his people in Old Testament days and yet transformed into the new Israel through the life, death and resurrection of Christ and the outpouring of his Spirit.*

Whatever our critical judgement about the promise to Peter (Mt. 16. 18) as an authentic utterance of Jesus, at least on the recorded occasion, there can be no doubt of its essential significance in the New Testament revelation. 'On this rock I will build my *ecclesia*, my *qahal*, my people of God.' The basic word for 'Church' is that which the Septuagint used to translate the Hebrew word that was applied to the assembled people of God, Israel gathered together in its totality before God. 1 Peter has a close link with catechetical instruction for Baptism; the new members are taught the high calling that will be theirs as members of Christ's Church—'a spiritual house, a holy priesthood, . . . a chosen race . . . God's own people' (2. 5 and 9). Everyone of these phrases has an Old Testament background. Just as God had in past days his dwelling place in the Holy of Holies in the innermost part of the Temple at Jerusalem, so now his presence is to be manifested in the Church, his new spiritual house, of which new members, added by Baptism, become living stones. Just as the old Israel was 'a kingdom of priests and a holy nation' (Ex. 19. 6), so now the Church is a royal priesthood and a people set apart for God, called to offer spiritual sacrifices to him through Jesus Christ and to declare his wonderful deeds to all the world. If God had delivered old Israel 'with a mighty hand and a stretched-out arm' from bondage in Egypt and had brought his people into covenant relationship with himself at Sinai, so now Christ in the Upper Room at the Last Supper had demonstrated in word and action that by his death the next day he was delivering his people from the far greater bondage of sin, and establishing a new covenant with a new people of God. The Old Testament records spoke of what could be described as a universal baptism of old Israel 'under the cloud' and as they passed through the Red Sea. They told also of God's provision of supernatural food for them in the manna and of supernatural drink in the water from the rock. These prefigured the two great sacraments of the Gospel. Yet, says St. Paul, these gifts must not lull us into a false sense of security. In the case of old Israel most of them were overthrown in the wilderness through faithlessness, and the same can happen to us (1 Cor. 10. 1-14). Judgement begins at the house of God, and the Lord can remove the lampstand of the faithless Church as well as bring judgement on the faithless individual (1 Pet. 4. 17; Rev. 2. 5).

At the same time the Church is profoundly different from the old Israel. For it stands on the other side of the great divide in history represented by the coming of Christ. It is the people of God refounded and reconstituted by Christ and empowered by his Spirit, and because of this fact it is the true Israel. As such, it is set free from the obligations of obedience to the Jewish Law, of which circumcision was the sign and initiatory rite, and from the limitations of race and nationhood, which attached inevitably to the Jewish people. Much of the New Testament is concerned with the Church's disentangling of itself from the position of a Jewish sect, distinguished from the rest of Judaism only by its confession of faith in Jesus of Nazareth as the Messiah come in the flesh, and its discovery of its true character under God as a Catholic society. Thus Acts tells the story of the Spirit's guidance in compelling the Church to leap over the barrier of Palestinian Judaism and embrace first Jews of the Dispersion, then Samaritans and finally the Gentile world. St. Paul in various epistles, notably Galatians, Romans and Philippians, battled with all his might against the powerful forces of Jewish Christianity, with their insistence that Gentiles could only become full Christians by accepting the requirements of the Jewish Law. This, he asserted with passion, was to cut at the very heart of the Gospel. For the good news, the kerygma, which the Church was commissioned to proclaim was the announcement of God's gracious action in his mercy and love in Christ to meet men and women where they are in all their bewilderment, weakness and sin and to accept them as they are on the basis of faith and trust alone. This meant a complete repudiation of the heavy burden of legal observance which the developments of the Mosaic Law, and still more the scribal and Pharisaic elaborations of it, involved—a repudiation of justification by works; it meant a return to the covenant relationship of promise and faith expressed in God's relationships with Abraham. Baptism, says St. Paul, is the sacramental expression of this relationship and the way of entry into the Israel of God that knows it has no grounds of its own to claim God's acceptance, but lives only by the grace of God (Rom. 6. 1-4).

The Church, then, is the people of God, a society that lives by the power of the Spirit yet also has an outward and visible character. Continuous with the old Israel, we know Abraham to be our father, the promises made to him to be promises of which we are the heirs. The Old Testament with its long record of God's dealings with his people is included in our Scriptures and the revelation of God conveyed through prophet and psalmist, historian and chronicler, wisdom writer and apocalyptist, is part of the total revelation of God which the Church has received and to which it bears witness before the world. Yet the Church has been recreated in Christ, it has left behind the burden of legal relationship and lives by the grace of God alone, it has shed the particularist character that attached to the old Israel as a nation and become a catholic society, it accepts the Old Testament as Scripture because it looks back on the old Canon from our side of the Incarnation and sees it as pointing forward 'in many and various ways' to the coming of Christ, the Son, in whom God has spoken his final and decisive word to man.[1]

3

Secondly, *the Church is both a society with a continuous history down the centuries from the days of the Incarnate Christ (and indeed*

[1] See Section A, chap. II above.

through the old Israel from the time of Abraham), *and also a society which each moment depends for its life and renewal and guidance on the presence of the risen Christ and the operative power of his Spirit.* It has a 'horizontal' dimension of continuity through the years, which bears witness to the significance of history as the sphere in which God's revealing and redeeming purpose has been and is being worked out, and also a 'vertical' dimension of dependence on the living Lord, its life hid with Christ in God. Here is one of those places where Catholic and Protestant approaches have so often been one-sided.

On the one hand, many Catholic theologians with their emphasis on the taking of our manhood by the Son of God, on Mary's place in the economy of salvation and on the significance of Bethlehem in the story of our redemption, have found it congenial to speak of the Church as 'the extension of the Incarnation.' Just as Christ became incarnate of the Blessed Virgin Mary and showed the glory of God through the medium of an earthly life, so he has provided a Church to be his Body through the centuries until his coming again. To this Church he has given certain spiritual gifts and powers, and these the Church passes on from generation to generation. Sometimes this way of approach can be expressed crudely, as in the hymn of J. M. Neale,[1] but among many theologians in the Catholic tradition there has been a tendency to identify Christ with his Body. Fr. Gregory Baum, O.S.A., for instance, commenting on the teaching of Vatican II's *Constitution on the Church*, frankly recognizes this past identification. 'We must note the change of emphasis that has taken place since *Mystici Corporis* of Pius XII, in regard to the historical existence of Christ's body. Pius XII, beginning with *body equals body social*, identified, without any qualifications, the mystical body of Christ with the Catholic Church. The Constitution, beginning with mystical body as communion of life with Christ,

---

[1] So age by age and year by year,
His grace was handed on;
And still the holy Church is here,
Although her Lord is gone.
                    E. H. 166.

does not come to the same conclusion. . . . Instead of simply identifying the Church of Christ with the Catholic Church, the Constitution rather says more carefully that the Church of Christ "subsists in" the Catholic Church.'[1] Certainly in much past teaching the one, holy, catholic and apostolic Church, continuing its unbroken life down the centuries, has been thought of as *simpliciter* the Body of Christ, identical with his Body born of Mary, the shrine of his continuing presence.[2]

On the other hand, there is the kind of language which sounds so strange to Anglican ears, which speaks of the Church as an event. As Lesslie Newbigin has put it, 'It makes of the Church practically a series of totally disconnected events in which, at each moment and place at which the word and sacraments of the Gospel are set forth, the Church is there and then called into being by God's creative power.' He admits that he is exaggerating to make the point clear, but illustrates it from Karl Barth's paper in the Amsterdam volume on the Church, in which 'he introduces all his key paragraphs with the phrase "The congregation (*ecclesia*) is an event (Ereignis)." '[3] This point of view could equally well be illustrated from what is taking place all over the world today, where evangelists concerned only to preach the Gospel bring into being congregations of Christians quite isolated from the historic churches or even from each other by any constitutional bond. Such congregations are only too easily swayed by the coming of some other strong personality. Schisms quickly arise and the fissiparous character of undenominational Protestantism is displayed in all its deplorable weakness.[4]

And, whatever sympathies one may have with the motives of those who in rebellion against current patterns of church life advocate a non-Church movement, it is difficult not to think that

[1] Comm. on *The Constitution of the Church*, pp. 23–24.

[2] For criticisms of 'extension of the Incarnation' terminology see L. Newbigin, *The Reunion of the Church, passim*, and *The Household of God*, pp. 80 ff.

[3] *The Household of God*, p. 80.

[4] One seceder in a recent series of such splits in Malaya is said to have carried off to the new meeting place the organ and chairs he had originally donated to the old!

the end-result will be either fragmented and disorganized groups
or a new denomination.

Error certainly occurs when either the 'horizontal' or the
'vertical' dimension is emphasized to the exclusion of the other.

On the Catholic side there is need to recognize that with all
its long and splendid history, with its wonderful record of
martyrs and doctors, confessors and missionaries, with its continuous life down the centuries and its nourishing of Christian
life and devotion in all cultures and all social levels through
word and sacraments, yet the Church stands under the judgement
of its Lord, who is head over the body as well as its life and
strength. God can speak a fresh word and give new guidance
to his Church through the action of his Spirit in many different
ways. The whole *aggiornamento* now going on in the Roman
Catholic Church through the initiative of the late Pope John
and the action of the Vatican Council bears witness to this fact
of renewal. And while we thank God for the way in which that
Church is giving heed to what the Spirit is saying to it, we have
also to acknowledge that the Church in the time of the Reformers
was not so ready and that it could not hear what we believe were
the authentic utterances of the Spirit in a day of worldliness and
corruption. One of the most significant acts of the Vatican
Council has been its readiness to accept its share of blame for
the break-up of Christendom in the Reformation period.

It is important in this connection to understand St. Paul's image
of the Church as the Body of Christ correctly. It is easy enough
to think of the image as simply concerned to emphasize the
organic nature of the Church's life. Just as in a human body
there are many members—eyes, feet, hands—which despite their
differences of function are yet bound into a unity by sharing
in the life of the one organism, so the many members of the
Church are bound together with each other across the differences
of function and ministry by participating together in the common
life of the Body of Christ. This is, of course, one of the things
St. Paul has very much in mind as he faces the rivalries and
jealousies of those with different gifts in the Church in Corinth.

But it is easy to interpret his words in such a way as to suggest that the Church has an organic life of its own and to forget the complementary truth that its organic life is entirely dependent on Christ.

E. Schweizer has recently emphasized this point. When the early Christians met Sunday by Sunday for the Breaking of the Bread, he says, and heard the words 'This is my body for you' they were first reminded of their dependence on the redemptive work of Christ on the Cross, on 'the crucified body in its for-our-sake-ness.' Yet 'this is not to be severed from the risen body, since the crucified body of Jesus is only important in its blessing and challenging effect which meets us in the blessing and challenge of the risen Christ.'[1] Similarly, Lesslie Newbigin, commenting on the crucial phrase 'through the body of Christ' in Romans 7. 4, says that it refers *both* to the death of Christ's body of flesh once for all on the Cross, *and* to the union of believers with him in his risen body of which they have been made members.[2] Secondly, says E. Schweizer, the phrase 'the body of Christ' implies a demand on the Church. As he puts it at the end of his book, 'the church can be the body of Christ only if it is willing to suffer and thereby to be the body of its Lord, who in his body, goes into the world, serving all mankind. If the Church is willing to live in this way as Christ's body, often suffering and dying, it will experience time and again that he himself creates in it that obedience and that readiness for self-sacrifice, in which he, as its Lord, encounters the world and converts Gentiles into members of his body.'[3]

The image of the body thus has an essentially 'vertical' dimension. It represents the union of the Church with its Lord who is Head of the Body in its dependence on his dying and rising again as the saving events by which it is constituted, in its life 'in Christ' through the power of his indwelling Spirit, and in the insistent demand that its character as the Body of Christ shall be manifested 'in the concrete brotherhood in which obedience to the Lord is manifest in love to the brother . . . in its

[1] *The Church as the Body of Christ*, pp. 43 and 46.   [2] *Op. cit.*, p. 68.   [3] *Op. cit.*, p. 78.

openness for others, for the world, therefore in its mission to the nations and its self-sacrifice to those who are outside of it.'[1]

Equally on the Protestant side there is need to recognize the 'horizontal' dimension. The revelation of God, culminating in the Incarnation, the life, death and resurrection of Christ took place in history, though we may differ as to how far the events of our redemption are open to historical investigation as such, and how far they depend on the response of faith to those events. For Christianity history is not just a meaningless series of happenings, not an illusion from which we seek escape into some timeless world of religion, but the sphere of God's action, originating in his creative purpose, redeemed by Christ, and destined to reach its climax and completion in the regeneration of all things. The continuous life of the Church down the centuries is an essential witness to the positive significance which the Christian God gives to history.

We are not surprised, therefore, to find the Church in the New Testament, as it passes from the first creative days of the apostles to the second generation, taking steps to safeguard the passing on of the apostolic tradition in its completeness. 'Guard what has been entrusted to you' (1 Tim. 5. 20), 'the faith once for all delivered to the saints' (Jude 3) were the battle-cries, as the Church of the sub-apostolic generation plotted its course through the dangerous waters of heresy. We can trace a continuous tradition of teaching from the earliest days, when St. Paul received the kerygma (1 Cor. 15. 1 ff.), through the later books of the New Testament to its formulation in the Apostles' and Nicene Creeds.

It was in this context that the phrase 'apostolic succession' was first used, for it meant, as we have been often enough reminded,[2] the faithful witness to the Gospel of the occupants of the apostolic

---

[1] Op. cit., p. 77. E. Schweizer's points are very illuminating, though with his Protestant shyness of mysticism he underestimates the significance of St. Paul's language about being 'in Christ.'

[2] Cf. e.g. A. C. Headlam, The Doctrine of the Church and Reunion, passim.

sees down the years, as opposed to the claim of the Gnostics to a secretly handed down tradition of teaching from the apostles.

Similarly, the defining of the Canon of the New Testament cannot be divorced from the ongoing life of the historic Church.[1] The purpose of that definition was not to provide a book from which any religious enthusiast, however one-sided or crack-brained, might confidently construct a brand-new religion. The Canon was closed so that the Church of succeeding generations might have the witness of the apostolic generation to the apostolic Gospel by which the Church lived and to which it must always be faithful.

And always the Church celebrated the two great sacraments of the Gospel—Baptism and the Eucharist; the first whereby the new member was admitted into the universal fellowship of Christ's Church and the second whereby the Church renewed its life in Christ and experienced afresh the meaning of the communion of saints back over history, across the world and over the barrier of death. Here in visible and dramatic form the realities of redemption were made present to those who belonged to the actual society of Christ's Church with its interior life hid with Christ in God and its exterior life set in the tangible realities of a continuing historical existence.

There is a further consideration to which Bishop Newbigin has called attention, namely that 'the Church cannot live except as a visibly defined and organized body with a continuing structure.'[2] All new movements which have represented an upsurge of the Spirit in revolt against the historic churches have themselves proceeded to develop their own means of continuing survival. 'The followers of Calvin and Knox, who had both absolutely denied that ministerial succession is a mark of the true Church, are found asserting a perpetual succession of presbyters. And the followers of John Wesley, who had performed an act of ordination for which he had no ecclesiastical authority, would probably be more horrified than any other body of Christians if one of their members today did the same.'[3] Only

---

[1] See Section A, chap. III above.   [2] *Op. cit.*, p. 72.   [3] *Op. cit.*, p. 73.

theologians writing their theses apart from the realities of the Church's everyday life, and evangelists of the kind referred to above, can, in fact, ignore the truth to which Scripture and the actual course of ecclesiastical development point, namely that the 'horizontal' dimension along the course of history belongs to the nature of the Church as essentially as the 'vertical' relationship with the living Christ in each moment of its existence.

To do them justice, the leaders of Protestant Churches today are as aware of the importance of historic continuity as leaders in churches of a Catholic tradition are increasingly sensitive to the criticisms of a too close identification of the empirical Church with Christ. Thus the Statement of Agreed Principles between representatives of the Anglican Church of Canada and the United Church of Canada begins its section on the Church with the words 'God in his Word not only teaches men but calls them into a visible fellowship in which redemption is given and received.' It goes on, 'Christians are therefore one not only in faith but also in orders, united not only by Scripture and doctrine, but by Church, Sacraments and Ministry.' At the same time, it emphasizes that the living Word which the Church hears in the Bible is to be received 'as the supreme rule of faith through which its life, teaching and worship are to be tested and renewed.'[1] Similarly, the Proposed Basis of Union for the Congregationalist, Methodist and Presbyterian Churches in Australia speaks of God having given 'to men in Scripture, in the teaching, worship and ordered fellowship of the Church means whereby he draws men to Himself.' The Church is 'of God's making and not of ours' and the uniting churches 'seek the fullness of the Church's ordered life and worship.' Yet also 'the Church's message is controlled by the Word spoken in Jesus Christ and mediated through Holy Scripture, which is the unique earthly instrument through which the Church hears the living Word, and the decisive measure by which her life on earth is tested and through

[1] *Canadian Churchman*, June 1965, p. 10. The United Church of Canada is a union of Methodists, Congregationalists and two-thirds of the Presbyterians.

which it is renewed.'[1] Similar statements could be quoted from most, if not all, Church unity schemes at the present time.

4

The third paradox in the life of the Church arises from the fact that it is a Body, 'upon whom the end of the ages has come' (1 Cor. 10. 11) and yet is still involved in the ambiguities of our earthly existence. On the one hand, the Church is that part of the human race which has already been redeemed by Christ. Christians are those who have already passed from darkness to light, have already died to sin and risen again to newness of life in Christ and already live in the heavenly places. Our commonwealth is in heaven, and we are one with the Church triumphant and the Church expectant on the other side of death. In one sense all the constituent elements of the hope of the End have been realized already. We shall not come into judgement, Christ's victory over evil is a present experience, his coming again has already taken place in the gift of the Spirit to inspire and direct the Church. 'Christ loved the Church and gave himself up for her, that he might sanctify her, having cleansed her by the washing of water with the word, that the church might be presented before him in splendour, without spot or wrinkle or any such thing, that she might be holy and without blemish' (Eph. 5. 25–27). It is easy to see how Catholic theologians can assert that in its essential nature the Church's unity, holiness, catholicity, and apostolicity cannot be lost or impaired. Individual members or groups may quarrel, and their sinfulness and faithlessness can bring scandal to the Church's life, but the Church as such cannot sin or err.

But the New Testament makes clear that the Church is still involved in the old order of sin and death. There is always a 'not yet' about the life of the Church on earth. Its unity is broken and the Church is called to its recovery. Its holiness has time and

---

[1] *The Church—Its Nature, Function and Ordering* together with the *Proposed Basis of Union*, pp. 75 and 78.

again been marred by worldliness, compromise and the pressures of power politics, and constantly needs renewing. Its catholicity can be impaired by the sectarian temper and its apostolicity lost when it has settled down comfortably in a position of security in a particular culture. The New Testament call to the Christian individual to 'become what you are' applies equally to the Church.

If the Catholic tends to resolve this paradox by insisting on the perfection of the Church in itself as distinct from its members, the Protestant has tried to solve the riddle by drawing a sharp distinction between the visible and the invisible Church. Lesslie Newbigin writes of 'the virtual disappearance of the idea of the Church as a visible unity' in the Reformers' doctrine of the Church. He quotes Luther's words, 'The essence, life and nature of the Church is not a bodily assembly but an assembly of hearts in one faith' and again 'A spiritual unity is of itself sufficient to make a Church' and comments (very justly in my view) 'This language is uncomfortably unlike that of the Bible with its stress upon an actual visible fellowship. . . . The one body spoken of in the New Testament is not the contrary of the one Spirit, but its implicate.' While we must recognize the pressures under which Luther was working in his great protest against a corrupt Church, yet this sharp division between the true Church and the Church as it appears in history is destructive of its true nature as 'a continuing historical society, that society which was constituted and sent forth once for all by Jesus Christ.'[1]

Similarly, the negotiators of the scheme for a united Church in Australia write, the 'duality which must be kept in mind if we are to grasp correctly the relationship of Christ to his Church, must not be seen as suggesting that the outward Church we see (visible) is not the true Church; and that only the inward (invisible) faith of true believers is the real Church. As the Body of Christ, the Church is a visible community, with its essential, external forms—sacraments, ministry, worship. By these she lives and grows.'[2]

[1] *Op. cit.*, pp. 54–59 *passim*, an important passage.   [2] *Op. cit.*, p. 16.

The Church has indeed its inward aspect, its life in Christ, but also its outward aspect in history. Between the two there is always tension. For the Church on earth is caught up in the 'not yet' of its earthly existence, and it must always be growing 'with a growth that is from God' (Col. 2. 19). God's gifts of ministry to his Church are 'for the building up of the body of Christ, until we all attain to the unity of faith and the knowledge of the Son of God, to mature manhood, to the measure of the stature of the fullness of Christ' (Eph. 4. 12–14). But it is the same Church, God's new Israel, with its continuing life and its immediate dependence upon its Lord, with its eternal inheritance and its earthly failings, its given character and its future completeness, its rejoicings in the good heritage of faith, worship and witness it has received from the past and its striving to be in ever-increasing measure the unspotted Bride of Christ, the embodiment on earth of the Kingdom of Heaven.

5

With this understanding of the paradoxical nature of the Church's life, we who are Anglicans must recognize *the inadequacy of Article XIX 'Of the Church.'* Closely resembling as it does the corresponding Article in the Augsburg Confession, it confines itself to the 'vertical' dimension, to the preaching of the pure Word of God and the due administration of the Sacraments in the visible Church, the congregation of faithful men. In so far as it speaks of the 'horizontal' dimension, it is merely negative, only saying that like various ancient churches the Church of Rome has erred both in ceremonies and matters of Faith. However understandable such a statement is in the context of the sixteenth century, it is not a balanced definition of the Church and needs supplementing by a much more positive affirmation of the Church's character as a continuing historical society through the centuries with a duty of witness to the world. The definition of the Church in the Revised Catechism is a necessary supplement, if our formularies are to be adequate both to the teaching of the New Testament and to the facts of Anglican history, which, as we all know, included great care to maintain all the elements of continuity with the historic Church which our Reformers could regard as compatible with the Gospel—more than most of the other Reformed churches felt possible.

But the evidence of the New Testament and the facts of our contemporary situation must make us equally aware that many of the old 'Catholic' slogans are inadequate for our day. There can be no tidy ecclesiologies, in which we are quite sure who belong to the Catholic Church and who do not, even if we are prepared to show charity by talking of God's uncovenanted mercies. As the Roman Catholic Church has recognized, the one basic fact of our belonging together with separated Christians is the one Baptism for the remission of sins, and we Anglicans must learn similarly to abandon the persistent survival in the background of our thinking of the old Tractarian 'three-branch' theory of the Catholic Church. Within the company of the baptized division is schism within the Church and the work of Christian unity is not just the attempt to bring back to the fold those who have broken away, but the recognition that in our divisions we have all of us become lop-sided, seeing some truths of the Gospel clearly, but sometimes being only half aware of aspects of Christian truth which other Christian bodies have preserved better than we have.

The Proposed Basis of Union in Australia sums up admirably the right approach to the whole quest for Christian unity:

Together we seek the fullness of the Church's ordered life and worship. Again we look to the past, and ask what God has revealed of the true life of the Church, and what he has been teaching her through the ages. Into this heritage, catholic and reformed, we would enter anew. But we would listen also to the call of God in the present, his call to us to represent the Church as a reconciled Body so that the world may hear of its salvation. And we look to the future, praying and believing that God will maintain his Church in fellowship with himself, purging her and enabling her to fulfil the mission to which in each generation she is called. . . . It is their (sc. the churches) hope and prayer that those who come after them will say and do things better than they, that God will lead his Church into a greater manifestation of her Unity, that in every way the Bride may be made the more ready for her Lord.

I

To that statement of Congregationalists, Methodists and Presbyterians members of the Anglican Communion can only add a fervent Amen.

6

'The call of God in the present.' On many sides the call of God is being proclaimed as a call to be a Servant Church, following the example of its Master, the Man for others. Hugh Montefiore has criticized that phrase as the key to the understanding of Christ. 'Isn't obedience rather than service of neighbour the key note of his life? Would he not more accurately be described as "the Man for God"?[1] I believe he is entirely right, and the Church will no longer be the Church if it concentrates so much on the second commandment of the Law as to forget or at least soft-pedal the first. That way it becomes just another do-gooding organization in the world. But it is equally true that directly as a result of being the Man for God Christ was the Man for others. All men everywhere, and not least those in need and sickness, were for him within the Father's care and redemptive concern, and in his service and suffering, his identification with men and women in their sinful and broken situations, he served the will of his Father in and through his service of others.

As the Christian Church faces the end of the Constantinian age, as its accepted and recognized position in society is questioned or ended, either with the growth of secular humanism in the West and the increasing neutrality of Governments or with the rise of independent nations in Asia or Africa which seek to build their new lives on a basically non-Christian cultural heritage, many of the spheres of service—education, hospitals, social welfare—pass from its control. To a decreasing extent will the Church be able to enjoy the position of power and prestige which was natural in a *corpus Christianum*, a Christian civilization. More and more must it be ready to 'strip down,' to involve itself

---

[1] *Frontier*, Spring 1965, p. 69. The comment comes in a review of the Cambridge lectures *Faith, Fact and Fantasy*.

positively in the great moral and social issues of the time, and to serve humbly men and women in their need in all the mixed-up situations of modern society. The Bishop of Woolwich in *The New Reformation* explains (perhaps in over-sharp tones) some of the factors in the modern scene which the Vatican Council had to face, which an increasing number in the Anglican Communion and elsewhere are facing, and which the whole Church must face sooner or later. The questions thus posed to us are searching, and to find the right answers is anything but comfortable. But the stark truth remains that it is never without travail that the whole structure of the Church 'is joined together and grows into a holy temple in the Lord' (Eph. 2. 21).

THE SACRAMENTS OF THE GOSPEL

The two Sacraments ordained by Christ himself—Baptism and the Supper of the Lord—ministered with unfailing use of Christ's Words of Institution, and of the elements ordained by him

INTRODUCTION

SACRAMENTS are essentially acts of the living Christ within the Church which is his Body. Hence a right understanding of the sacraments depends on a right doctrine of the Church. Yet in a wider context that understanding depends also on a right grasp of the relation between the whole material world and God its Creator, between the physical universe and the Son of God, the Logos, through whom all things were made. There are many religious creeds which are suspicious of or despise this world and all that belongs to it and whose *raison d'être* is to offer men a way of release. For many in the Hindu tradition this earthly order is an illusion and the practices of mysticism are designed to help men escape from its chains. For the authentic Buddhism of Gautama the root of all evil is found in desire— not necessarily evil desire, but the sheer positive desire that keeps one bound to the chain of existence and so involves one in the suffering that is an inevitable concomitant of earthly life. The aim of true living is to slough off desire and so finally to attain Nirvana, to enter the bliss of being absorbed like a drop of water into the ocean of being.

The Protestant tradition in a different way has often been highly suspicious of the material, the tangible, the earthly. For one thing these elements have too frequently been the focal points of superstition and something not far removed from magic in Catholic devotional practice; for another they have seemed, even when free of such abuse, to be dragging the Christian Church back from the level of the New Testament with its apparent emphasis on the inward and spiritual to that of the Old Testament cultus with all its elaborate externals. Did not Christ say that the hour had come when men would no longer worship God in the temple at Jerusalem or on Mount Gerizim, but in spirit and in truth (Jn. 4. 21–24)? Paul Tillich once wrote of 'the death of the sacraments in the Protestant tradition'[1] and Lesslie Newbigin

---

[1] *The Protestant Era*, p. 95.

speaks of 'the whittling away of the sacraments at many times and places in Protestant history.'[1] They have seemed an uncomfortable element in what to many people is essentially a 'purely spiritual' religion.

The first answer to this lies in the Biblical doctrine of creation, in the assurance that 'God saw everything that he had made, and behold, it was very good' (Gen. 1. 31). The material universe is God's handiwork and though infected, like man in his inmost nature, with evil, it yet bears upon it, as man's nature does, the marks of its Creator. Further, the Christian gospel of redemption is not good news of deliverance from the material world, it is good news of deliverance from *sin*, and it embraces in its compass the whole universe. God's purpose was that through the Cross all things, whether on earth or in heaven, might be reconciled to himself (Col. 1. 20). It is right then to see certain parallels between the world of nature and the world of spirit, for both derive their existence from the same God. And because this is a 'sacramental universe,' we must acknowledge 'God as the Lord and Governor of Nature, who uses all the elements according to his will for the promotion of his own glory.'[2] Calvin wrote that in the course of a comment on the giving of the rainbow in the Genesis story as a sign to Noah and his descendants that he would never again destroy the human race. He knew as well as we do the natural character of the rainbow, but for him the meaning given to it derives from 'God's power to mark his creatures with his Word, that they may become sacraments, though before they were mere elements.' It is for this reason that the Revised Catechism recognizes a wider use of the word 'sacrament,' as well as the stricter use in relation to the two sacraments of the Gospel.[3] Sacraments are in harmony with the basic Christian understanding of God's relation to the material universe.

---

[1] *The Household of God*, p. 75.

[2] Calvin, *Institutes*, Bk. IV, xiv, 18 quoted D. Baillie, *The Theology of the Sacraments*, p. 45.

[3] 36. Q. What do you mean by a sacrament?

A. By a sacrament I mean the use of material things as signs and pledges of God's grace, and as a means by which we receive his gifts.

Secondly, sacraments correspond to the nature of man. We are not souls temporarily housed in bodies of flesh, but to the Hebrew and Biblical way of thinking animated bodies, or in the modern jargon, psycho-somatic unities. Our bodies link us with the whole world of matter, with God's creation. Redeemed by Christ, they have become his members (1 Cor. 6. 15) and it is in our bodies that we are to glorify God (v. 20). Life cannot be lived on a 'purely spiritual' level in this world, but only in and through the body. Sight, hearing, eating, drinking, movement and action all have their part to play in our reception of the realities around us and in our response to them. That is why the tremendous emphasis in classical Protestantism on the centrality of the preached Word is to narrow unduly the channels by which God can work in us. Of course the preached Word is vitally important, for through it the Gospel reaches home to our understanding. But the Gospel confined to the preached Word becomes only too easily an intellectualist formulation, as can be seen from the way in which Protestant scholasticism has not infrequently substituted acceptance of the dogma of justification by faith for trust in the God who justifies.

Protestantism has indeed found a splendid outlet for the response of faith through the great chorales of Bach and the hymns of Watts and Wesley. They give expression to elements in the human personality other than the intellectual, and the same thing is true of ceremonial, colour and movement in the Catholic tradition of worship. These can obscure rather than illuminate the truth when they become over-elaborate and fussy, but it is merely partisan to decry their use altogether in days when all educational methods recognize how much more most people receive through the eye than the ear and when in consequence audio-visual materials are essential teaching aids.

Sacraments fit naturally into this understanding of human nature. From time immemorial and over a vast number of countries washing with water has been the natural form for rites of purification. It is so elemental to all human experience that it speaks to man at a deeper than conscious level of his being.

How natural then that the first Sacrament of the Gospel should be Baptism, washing with water in the name of the Trinity! Similarly, the common meal has been a universal way of expressing and increasing fellowship among the participants, not least in societies where the sharing of meat together is thought of as uniting the participants, not only with each other but with the god whom they worship together in the sacrificial feast. How appropriate then that at the heart of Christian worship there should be the sharing of bread and wine, blessed and consecrated to be the channels of the life of the One who gave his life as a ransom for many! To participate in the sacraments of the Gospel is not to participate in meaningless rites, nor are we excused the task of understanding as fully as we can their rich and varied significance. But to share in them is to share in mysteries in which God touches our lives in more ways than our conscious minds can grasp and gives more than either we desire or deserve. The inward-outward character of the sacraments makes them particularly appropriate means by which the living God can touch our psychosomatic personalities at every level.

Thirdly, sacraments bear witness to the Christian life as a life-in-fellowship. They are social acts. 'Inasmuch as the Sacraments belong to the Church, they afford in special measure an instance of that corporate action without which the corporate life of the Church as of any other society must atrophy.'[1] Too often they have been minimized by those whose main concern is with the faith of the individual, and even in circles where they have been properly valued there has frequently been an individualistic approach. The Doctrine Report is right in criticizing this as misleading. 'The way . . . to attempt to reach an understanding of the Sacraments is to consider their place in the corporate life of the Christian society, and to proceed from this to their value for the individual. To invert this process, and to ask first (e.g.) what is the difference between a baptized infant and an unbaptized, is to confuse the problem in advance. The Sacraments are social and corporate rites of the Church in which

[1] *Doctrine in the Church of England*, p. 126.

by means of divinely appointed signs spiritual life flows from God.'[1] This emphasis on the corporate needs making, for it is, as we have seen, only in the setting of the family life of the people of God that the authentic New Testament understanding of what it means to be a Christian is found. It is through sharing in the organic life of the Body of Christ, through being brought into the blessings of the New Covenant that the individual Christian finds the fullness of Christian life.

[1] *Op. cit.*, p. 128.

I. BAPTISM AND CONFIRMATION

I

IN his recent book, *The Central Message of the New Testament*, J. Jeremias writes of *the central importance of Baptism* in the teaching of St. Paul. The apostle, he says, 'uses a multitude of illustrations to show to the newly converted what this rite means to them. He tells them:

"When you are baptized you are washed; you are cleansed; you are sanctified; you are buried in the water and by this burial you get a share in Christ's death and resurrection; you are putting on Christ like a garment; you are incorporated into his body; you are adopted and you become sons of God; you are circumcised with the circumcision made without hands, that is, you are made members of God's people; in short, you are included in the Kingdom." '[1]

It would be difficult to find anywhere such a succinct and comprehensive summary of the teaching about Baptism, not only of St. Paul, but of the whole New Testament. Here in a few words are the main pieces of imagery used to convey the meaning of transference from the old life to the new, from the Kingdom of darkness to the Kingdom of the Son of God's dear love, from the stain, guilt and bondage of sin to the freedom and newness of life of those who have received from God the forgiveness of sins and now live in the Spirit, from the bondage of the past to being sealed for the final redemption. This is the language that permeates the services of Holy Baptism in the Prayer Book, and it is picked up in the statements of the Doctrine Report:

'Baptism signifies and effects spiritual cleansing, "death unto sin and new birth unto righteousness," through incorporation into the Body of Christ the Church. This is the fellowship of the redeemed in whom the power of the Holy Spirit as given through the revelation of God in Christ is at work, in distinction from "the world" . . . Baptism, standing at the beginning of the Christian life, on the one hand signifies a state of salvation which is fully reached only through the whole process of life, and on the other effects forthwith the necessary first stage of that life.'[2]

[1] P. 60.   [2] Pp. 136–137.

122

The Doctrine Report emphasizes that Baptism admits not just to the visible Church on earth, but to the Body of Christ which includes the Church beyond the grave. 'It is into this eternal fellowship that Baptism gives admission.'[1]

Similarly, the Canadian Church Union Scheme states 'Baptism with water and with the Spirit, in the name of the Father and of the Son and of the Holy Ghost, is a divinely instituted sacrament whereby we are made children of grace and incorporated into the Body of Christ, and receive forgiveness of sin and a new birth unto righteousness.'[2] And the Proposed Basis of Union of the three Churches in Australia includes the following definition:

'By Baptism men are incorporated into the one Body of Christ through participation in his Baptism accomplished once on behalf of all in his cross, burial and resurrection, and made available to all by the outpouring of the Holy Spirit at Pentecost. Baptism into the Body of Christ initiates men into the life and mission of Christ, under the universal name of the Father of heaven and earth and in the power of the Holy Spirit poured out on all flesh.'[3]

These definitions would find widespread acceptance in the historic churches, as is shown, e.g., by the Faith and Order Report, *One Lord, One Baptism*, and by the papers produced by writers from different communions in *Crisis for Baptism*,[4] the report of a conference sponsored by Parish and People.

There would also be general agreement among theologians that for the dominical origin of this sacrament we should look, not just to the familiar passages at the end of the Gospels according to St. Mark and St. Matthew, which may not go back to the first days of Christianity,[5] but to a wider background. First, there was our Lord's baptism in the context of the preaching of John the Baptist. There can be no doubt of the close connection between John's mission and that of Jesus. The former preached repentance in preparation for the coming of the Kingdom of God, and those who responded to his message were baptized in the

---

[1] P. 137.   [2] *Canadian Churchman*, June 1965, p. 10.   [3] P. 79.   [4] Basil S. Moss, ed.
[5] Mk. 16. 16 belongs to the post-Marcan addition to the Gospel; Mt. 28. 19 includes the developed Trinitarian formula, which in all probability dates from the Gentile mission—baptism into the name of Jesus the Messiah (Acts 2. 38) was adequate for the early Jewish days.

Jordan and thereby sealed as among those ready for the Kingdom when it came. Jesus came to hear John, identified himself with his people and received baptism also. As he came up from the water, the Gospels tell us, the Spirit descended upon him and he received the divine assurance of his Messianic character and vocation. Karl Barth has found here Jesus' institution of Christian baptism,[1] and though this may be going too far there can be no doubt that it was one of the main factors in the universal and un-questioned acceptance of Baptism by the whole Church. 'It seems obvious that when the early Christians baptized into the name of the Lord Jesus, their thoughts went back to the incident which in the Synoptic tradition stood immovably at the beginning of his public ministry—the baptism of Jesus himself by John in the Jordan.'[2] Indeed, some scholars hold that the particular form in which the baptism of Jesus, the gift to him of the Spirit and the divine attestation of him as Son, are recorded reflect an early pattern of Christian initiation. The Liturgical Commission of the Church of England in the services *Baptism and Confirmation* which it presented to the Archbishops of Canterbury and York in 1958 was certainly in line with modern study of the New Testa-ment in beginning a collect, 'Almighty God, our heavenly Father, who at the Baptism of thy Christ in the river Jordan didst declare him to be thine only-begotten Son . . .' and in including as one of the lections St. Mark i. i–ii.

Secondly, there was the strange language in which Christ spoke of his coming death as a baptism. 'Are you able to drink the cup that I drink, or to be baptized with the baptism with which I am baptized?' 'I have a baptism to be baptized with; and how am I constrained until it is accomplished!'[3] His death was as it were a drowning, a passing beneath the waters, though beyond was the rising again and the victory of the Kingdom. It was from such imagery as used by Christ that the New Testa-ment terminology of dying to sin in the waters of baptism and

[1] *The Teaching of the Church regarding Baptism*, pp. 18 ff.
[2] D. Baillie, *op. cit.*, p. 77.   [3] Mk. 10. 38; Lk. 12. 50.

rising again to newness of life in him would seem to derive (cf. e.g. Col. 2. 9–15; I Pet. 3. 18–22).

Thirdly, there was the fulfilment of Christ's promise in the outpouring of the Spirit on the assembled disciples on the day of Pentecost. This was 'the counterpart for the Church of the baptism of Jesus and the descent of the Spirit upon him' (Jn. 1. 31–32; Acts 2. 1–3, 38; Acts 10. 44–48).[1] For the author of Acts the events of the first Whitsunday were 'Pentecost' for the Jews, the outpouring of the Spirit upon the first disciples and their commissioning for the mission that began immediately among their fellow-Jews who were challenged to share in this gift of the Spirit through repentance and baptism. The events at Caesarea were for Luke 'Pentecost' for the Gentiles, the out-pouring of the Spirit upon the first Gentile Christians and their admittance through baptism into the one Church of Jews and Gentiles.

The organic relationship between the person and mission of Christ and the sacrament of Baptism is thus clear and we are thereby justified in continuing to speak of it as a dominical sacrament.

Hitherto, we have concentrated on the Divine action and gift in Baptism. But if there is general agreement about this, there is equal agreement about the requirement of repentance and faith in the recipients, if the benefits are to be received. The Catechism is insistent on this, and so are all statements about the meaning of this sacrament in all the churches.[2] Faith does not create the sacrament, but it is an essential for receiving its benefits. More-over, as O. C. Quick emphasized, 'Baptism symbolizes much more than what at the moment it effects.'[3] The Christian indivi-dual, like the Church on earth, lives in two worlds at once. He has died with Christ, but he must go on mortifying the members that are on the earth, he has risen with Christ, but he must go on

[1] *The Church—Its Nature, Function and Ordering* (Australian Church Union Report), p. 21.
[2] Cf. e.g. *The Theology of Christian Initiation*, p. 12, and the Australian Church Union document, p. 22.
[3] *The Christian Sacraments*, p. 173.

seeking the things that are above. He must, in the old phrase, 'improve his Baptism.' 'The Christian life is thus a continual "becoming what we are": what we are rests upon a creative action of God, inwardly received by the action of faith which it elicits.'[1] Baptism then sets the new member in the environment of the Church's life, it brings to bear on him all the influences of the new life in Christ as he responds in faith, and what it sets out in its symbolism as a complete whole is worked out effectively in the life of the Christian as he grows in grace. 'Baptism ... in symbolizing the ultimate end of salvation, symbolizes also by anticipation all those many purifications from sin and gifts of new life, of which the progress towards final salvation is made up.'[2]

We may conclude then that in the historic churches there is widespread agreement about the significance of Baptism. But there are some differences of emphasis in doctrine, serious disagreements between Baptists and others on the rightness of Infant Baptism, various views about the significance of Confirmation, and much heartsearching about the practice of Baptism and Confirmation in the Church today. We will take these matters in turn.

2

First, then, we consider *the relative place of faith and of baptism in the making of a Christian.* This is an issue which has been raised recently by my friend and colleague in Singapore, Alan Cole, in his book *The Body of Christ*, one of the Christian Foundations publications of the Evangelical Fellowship in the Anglican Communion. What he says would be subscribed to presumably by many Conservative Evangelicals. Alan Cole raises the question squarely enough by heading chapter 3 of his book, 'How do I become a member of Christ's Body?'[3]

[1] *The Theology of Christian Initiation,* p. 12.
[2] O. C. Quick, *op. cit.,* p. 173. Cf. also, 'What is given to us in baptism in an anticipatory way and as an "earnest" is "fulfilled" only on the day of resurrection. What happens in baptism is that my little life is taken up into God's plan of salvation, the mighty movement of salvation-history, whereby it is carried along towards its eschatological fulfilment at the *Parousia* of Christ.' *One Lord, One Baptism,* p. 57.
[3] Pp. 30–39.

'What makes a man a Christian?' he asks. 'Is it baptism, or faith, or both? and if so, in what relation do these stand to each other?' And he goes on to point out the importance of the issue. 'Ultimately, the nature of the Church, the nature of the ministry, and the nature of the sacraments are all involved here.'

He himself has no doubt that it is 'the inward, Spirit-given faith' which makes a man 'a Christian, a member of the Body of Christ.' And he argues for this, first on the basis of Peter's confession at Caesarea Philippi and secondly on the basis of the experience of Paul. What brought Peter his beatitude, his position as a foundation-member of the Church, was his acceptance of a divine revelation attesting the true identity of Jesus of Nazareth, not the reception of Christian baptism—there is indeed no evidence that he ever received any baptism other than perhaps John's. Similarly, 'Paul's appeal when explaining his position as a Christian is not to his baptism, but to his conversion: his great cry is not "I am a baptized man," but "I am a converted man," ' though it is admitted that, when the apostle 'appeals to Christians for moral living, it is often on the grounds of the symbolism of baptism that he does it.'

What are we to say about this? First, I believe that this interpretation of Peter's confession at Caesarea Philippi is open to serious question. Even on the strictest form-critical principles of interpretation, this great central moment in the Synoptic Gospels is surely not a demonstration of how a man becomes a Christian— indeed I would deny the legitimacy of calling anyone a Christian before Pentecost. What in my view it is designed to make clear is the faith in Jesus as the Christ which is the foundation of the Church's life. At the same time it reveals how at that stage of Jesus' earthly ministry this faith was still partial, limited and indeed in many respects wrong-headed. Only on the other side of the Cross and Resurrection would the Church come to understand and confess Jesus as the Christ who came to the glory of his Kingdom by way of suffering and death. The confession at Caesarea Philippi is indeed part of the essential confession of faith made by the new member of the Church, but it is surely

K

illegitimate to treat the episode as a blueprint for Christian initiation in post-Pentecost days.

Again, can we be so sure that St. Paul came down decidedly on the 'faith' rather than the 'baptism' side of the fence? Lesslie Newbigin asks the same questions about the relation of faith to baptism, but he answers, 'So far as I can see, the New Testament writers are totally unconscious of these difficulties. It is simply taken for granted that baptism is that by which we were made members of the body of Christ and participants in the Spirit. St. Paul in the midst of his tremendous arguments in Galatians and Romans, when he is battling for the truth that faith alone justifies, can without the slightest awkwardness refer to baptism as that by which we were incorporated in Christ.'[1] Similarly, J. Jeremias in his illuminating chapter on 'Justification by Faith' in his book already quoted writes, 'How is justification bestowed? How does God accept the ungodly? In this matter we see things more clearly today because we have learnt in the last decades that it is in baptism that this bestowal takes place' and he illustrates this from 1 Corinthians 6. 11. 'Paul does not stress explicitly the connection between justification and baptism for the very simple reason that in the justification formula the term "by faith" includes baptism by way of abbreviation.'[2]

Alan Cole admits indeed St. Paul's use of 'realistic' language, but says that it was easier for him to do so than for us. Only some two centuries later did the danger arise 'of treating the physical act as automatically conveying the symbolized reality,' which is still present with us today. Here is the fear which always lurks in the Conservative Evangelical breast, a genuine and wholesome fear of sacraments being regarded as conferring spiritual gifts automatically, of a minimizing of the need for personal response and commitment to Christ. Those who take a high view of the sacraments must respect such fears and understand such hesitations.

Further, they must recognize that the Church on earth has ragged edges. Within its membership there have been from the

---

[1] *The Household of God*, p. 66.   [2] *Op. cit.*, p. 59.

first days unworthy members such as Ananias and Sapphira. On the other hand, martyrs who died unbaptized were regarded as having received a 'baptism of desire,' and the same charity must be extended to many young people in non-Christian lands who have accepted Christ but who are not allowed by their parents to be baptized. 'It is always to be recognized that (in the Augustinian phrase) many who seem to be within are without, and many who seem to be without are within' (De Bapt. v. 38).[1]

Yet to emphasize the moment of the response of faith as the moment of becoming a member of the Body of Christ and to regard Baptism as just a symbolic witness to this is consonant only with the pietistic doctrine of the Church as the invisible society of true believers which we have seen reason to reject; it can lead easily to a view of Baptism as a helpful but in the end optional extra rather than as one of the 'sacraments generally necessary to salvation'; and not infrequently it can lead to a narrowing of the name Christian to those who have passed through a characteristically Evangelical experience of conversion.

Surely the right way is to recognize that the response of faith to the proclamation of the Gospel is the beginning, but because the Christian life is not just an individual relationship to God but membership of Christ's body, the Church, with its outward and inward aspects, the decisive moment of becoming a Christian is the moment of baptism. Here God's free and unmerited grace meets our human response of faith in the sacramental act of washing within the setting of the Church's life, and we are made 'members of Christ, children of God and inheritors of the Kingdom of heaven.' It is surely not without significance that in the periods of his life when he felt oppressed by the sense of sin and the reality of judgement, Martin Luther, the great rediscoverer of the New Testament doctrine of justification by faith, brought reassurance to his heart with the words 'Baptizatus sum, I am baptized.'

---

[1] Doctrine in the Church of England, p. 139.

3

We now come to consider *the place and validity of Infant Baptism and, closely connected with it, the relation between Baptism and Confirmation.* The former is the subject of considerable controversy among Biblical scholars at the present time, Karl Barth and K. Aland being the protagonists in the attack on Infant Baptism, O. Cullmann and J. Jeremias being its defenders.[1] The case for Believers' Baptism in the light of New Testament teaching has also been powerfully presented by G. R. Beasley-Murray in *Baptism in the New Testament.* What conclusions emerge? In the first place, I think we must frankly recognize that, while there is a high degree of probability that the children of converts were baptized along with their parents, the New Testament give us no instance in which the evidence for such a practice is absolutely clear-cut and undeniable. It may be that the story of Jesus blessing the children (Mk. 10. 13–16 and parallels), with its inclusion of the allegedly liturgical word 'hinder,' is included in the Synoptic Gospels as dominical justification for the practice, but we cannot be sure. The argument about the word 'household' in, e.g., the story of the Philippian jailer (Acts 16. 25–34) can never be conclusive. Further, even if there were unmistakable evidence of the baptism of whole households (including children) into the Church, this still would not answer the question whether children born subsequently to their parents (or one of them) becoming Christians were baptized or whether, as 1 Corinthians 7. 14 seems to imply, the Christian status of one partner in a marriage in some sense consecrated the other partner, with the result that the children of the marriage were 'holy' by physical descent.

In the second place, we must recognize, as we have already done, that the teaching of the New Testament about Baptism treats it as part of a complex whole. The redeeming love of God welcomes the new convert on his profession of faith and transfers

---

[1] K. Barth, *The Teaching of the Church regarding Baptism;* K. Aland, *Did the Early Church Baptize Infants?* O. Cullmann, *Baptism in the New Testament;* and J. Jeremias, *Baptism in the First Four Centuries.*

him from the realm of sin, darkness and death to the new realm of light, life and joy in the Holy Spirit. This has been made clear in official Anglican pronouncements in the post-war years. 'It is assumed in all the New Testament language about the rites that the convert receives them with a lively faith and a renunciation of the old world.'[1] 'It is clear that the doctrine of baptism in the New Testament is stated in relation to the baptism of adults, as was also the case (with two or three exceptions) in the writers of the first three centuries. In every recorded case of baptism in the New Testament, the Gospel has been heard and accepted, and the condition of faith (and presumably of repentance) has been consciously fulfilled prior to the reception of the Sacrament.'[2] The Liturgical Commission of the Church of England (of which I was then a member) felt, therefore, that it was closely following official Anglican thinking, when it placed first in its 1958 Order of Services the full complex of rites—Adult Baptism, Confirmation and Holy Communion, and said in its Introduction, 'In the New Testament Adult Baptism is the norm, and it is only in the light of this fact that the doctrine and practice of Baptism can be understood.'[3] The severe criticism which that remark evoked in the Convocations and elsewhere was a good example of how people will accept something in principle, but react against it when they see its consequences in practice.[4] I am quite prepared to believe in the light of later discussion and experience that revised Services of Baptism and Confirmation will only be acceptable to the main body of Anglicans if they can be seen to derive organically from what we have in the Prayer Book, and if they avoid introducing more theological ideas than most people can digest; but I am also sure that any such revision will be on the wrong track, if it does not place first Adult Baptism, Confirmation and First Communion as the theological

---

[1] *The Theology of Christian Initiation*, p. 9.   [2] *Baptism and Confirmation Today*, p. 34.
[3] *Baptism and Confirmation*, p. x.
[4] The phenomenon is familiar to every parish priest with a conservative congregation. His people will accept what he says about the need for good music in the worship of the Church, provided he confines himself to the talking stage: but let him introduce a new hymn-tune in place of an old one. . . .!

norm for Christian Initiation and then modify it for Infant Baptism rather than the other way round as in the 1662 Prayer Book.[1]

Ought we, however, to continue Infant Baptism at all if the two points made above are valid? There have been a few secessions of ordained men from the Church of England on this very issue in recent years, and there are a few others—a vocal group—who have announced that they no longer feel able to baptize infants, though in most cases it would probably be true to say that they have been driven to this conclusion less for doctrinal reasons than because of the problems of 'indiscriminate baptism.'

In reply, I would point again to the Anglican appeal to Scripture. We hold to the authority of Scripture on all matters of fundamental and essential doctrine; only such matters may be taught as 'of necessity for salvation.' But we do not believe, as the Puritans did, that the Bible provides a blueprint of Church practice valid for every age. The Anglican appeal is to Scripture as interpreted by the Church of the first centuries, and in the light of modern scholarship we understand that principle dynamically and not statically. As we have seen, the New Testament itself is a book in which we find growth taking place in the realms of both doctrine and practice, and it is natural that we shall find that growth continuing after the New Testament is closed. In particular, when Christians came to recognize that the Parousia would not take place immediately and that the Church in all probability must face a long history down the centuries, it was inevitable that greater attention should be given to the problems of one generation succeeding another in the life of the Christian family. It is in this context that prayer for the faithful departed and infant baptism must be understood—the one concerned with the continuing membership in the Body

[1] The complete Christian Initiation Service in the Liturgical Commission's Report was an attempt to follow the line advocated in the Report *Baptism Today* under the heading 'Adult Baptism' (pp. 34 and 35), where the recommendation of W. H. Frere in *Some Principles of Liturgical Reform* (pp. 199 ff.) is quoted in support.

of Christ of the generations that have passed, the other with the bringing into membership of the new generation just born.

With all such developments the question that has to be asked is—does this new practice accord with the basic revelation of the Gospel or not? In both matters, I believe, the answer is in the affirmative, though that is not to approve 'the Romish Doctrine concerning Purgatory,' nor to assert that all the arguments which have been used in support of Infant Baptism are sound.

Perhaps the most concise statement in defence of Infant Baptism was given in the Lambeth Conference 1948 Report of the Committee concerned with Christian Initiation:

'We particularly value the practice of Infant Baptism for the emphasis which it lays upon the initiative of God in man's redemption, and in his translation from the Kingdom of darkness into the kingdom of light, and also for the welcome which it gives to little children on their incorporation into the family of the Christian Church. . . .'[1]

The whole New Testament emphasizes that God's grace is always prior to our response, that it was while we were yet sinners that Christ died for us. St. Paul also makes clear in Romans, chapter 5, that there is a solidarity of mankind in his natural-born state of alienation from God and a solidarity of mankind in Christ, the head of an already redeemed and reconciled humanity. As F. D. Maurice was never tired of emphasizing, conversion is an awakening to our true status before God as already in principle his sons and daughters in Christ, it is claiming the heritage that by the grace of God is already ours. In the Baptism of Infants the Church claims this heritage for those brought to the font. It sets forth the link between the Incarnation and the Atonement and the individual life now brought into vital relationship with Christ's redeeming work. Further, it recognizes the unity of the human family and the rightful place of all its members within the family of God. Just as the Jewish child was brought into the Old Covenant by circumcision, so it was natural that the Christian child should be brought within the

1 Pt. II, p. 109.

New Covenant by baptism. And it must frankly be recognized that Infant Baptism is a more satisfactory way of bringing the child into God's family than the method referred to in 1 Corinthians 7. 14, if the interpretation given above is the correct one. 'Holiness' by virtue of physical relationship suggests the level of *mana* and *tabu*, not the level on which the New Testament normally moves.

What then 'happens' to the baby at the font? Here I think we must be content to be agnostic. The child is brought from the old uncleansed order into the new order of Christ's kingdom, the life of the Spirit at work in the Church can start to work in the life of the new member, the wholesome influences of the new environment can begin to operate on the child's unconsciousness. Donald Baillie speaks of the need a helpless infant has to be loved and cuddled, not just to be brought up in an impersonal atmosphere of aseptic care.[1] So the love and care of Christ-in-his-Church can influence the life of the baptized child, though it is wise not to try to define this too exactly. We just do not know enough about the effect of influences on a child before it is able to grasp what is going on, though we have learnt enough from Freud to know that the effect of such influences can be great.

Two arguments for Infant Baptism which became dominant as a result of St. Augustine's teaching must frankly be abandoned. As we have already seen, a new-born child, while born into an estranged human race, cannot be held 'guilty' before God, for guilt only attaches to the person who has wilfully consented to the pull of his lower nature and has committed actual sins. The doctrine of 'original guilt' must be abandoned, and the fact recognized that in Infant Baptism the emphasis is all on the future, on the new relationship in Christ, and on the working out of that new relationship in Christ in coming years. There can be no question of Infant Baptism being for the forgiveness of past sins, and future revisions of the service must stress the bringing of the

[1] *Op. cit.*, pp. 86–88.

child into the life of the Church wherein among other gifts to be received will be the forgiveness of sins as and when committed.[1]

The other argument which followed from the doctrine of original guilt was that, if a child were allowed to die unbaptized, he was thereby deprived of eternal bliss. Either he must face the condemnation of hell as a 'child of wrath' or, as a more merciful doctrine taught, he could only enter the state of natural happiness called Limbo, but would for ever be deprived of the supernatural joys of heaven. The Prayer Book gives some countenance to such doctrines, when it states in one of the rubrics preceding the Order for the Baptism of Infants, 'It is certain by God's Word, that children which are baptized, dying before they commit actual sin, are undoubtedly saved.' The statement in itself is unexceptionable, but it leaves uncomfortably open the fate of children who die unbaptized. Today we have learnt a wider charity and, if we are prepared to leave to the love and mercy of God those who die without ever having heard the name of Christ, we can do no less for children in a culture where Christ is known who die without having received baptism. 'We are . . . agreed,' said Section III, on Membership, of the Nottingham Conference, 'that infant baptism is not to be defended by any argument asserting that the child is thereby saved from being penalized eternally.'[2]

Infant Baptism, as is already apparent, cannot have 'the full meaning which the New Testament ascribed to adult Initiation.'[3] The child is too young to have been able to commit any 'actual' sins, for which Baptism would be the sacrament of forgiveness. He is too young also to be able to make a personal response of faith. Nevertheless, the Church has historically tried to retain this element in its baptismal liturgies. In the medieval Church and in the 1549 Service the questions were put to the child and the godparents answered; in 1552 they were addressed to the god-parents; in 1662 the form with which we are familiar 'Dost

---

[1] Cf. *Baptism Today*, app. II, 'The Theology of Original Sin and Original Guilt' by F. C. Tindall; also *supra*, Part II, ch. 2.

[2] *Unity Begins at Home*, p. 65.   [3] Lambeth Conference 1948 Report, Part II, p. 109.

thou, in the name of this child . . .?' was adopted. In all services the godparents were regarded as making the vows and promises on behalf of the child baptized. It is interesting to note that in at least one ancient baptismal rite[1] the reply given to the questions about faith in Father, Son and Holy Spirit was 'Credat—May he believe!' and this idea of the godparents' answering not as proxies but in terms of prayer and support for the child is adopted explicitly in the baptismal liturgy of the Church of South India. The Lambeth 1948 Committee stated that such a break from a centuries-old tradition 'would upset the doctrinal balance of the 1662 Service, which requires the conditions of Baptism to be put in evidence and as it were guaranteed, before the child is received into the Church,'[2] and most members of the Commission that produced *Baptism Today* endorsed that view. Nevertheless, I believe that, provided Infant Baptism is clearly recognized to be only the first stage of Christian initiation, there is much to be said for the C.S.I. approach, and at the Parish and People Conference of which *Crisis for Baptism* is the report the Commission on 'The Liturgical Setting of Initiation' took the same view.[3]

Whatever one thinks about this particular matter, there can be no doubt that our Anglican reformers did well to preface the rite of Confirmation with a renewal of baptismal vows, however mistaken they may have been in thinking they were following ancient precedent.[4] Such a renewal is, of course, unnecessary in the case of Adult Baptism, where the candidate has already taken the vows himself, for Adult Baptism should be administered wherever possible in close association with Confirmation, but for those baptized in infancy it provides the element of personal response which was not possible at their baptism.

[1] The *Bobbio Missal*.   [2] *Op. cit.*, p. 114.

[3] 'The Commission as a whole was not ready to regard the duties of those sponsoring the child in terms of vicarious identification. . . . The parents and sponsors should make the promises for themselves, without the "fiction" of making them for the baby.' *Op. cit.*, p. 17.

[4] G. Dix, *The Theology of Confirmation in relation to Baptism*, p. 28; F. J. Taylor, *Baptism and Confirmation* (A collection of papers by Evangelical scholars), pp. 53–54.

4

We now come to consider *the significance of the rite of Confirmation itself.* Certainly it is no easy task to trace its origin and development. Was baptism a sacramental rite in which washing or immersion in water was the only outward feature in New Testament times? Or did the practice of anointing with oil and laying on of hands which are integral parts of the rite of Initiation in e.g. Hippolytus' *Apostolic Tradition* ante-date the New Testament, come into being during the New Testament period or develop in the sub-apostolic age? Why is it that the Orthodox Churches of the East transferred baptism, anointing and first communion to infancy, while the Western Church kept Confirmation normally to the bishop and so made inevitable in the vast dioceses of northern Europe an increasing gap in time between Baptism and Confirmation? Why has the familiar passage from Acts, chap. 8, which the 1928 revision adopted as the lesson to be read in the Introduction to Confirmation not been associated in the East with the completion of Baptism in what they call Chrismation or unction? How should we think of the action of the Holy Spirit in Baptism and Confirmation respectively?

It would need a treatise to answer such questions in full, and I can only make a few comments. First, I believe we can see a providential ordering of our pattern of the Christian Initiation in the delay of Confirmation, not only to the earliest time the bishop comes round but till years of discretion. It not only means that Confirmation takes place at a time when the candidates can take over the promises for themselves, but also that God who has begun a good work in those who were baptized in infancy touches their lives afresh at this moment of self-dedication in response to the prayer of the Church and through the laying on of hands.

Secondly, whatever the history of and the justification for the practice of anointing which was held to be the 'matter' of the Sacrament in the medieval Church and has a continuous history in Eastern Orthodoxy, we may surely be glad that at the Reformation the laying on of hands was made the central act of the rite. This has clear Scriptural precedent in a variety of contexts, and is an outward and visible act that conveys a clear meaning. We may be glad, too, that the Anglican Communion has retained the practice of episcopal confirmation as the rule, for thereby the truth is set forth that the Christian becomes a member not just of the local congregation, but of the whole Catholic Church.

Yet a bishop is not absolutely essential to the rite in person, as he is in Ordinations in the Catholic tradition. In the Eastern Churches the patriarch blesses the oil, but the parish priest carries out the anointing. In the Roman Church the bishop can in certain circumstances authorize a priest to act on his behalf. And the question needs asking whether with us also a bishop should not be able in emergencies to commission a priest to confirm by delegation.[1] Further, while we can commend episcopal Confirmation to churches with whom we enter into union, we must remember that 'the insistence that in all cases the minister of Confirmation must be a bishop' without any exception 'is a peculiarity in Christendom of the specifically Anglican tradition.'[2] We can therefore accept in a united Church the existence side by side of episcopal Confirmation and Confirmation by duly authorized presbyters without any betrayal of our Catholic heritage.

Thirdly, what is the gift received in Confirmation? In the immediate post-war period the Church of England was in danger of being dazzled by the brilliant, but often unreliable, scholarship of Gregory Dix, who in this sphere was supported by the highly typological Biblical scholarship of Fr. L. S. Thornton.[3] Both

---

[1] I can illustrate the need from the position of the Anglican/Episcopal congregation in Saigon, set in the hazards of war and with a constantly shifting membership. A Bishop of Singapore and Malaya can visit Saigon at most once a year, and for the rest must rely on American bishops to help out, when any happens to be visiting Vietnam.

[2] A. E. J. Rawlinson, *The Anglican Communion in Christendom*, p. 69.

[3] G. Dix, *The Theology of Confirmation in Relation to Baptism*; L. S. Thornton, *Confirmation: Its Place in the Baptismal Liturgy*.

revived a theory championed in a previous generation by Fr. Puller of Cowley and A. J. Mason of Canterbury, that the second-century pattern of Christian Initiation in which Baptism was particularly associated with the regeneration and the anointing and laying on of hands with the gift of the Spirit should be regarded as definitive for thought and practice today. They regarded the pattern fully described in Hippolytus as part of the tradition of practice which the Church inherited from a time anterior to the New Testament and found evidence for it in unexpected places in the New Testament. And they were prepared to maintain that those who had been baptized but not confirmed had received regeneration but not the gift and sealing of the Spirit. Gregory Dix was always the advocate pleading a cause, and it is hard to resist the conclusion that one of his purposes was to draw a distinction between 'Catholic' churches which had retained Confirmation and 'Protestant' ones which had not, and so forge a fresh weapon with which to defend the old Tractarian 'three-branch' doctrine of the Catholic Church.

Now whatever justification there may be for so understanding the various parts of a complex rite of Christian Initiation which is celebrated as a complete whole—and G. W. H. Lampe has shown that Dix and Mason have misinterpreted some of the New Testament evidence and underestimated the variety of teaching in the Fathers[1]—the fact remains, as O. C. Quick had already said, that 'a theory which declares that Confirmation marks the first gift of the indwelling Spirit, and a practice which places Confirmation a dozen years or more after Baptism, point, when taken together, to conclusions which are intolerable.'[2] The Lambeth Committee of 1948 endorsed the statement that 'the dissociation of the Holy Spirit's operation from any part of the Initiation is strongly to be deprecated.'[3] As The Theology of Christian Initiation put it, 'we stress the positive conviction that from infancy onwards the Holy Spirit gives the baptized the utmost that they are capable of receiving at whatever stage of growth they may have reached.' The Report continued, 'We believe, however, that

[1] The Seal of the Spirit, passim.   [2] The Christian Sacraments, p. 184.   [3] P. 110.

there is a fullness of his power within a baptized believer which can only be received after he has made deliberate and open confession of his personal adherence to Christ.'[1] Finally, in the Schedule attached to the concluding Convocation Reports entitled *Baptism and Confirmation Today* (1955) 'the Mason-Dix line,' as it has been called, was set aside by the majority of the signatories and this verdict was endorsed by the Convocations.[2]

Confirmation retains indeed an initiatory character as the gateway to fully committed Church membership, it brings the strengthening power of the Holy Spirit for Christian service and witness in the world to those who have made their full profession of loyalty to Christ, it introduces them to participation as communicants in the great Sacrament of Holy Communion. Even if it were conclusively proved that in the first generation situation of the New Testament, baptism was always baptism of believing adults, we can surely see all the essential elements of New Testament Initiation represented in our tradition of Infant Baptism—Renewal of Baptismal Vows—Confirmation, and believe that in this development the Church has acted under the guidance of the Holy Spirit.

In a united Church we shall certainly be right, in the spirit of the Nottingham Conference,[3] to allow for variety of practice, but we shall also hold that the Anglican Communion has in its traditional practice in regard to Christian Initiation a valuable contribution to make to the life of such a united Church.

5

In conclusion, I add a few comments about *the administration of Baptism and Confirmation.* I am sure it is good that at least once

[1] P. 15.

[2] If the quotations in this paragraph represent the truth of the matter, then clearly Acts 8, vs. 14–17 is a misleading lection for a Confirmation service, for its clear implication in such a context is that the Holy Spirit was not operative at all in the candidates' baptism.

[3] 'We believe that in a united Church the co-existence of patterns of initiation, including both believers' baptism and infant baptism, will itself lead to a fresh appreciation of the insights they reflect, without being destructive of the unity we wish to attain or compromising the question of achieving a common practice subsequently' (*op. cit.*, Section III—Membership report, pp. 64–65).

or twice a year the full pattern of Christian Initiation—Baptism, Confirmation and First Communion—should be set forth in one Service, preferably on Easter Even. The Liturgical Commission's 1958 proposals made clear how this can be done without wearisome repetition, and their proposals about structure can be followed, even where the 1662 and 1928 rites are used. In St. Andrew's Cathedral, Singapore, for instance, it is customary to hold such a service at regular intervals. It begins with the Ante-Communion, using the Nicodemus lection from the Adult Baptism Service for the Gospel. The candidates for Baptism and Confirmation are then asked the three questions from the 1928 Confirmation Service. Then comes the procession to the font, the Blessing of the Water and the Baptism and Reception. The procession then returns to the chancel in the middle of which the high altar now stands and the Confirmation proceeds from the versicles to the laying on of hands, for which the candidates kneel at the altar rails. Their first act thereafter is joining in the Nicene Creed as full members of the Church, and so the Eucharist proceeds as usual, with the post-Confirmation prayer said by the Bishop before the final Blessing.[1]

It is good also that increasingly the practice is growing of administering Infant Baptism publicly, say, once a month either in the setting of Mattins or Evensong or at a special Baptismal service. This becomes *the* celebration of the sacrament for the parish for the month to which all infants to be baptized are brought. Only in special situations is Baptism administered privately. One welcomes too the increasing care taken to provide preparation instruction and to do everything through the use of cards, interviews and baptismal rolls to ensure that the parents and godparents understand and accept their responsibilities.

The fact remains, however, that despite every effort being made by conscientious parish priests there are still many parents and godparents with no obvious Christian faith, no attachment to

[1] I regularly followed a similar Order in the diocese of Singapore and Malaya when confirming in the course of a parish communion. I found that it worked out best when the maximum number of candidates was about thirty.

the Church in any sense that matters—people who will make no promises about ensuring any sort of Christian upbringing for their children—who still want their babies 'done.' What should be the duty of the parish priest?

Here a bishop who has been serving overseas till recently must walk warily. Perhaps, however, the fact that I was a proctor in Convocation for ten years during which most of the important Reports were published may be accepted as adequate ground for saying something on the subject, particularly when it is remembered that the same problem exists in non-established parts of the Anglican Communion, wherever the phenomenon of nominal Christianity appears.

The Report, *Baptism Today*, gives an excellent summary account of the three positions which are held in regard to the problem of 'indiscriminate baptism'—the position of those who would not refuse or delay Baptism, the standpoint of those who advocate reform, and the waiting position of those who stand in the middle.[1] A Report, *Focus on Baptism*,[2] contains papers setting out the two opposite points of view by M. G. Hare Duke and N. O. Porter; and the Parish and People Conference had a Commission concerned with this whole problem.[3] The successive changes in the relevant Canon B.22 show that the arguments of those who believe baptism should be administered only after proper preparation and with the requirements in regard to godparents have been effective. If the House of Laity gives its approval, parish priests will have authority at least to postpone the baptism of infants.

Two factors in the historical situation must always be borne in mind in the Anglican Communion, and not least in the Church of England. First, our tradition is that of a national church. Unlike the sect-type bodies of the Reformation period and the 'gathered church' concept of subsequent times, the Church of England in the sixteenth century was consciously modelled on

[1] Pp. 24–32.

[2] Papers read at the Children's and Provincial Councils' Conference, Swanwick, 1963.

[3] *Crisis for Baptism*, pp. 22–39; cf. also the paper by Eric James in the same report, pp. 128–139.

the pattern of the Jewish people—the godly prince (or princess), the anointed of the Lord, at the head of a nation-church, to which all citizens belonged. In the days when Christian presuppositions were generally accepted, if not always followed, there was a logic about this which Hooker makes clear in the *Ecclesiastical Polity*. And the ideal of a nation in all its corporate life and activity having its place in the Kingdom of God was a noble one, however short-lived was the period in which the boundaries of national church and national state could be held to coincide. It was entirely natural at such a time that all babies should be brought to baptism in the established Church and it is this long-established tradition which still leads so many parents to bring their children to be 'christened,' even where there is no other effective link with the Church.

Secondly, our Prayer Book tradition, based as it has been on Augustinian teaching, has urged the baptism of infants upon parents as soon as possible after birth. 'For centuries the clergy have been solemnly charged "to seek out any unbaptized child and bring it to Holy Baptism,"'[1] while the rubric about the salvation of infants who have been baptized has, as we have seen, left an uncomfortable question mark over these who die unbaptized. We cannot be surprised if centuries of teaching have borne fruit in practice, however debased or superstitious the conscious reason for wanting a child baptized may have become.

Clearly these two facts of history must lead to immense patience and charity. You cannot destroy a long-standing tradition overnight, nor condemn people for doing today what they were told they must do yesterday. Yet when every allowance has been made, the fact remains that there comes a point when the presuppositions of a Christian nation can no longer be stretched without wilful blindness to cover a situation that has radically changed. Infant Baptism cannot be justified theologically except in the context of a Christian upbringing, and I venture to think that the more the parish clergy feel themselves forced up against the harsh facts of indiscriminate baptism, the greater will be the

[1] *Baptism Today*, p. 24.

L

number who will be drawn to favour believers' baptism. If the age-long tradition of the Church in favour of Infant Baptism is to survive on a theologically defensible basis, then serious consideration will have to be given by authority to the kind of proposals put forward by N. O. Porter. He advocates some restriction in the administration of the Sacrament and the use in other cases of a 'form of blessing, thanksgiving, intercession, for and with the child and the parents in order that there may be no doubt at all in their minds that even though they are not in a position to enter into any kind of covenant relationship with God for the child, yet God's love for them and the Church's care for them are undiminished.'[1] Such a development could safeguard the Sacrament from abuse and would yet retain the link between the Church and the nation at large which is rightly desired by many. The Bishop of Woolwich, who is certainly no advocate of a Church that is a pious group on the sidelines of the national life, has suggested that in the new secular age we should think of the Church's relation to the nation as very much that of the Communist Party in a 'people's republic', i.e. it should be a committed group concerned to be a leaven in the whole lump of society.[2] The proposals outlined by N. O. Porter, which find an echo in much that was recommended at the Parish and People Conference, fit in well with this conception of the Church's role in the developing pattern of a secularized society.

'Indiscriminate Confirmation' is a much smaller problem, but a correspondence in *The Times* in the summer of 1965 discussed the question of the appropriateness of school confirmations in cases where some candidates, but more often their parents, have no links of worship or membership with their local church. The vicar of the home-parish who receives a letter of commendation from the School chaplain in such circumstances is bound to wonder whether in fact the school Confirmation Service is not just part of the school routine like taking the G.C.E., and it is easy for him to see a parallel with the case of parents who class 'christening' with vaccination.

[1] *Op. cit.*, p. 42.   [2] *The New Reformation*, p. 49.

Yet the parallel is not exact. As an editorial in the *Church of England Newspaper* expressed it, 'At confirmation the boy comes to the stage of making a profession of his own, and in doing so he frees himself from the crutches provided up till then by his godparents. He can now fulfil the baptismal vows himself and stand on his own feet.' Of course, the ideal is that the whole family should attend church, but the generations do not always agree, and 'to insist that his parents should attend church may be to impose conditions that are restrictive and irrelevant.'[1] The important thing is that no undue pressure should be put upon boys or girls at school nor should Confirmation be regarded just as 'the done thing.' Provided such dangers are avoided and school chaplains do all they can to ensure that their candidates sincerely intend to commit themselves to Christ and his Church, whatever the outlook and habits of their parents, the problem should be well on the way to solution.

Since the above was completed, two proposals have been made for a change in our Anglican practice in regard to Christian Initiation. The Bishop of Woolwich, in a Prism Pamphlet (No. 31), *Meeting, Membership and Ministry*, argues the case for the completion of Infant Baptism with an anointing with oil, administered by the parish priest. This rite would form the gateway to Communion. At a later age would come the episcopal laying on of hands regarded as a commissioning for mission or (as it has been called) 'the ordination of the laity.' A. H. Dammers has appealed for an inversion of our present practice. Because the laying on of hands with prayer in the New Testament is, he claims, a sign of God's free gift of the Holy Spirit, available for infants and believers alike and demanding no response from the recipients, let this be permitted as the rite for infants. And because the death unto sin and rising again unto righteousness which is the heart of the meaning of Baptism implies the confession of faith let this be allowed as the appropriate rite for the believer. 'Such a reversal would cut the Gordian knot of our difference

[1] August 13th, 1965.

with the Baptists and remove the scruples of a growing number in our church about the wellnigh indiscriminate administration of Infant Baptism.'[1]

I would make three comments on these proposals: (1) I doubt very much whether the New Testament makes anything like such a clear-cut distinction between baptism and laying on of hands, so far as the response of faith is concerned, as A. H. Dammers suggests. (2) The proposal put forward by the Bishop of Woolwich deserves consideration, for it would make possible admission to communion at an early age, while placing the commissioning for service at the time of entry into adult life and responsibility. It is interesting to note that quite independently Helmut Thielicke has made a closely parallel proposal for the German Evangelical Church situation.[2] (3) Nevertheless, it is not without significance that, though writers such as Fr. Jungmann in Germany oppose it, there is a growing movement in the Roman Catholic Church in France and Germany to restore the traditional order of baptism, confirmation and communion, which became disrupted in the nineteenth century.[3]

---

[1] *A.D. 1980—The Road to Christian Unity*, pp. 24-25.
[2] *The Trouble with the Church*, pp. 120–126.
[3] Charles Davis in *Crisis for Baptism*, pp. 100–102.

II. THE HOLY COMMUNION

THE tragic fact that the sacrament of unity has only too often in Christian history been a source of bitter dissension has been frequently noted. To repeat it is to utter a truism. Further, there are welcome signs in these ecumenical days of movement from the old entrenched positions. On the Roman Catholic side theologians have moved a long way from many of the accepted expositions of the Eucharistic sacrifice, and the Liturgical Movement has emphasized again the character of the Mass as a corporate act of worship that finds its climax in the communion of the people.[1] Some of the worst abuses of the late medieval period which aroused such violent, yet understandable, reaction among the Reformers were diminished by the Council of Trent, but much remained to be done which has been taking place in our own day. On the Protestant side also there has been fresh thinking. Books such as G. Aulen's *Eucharist and Sacrifice* and D. M. Baillie's *The Theology of the Sacraments*, to which reference has already been made, show the ecumenical dialogue in progress from the Lutheran and Presbyterian sides respectively, while the *Liturgy of Taizé* gives expression to freshly grasped ideas in the Reformed tradition on the Continent of Europe. L. W. Brown's *Relevant Liturgy* helps us to see how closely official utterances from various quarters (Lambeth Conference 1958; Montreal Faith and Order Conference 1963; Vatican II) resemble each other.

Yet it would be idle to pretend that considerable differences do not still exist. The reaction of Conservative Evangelicals to the statement of one of the Lambeth Conference 1958 Committee Reports that in the light of recent Biblical and liturgical studies 'the time has come to claim that controversies about the Eucharistic Sacrifice can be laid aside' and 'the tensions surrounding the doctrine transcended' shows that the members of the Committee

[1] Cf. E. L. Mascall, *Corpus Christi, passim*; L. Bouyer, *Life and Liturgy*.

concerned were unduly optimistic.[1] As Max Warren pointed out in the *Conversation about the Holy Communion* which he edited, some Evangelicals are still so conditioned by the sixteenth-century reaction to the abuses of the Middle Ages that, even though their experience is fuller, yet in language they are unwilling to go beyond phraseology that suggests a solemn memorial of Calvary.[2] And among those who are prepared to do some fresh thinking there is still a wide gap separating Catholic and Protestant teaching.

I

Behind the different approaches to the meaning of the Eucharist lie, I believe, *differing understandings of Christian worship*. It is important that these should be made clear, because too often discussions about the Eucharist fail to bring participants nearer to a common mind through failure to understand the hidden pre-suppositions.

The Protestant approach stems basically from the way in which the doctrine of justification by faith is worked out. In contrast to the involved religious systems by which he had sought to earn the favour of God, Luther found in the message of the Epistles to the Galatians and to the Romans the truth that God in his infinite mercy and grace declared to us in Christ was prepared to accept, acquit and forgive him without any question of his merit at all. The grace of God meeting the sinner in his utter unworthiness and clothing him with the righteousness of Christ—here was a revelation which delivered him from bondage and gave him the liberty with which Christ made him free. At the same time Luther knew that this was not the final deliverance from sin. The Christian is still *simul justus et peccator*, at once righteous before God and yet still a sinner, and this double truth of his situation conditions the Protestant approach to God in worship.

---

[1] Lambeth Report 1958, p. 2. 83.

[2] *Op. cit.*, pp. 57–58. It is encouraging that E. M. B. Green, in his book *Called to Serve*, one of the Christian Foundations series published by the Evangelical Fellowship in the Anglican Communion, should note, 'it will be disastrous for ecumenical advance if some churchmen take fright at the language others are using, without pausing to analyse whether such terms are necessarily to be construed in the most sinister way' (p. 83).

The Christian can bring nothing as he draws near to God. Like the taxgatherer in the parable he can only say 'God, be merciful to me a sinner' or in the words of the prodigal son 'Father, I have sinned against heaven and before you; I am no longer worthy to be called your son.'

Inevitably, therefore, the emphasis is on the manward aspect of worship. The initiative remains entirely with the free grace of God proclaimed in the faithful reading of the Scriptures and preaching of the Word and in the due administration of the sacraments, wherein is imparted to us the *Verbum visibile*, the Word in visible form. Only as the grace of God touches the Christian afresh can he respond in gratitude and dedication. In a good deal of the Protestant tradition, what may well be the entirely right approach of the newly converted or newly restored person is made the norm for every Christian at every stage of the Christian life. Thus, when Cranmer prefaced the offices of Mattins and Evensong with a long penitential introduction in which the worshippers were expected to confess twice a day 'there is no health in us,' he was not so much giving expression to a streak of morbidity in his own nature,[1] as putting into precise liturgical form the theology of the Reformation. So also when the revisers made the two post-Communion prayers in the 1552 Liturgy alternatives, they were not botching the rite, but making room in the Church of England for the extreme Protestant wing that refused to use any sacrificial language in connection with the Lord's Supper, even the Pauline language of the prayer of oblation after Communion. Certainly to suggest that the Christian might have anything to offer at the start of an act of worship except his penitence would be regarded by such Protestants as impugning the truth of justification by faith alone and opening the door to the peril of 'works.'[2]

[1] As suggested by H. A. Williams in his essay in *Soundings*, and by Leslie Weatherhead, *The Christian Agnostic*.

[2] This approach clearly underlies the structure of *An Evangelical Eucharist*, the product of Oak Hill, L.C.D., Tyndale Hall and Clifton Theological Colleges. In this Order the elements are placed on the table 'unobtrusively' and 'the offertory is removed to the post-communion' (*Studia Liturgica*, Vol. III, No. 3, pp. 175–77).

For the sake of making the distinction clear I have no doubt over-emphasized this very important aspect of the Protestant tradition. It is not of course the only one. D. M. Baillie in a chapter on 'The Eucharistic Offering' in his work already referred to points out the significance of the definition of prayer in the Westminster Shorter Catechism as 'an offering up of our desires unto God, for things agreeable to his will, in the name of Christ, with confession of our sins, and thankful acknowledgement of his mercies.' He also notes that in the very section which violently condemns the 'popish sacrifice of the mass,' the Westminster Confession includes as part of the meaning of the sacrament of the Lord's Supper 'a spiritual oblation of all possible praise unto God for the same' i.e. for Christ's once-for-all offering up of himself on the Cross.[1] Cranmer used similar language repudiating any idea of a propitiatory offering, but accepting the concept of an offering of praise and thanksgiving for the one oblation of Christ once offered.

Further, Evangelical piety has developed in subsequent centuries a richer and warmer devotion. The doctrine of assurance and the emphasis on the life in Christ and in the power of the indwelling Spirit have encouraged Evangelicals to claim that freedom of access to the Father which the New Testament proclaims as one of the blessings of the Christian life. Yet while such truths may be cherished and proclaimed at the Keswick Convention and elsewhere many Evangelicals are too much bound by the old fears of 'the sacrifice of the mass' to give them free rein in their approach to the Holy Communion. The basic pattern of Eucharistic worship is down from God to man, with man making his response only after God's word is proclaimed and his gift in communion received by faith with thanksgiving.

The Catholic tradition at its truest begins at the same point as the Protestant. It fully recognizes that, unless the priority of God's gracious action to all the Church's response of worship is kept clearly to the fore, there is an inevitable danger of Pelagianism—

---

[1] *The Theology of the Sacraments*, pp. 113–114.

the offering of worship in general, and of the Eucharist in particular, can come to be thought of as something which man does in his own strength. It acknowledges that in the Middle Ages popular piety fell into this error, and that the development of private masses and the chantry chapel system was due to the notion, wholly alien to the New Testament, of a commercial transaction between man and God, whereby through the mere performance of a rite paid for on a tariff scale man could build up claims for God to honour.

Yet having fully admitted such errors, those who stand in the Catholic tradition would say that the stark Protestant approach to worship outlined above in effect denies the transforming power of the grace of God by keeping the Christian in the same position as the newly penitent sinner. When a person repents and believes and is baptized, they would claim, his whole position before God is changed. He has come home, he now lives in the Father's house, he has been adopted as a son and can now say Abba, Father. In Christ we have 'boldness and confidence of access through our faith in him,' we can 'with confidence draw near to the throne of grace' and with confidence 'enter the sanctuary by the blood of Jesus.'[1] The Catholic is therefore not very happy with Luther's saying *simul justus et peccator*, for it seems to him to place the two aspects of the Christian's state on a level, sometimes indeed to stress the latter at the expense of the former. He recognizes, of course, that if he claimed to have no sin he would be deceiving himself and the truth would not be in him. But for the Catholic the basic truth about the Christian is not that he is essentially a sinner whom God continues to declare acquitted, but that he is essentially a person accepted by God, though there are still the marks of the old Adam about him. 'Father, I have sinned against heaven and before thee, and am no more worthy to be called thy son' is an entirely appropriate cry from the prodigal arriving home, but it is no longer appropriate once he has taken his place again in the family circle. Of course,

[1] Eph. 3. 12. Cf. Rom. 5. 2; Eph. 2. 18; Heb. 4. 16, 10. 19.

'see, Father, what wonderful progress I am making' would be as out of place as the prayer of the Pharisee. But penitence for continuing failures is now of a different kind. It is something experienced within the restored relationship with a loving parent. 'Thank you, Father, for all the help and encouragement. Please forgive me that I still fail at various points in living up to your expectations.'

The Catholic approach to worship, therefore, is Godward. Its background is the prior grace of God at work creating, redeeming and sanctifying, by which the Church has been brought into being and through which it is sustained. It is in that setting that Christians assemble for worship. They meet together, not just as men and women intent on a Pelagian offering to God of a merely human worship, but as those who are already 'in Christ' and already accepted in the beloved, to exercise their calling as 'a kingdom and priests to our God' (Rev. 5. 10). In this, the Catholic would say, he is truer to the full teaching of the New Testament than his Protestant brother with his unduly narrow interpretation of justification by faith. For the epistles are full of the recognition that the worship and life of Christians as the royal priesthood are to be directed *ad maiorem Dei gloriam*. They are called 'to offer spiritual sacrifices acceptable to God through Jesus Christ.' Having 'come to Mount Zion, and to the city of the living God, the heavenly Jerusalem,' they are to 'offer to God acceptable worship, with reverence and awe,' and 'continually offer up a sacrifice of praise to God, that is, the fruit of lips that acknowledge his name.' Benevolence and almsgiving are sacrifices pleasing to God, and in response to God's grace Christians are to present their bodies 'as a living sacrifice, holy and acceptable to God, which is their spiritual worship.' St. Paul sees his whole apostolic ministry as a 'priestly service of the gospel of God,' designed 'so that the offering of the Gentiles may be acceptable, sanctified by the Holy Spirit.' 'Whatever you do, in word or deed,' he writes to the Colossians, 'do everything in the name of the Lord Jesus, giving thanks to God the Father through him.'[1] Eucharistic worship has its proper setting in the eucharistic life.

Perhaps in the full pattern of the Liturgy we can see a reconciliation of Catholic and Protestant traditions. In the ministry of the Word there is the downward movement from God to man in epistle, gospel and sermon. Then through the offertory, the *Sursum Corda* and the *Sanctus* and into the prayer of consecration there is the upward movement from man to God as the Church lifts up the gifts of bread and wine for God to take and bless and transform, as he continually transforms and renews the life of his people. So in a fresh downward movement God gives us the gift of Christ's very life to knit us more closely to him and to each other in the unity of the one body, and to that gift we respond in a final prayer of thanksgiving and in a continuing life of witness and mission to the world. 'In the liturgy,' said Vatican II's Constitution on the Sacred Liturgy, 'God speaks to his people and Christ is still proclaiming his gospel. And the people reply to God both by song and prayer' (33).

There is a further difference between Catholic and Protestant approaches which applies particularly to their understanding of the sacrament of Holy Communion. Many in the Protestant tradition start from the presupposition that nothing can be true of the Eucharist which cannot be true also of the Last Supper. There and there alone in the Upper Room is to be found the whole meaning of the Lord's Supper. I remember well the Evangelical vicar under whom I was brought up insisting on this basic truth, as he believed it, and I recall too from my days in Japan a member of a Continental missionary society saying, 'Your triumphant Easter Communion Service is very strange to us; for us the Lord's Supper is always a sad service.' For Protestants of that type indeed it is little more than a memorial service for Calvary, a 'Zwinglian' service of pious remembrance.

The Catholic would claim that he has modern New Testament scholarship on his side in finding a wider background to the Eucharist in its pages. H. Leitzmann may have overpressed the

[1] 1 Pet. 2. 5, Heb. 12. 22 and 28, 13. 16, Rom. 12. 1, 15. 16, Col. 3. 17.

evidence in his *Messe und Herrenmahl*, when he argued for two types of Eucharist in early days—a Jerusalem-type eucharistic fellowship meal and a Pauline-type mystical commemoration of the Passion, but he called attention to facts which cannot be ignored. The truth is that the Eucharist as it developed in the Church derives from three sources in the New Testament. First, there were the common meals which Christ shared with his disciples and which developed on occasions into the feeding of the multitudes who had come to hear him. It is significant that this is the one miracle to be recorded in all four gospels (twice in Mark and Matthew), that the central action of Christ in taking, blessing, breaking and giving has already in the Gospel tradition assumed a liturgical form, and that in the Fourth Gospel the great eucharistic discourse on Christ as the Bread of life which follows provides the key to the meaning of the sign.

Secondly, there was the Last Supper with all its paschal associations, in which Christ invested his coming death with sacrificial significance and by which he associated his disciples with the fruits of his redemption. As often as they eat this bread and drink the cup, they will be proclaiming the Lord's death until he comes (1 Cor. 11. 26). It is not surprising that from an early date the solemn recital of the narrative of the Last Supper has formed part of the great eucharistic prayer as giving the warrant for the Church's celebration of this sacrament and as providing one of the main clues to its meaning.

Thirdly, there were the Resurrection meals of the living Christ with his disciples—whether with the two in the house at Emmaus when he was known to them in the breaking of the bread (Lk. 24. 35), or after the night's fishing when he invited them to come and have breakfast (Jn. 21. 12). The earliest title for the sacrament would seem to have been 'The Breaking of the Bread,' and the first summary statement of the life of the new Christian community after Pentecost says 'they devoted themselves to the apostles' teaching and fellowship, to the breaking of bread and the prayers' (Acts 2. 42).

The Eucharist, then, is a stream fed from various springs. In post-New Testament days other streams flowed into it also, and these of course must be tested. What matters is not whether warrant for them can be found in some explicit proof-text in the New Testament, but whether they are in general consonant with its teaching. Where the answer is 'yes,' we can gladly see the continuing guidance of the Holy Spirit enriching the Church's experience of the Eucharist. Where the answer is 'no,' then such developments must be rejected. Whatever our judgements on particular questions of that sort, however, the basic fact remains that a sacrament celebrated on our side of the Resurrection and Ascension and of Pentecost must have a fuller and deeper meaning than a meal shared, however solemn the occasion, by Christ with his disciples in the Upper Room when he was still in the days of his flesh. To insist otherwise is to carry Biblicism to an extent which conflicts with the evidence of the New Testament itself. In this sacrament we do not just remember the Christ who died, we are in communion-fellowship with the Christ who lives, who died, and behold, he is alive for evermore, our High Priest who now appears in the presence of God on our behalf (Rev. 1. 18, Heb. 9. 24).

2

We now come to the meaning of the Eucharist. Its first signifi-cance is to be found, I believe, in its character as *the Church's sacrifice of praise and thanksgiving for all God's gifts in creation and redemption, in which she shows forth and pleads Christ's all-sufficient work of atonement for the forgiveness of her continuing sins and those of her members and offers herself in union with him and in the power of the Spirit to become in ever-greater measure the Body of Christ, the first-fruits of a redeemed and renewed Creation.*

'When he had given thanks'—in the accounts of the feeding of the multitudes, of the Last Supper and of a post-Resurrection meal such as that of Emmaus, there is reference to our Lord blessing God over the food or giving thanks to him for it. He was following the normal Jewish custom of grace before meat, particularly as used on the more solemn occasions such as the Sabbath and great festivals. The procedure used by Jews in the first and second centuries—in all probability already in existence in the time of Christ—was as follows. The head of the household took bread and broke it with the words, 'Blessed be thou, O Lord our God, eternal King, who bringest forth bread from the earth.' He then received a piece himself and distributed the rest to each person at the table. A similar blessing was used over each course as it was served. If wine were served, each guest said over his wine cup each time it was filled, 'Blessed art thou, O Lord our God, eternal King, who createst the fruit of the vine.' At the end of the meal came *the* blessing, a long prayer of thanksgiving which began with a dialogue between host and guests and continued with praise of God for his supply of men's earthly needs and for his redemptive acts in delivering his people out of Egypt; in bringing them into covenant-relationship with himself and in giving them the Law.[1]

At the Last Supper our Lord introduced into the familiar ritual new thoughts which interpreted his coming death. He identified the bread with his body which was to be given for his disciples and the wine with his blood which was to be shed for them and for many. By his death God would give them a greater deliverance than any the Hebrews had been granted from Egypt, by the shedding of his blood God would bring his disciples into the New Covenant-relationship he was establishing with his new Israel. As they shared such sacred meals in the future, they were to do so 'as a memorial' of him (NEB). It is doubtful if they could then understand what he was talking about, but after the Resurrection it became clear. They were living in a wholly new relationship with the living, victorious Christ, and in the fellowship of his Spirit were already entering into the joy which was one of the marks of the kingdom of God. 'Breaking bread in their house, they partook of food with glad and generous hearts, praising God and having favour with all the people' (Acts 2. 46 and 47). Thankful remembrance of all God's good gifts in creation

---

[1] See G. Dix, *The Shape of the Liturgy*, pp. 51–54.

and redemption, joyful consciousness that they were already receiving the blessings of the Last Day—these were the dominant notes of the Christian common life.

It is entirely in accord with this picture of early Christian life that as soon as we pass from the New Testament to the sub-apostolic age we find the title 'Eucharist' attached to the sacrament[1] and that in all the early accounts of its celebration the emphasis is on the Eucharist as the Church's thank-offering. The *Didache* has sections which deal in all probability with the Agape, the common meal of Christians (chs. 9 and 10), and with the Eucharist proper (ch. 14). Forms of thanksgiving over the cup and the broken bread at the common meal are provided and they are clearly a Christian adaptation of the Jewish grace before food. The purpose of the public gathering for worship on the Lord's Day is 'to break bread and give thanks.' It is to be preceded by a confession of sins 'that your sacrifice may be pure.' Clement of Rome (A.D. 95) in a passage which, it is generally agreed, refers to the Eucharist speaks of each Christian 'giving thanks' unto God 'adhering to the appointed rule of his service (liturgy) with all reverence' (c. 41) and in reference to the trouble over the presbyters at Corinth warns against the rejection of those 'who have holily and without offence offered the gifts pertaining to the office of the bishop' (c. 44). Justin Martyr describes the celebration of the Eucharist in his day (A.D. 150), when it is already beginning to take the form familiar to us in later liturgies. After the ministry of the Word, the bread and a cup of wine and water are brought to the president, who then using his own words offers 'praise, prayer and thanksgiving . . . to the Father through the Son and Holy Spirit, for the creation of the world and all that therein is for man's sake, and for deliverance from evil, and redemption through the Passion,' to which the congregation replies *Amen*. The deacons then administer the 'eucharistized' bread and cup to those present and convey them to the absent.[2] Irenaeus (c. 180) speaks of Christians offering 'first-fruits to God from his creatures, not as

---

[1] *Didache* 9; Ignatius, *Philad* 4; *Smyrn.* 6.
[2] J. H. Srawley, *The Early History of the Liturgy*, p. 31.

though he was in need, but in order that they themselves may not be either unfruitful or unthankful.'

There are developments to be noted in the practice of the Eucharist from the first days. No doubt partly as a result of the kind of abuses which occurred at Corinth, the Eucharist proper has been separated from the fellowship-meals, the thanksgivings over the bread and wine have been brought together into one continuous prayer, and the blessing of God over the food and drink placed on the table in the Jewish tradition have been 'translated' in Gentile Christian circles into a thankoffering which includes the lifting up before God of the bread and wine for him to bless and give back for communion. Nevertheless, the thinking and action move in the circle of ideas and practice that run back through the New Testament to their Jewish antecedents.

What, however, of the relationship between 'the one oblation of himself once offered' whereby Our Lord made 'a full, perfect and sufficient sacrifice, oblation and satisfaction for the sins of the whole world' and the offering in the Eucharist? Here, it seems to me, two great truths of the Gospel and of Christian experience have to be held in tension. On the one hand, there is the completeness and sufficiency of Christ's work of atonement. Nothing can derogate from the ringing 'once-for-alls' of the Epistle to the Hebrews. Under the old covenant the Levitical priests had to offer repeatedly the flesh of bulls and goats as sacrifices which at best availed for the removal of ceremonial defilements. Under the new covenant Christ offered the perfect obedience of his wholly surrendered will and by that sacrifice of himself really did take away sin and opened a new and living way into the sanctuary by his blood (cf. Heb. 10. 19 and 20). 'By a single offering he has perfected for all time those who are consecrated' (10. 14). Christ's offering achieved what the sacrificial obedience of no other person achieved because, while he fulfilled the two qualifications of all earthly priests—he was taken from among men, sharing their experiences and temptations, and was also called by God, yet he was a priest of a different and eternal order, God's only Son, through whom the Father's love had acted to put right the broken relationship between sinful humanity and himself. Here indeed is 'the scandal of particularity,' the offence of the Cross and the incredibility of the Resurrection, which the Church has nevertheless proclaimed from the beginning as the means by which the salvation of the world has been won. Christ has indeed opened the kingdom of heaven to all believers, and this is the deepest ground for our thanksgivings.

But if the work of atonement was achieved once for all, it remains effective for all time and for all generations. The preaching of Christ to the spirits in prison (1 Pet. 3. 19 and 20) indicates the bringing into the orbit of the divine salvation of those who lived in Old Testament days. And it is equally 'through Jesus Christ our Lord' that the unbeliever and the sinner in all subsequent ages are brought back into fellowship with God. The Epistle to the Hebrews speaks not only of Christ as 'a priest for ever' (5. 6), but also of his having offered to God 'a spiritual and eternal sacrifice' (9. 14 NEB), while John the Seer in his vision of the adoration of the Lamb describes him as 'with the marks of slaughter upon him' (Rev. 5. 6 NEB). He is indeed our great high priest, who ever lives to make intercession for us, so that 'should anyone commit a sin, we have one to plead our cause with the Father, Jesus Christ, and he is just' (1 Jn. 2. 1 NEB). Through Christ alone the Christian can not only exercise freedom of access to the Father, but also find renewed forgiveness for the sins and failures that continue to mar his life in grace. Only in union with Christ's perfect offering of himself can he offer the still imperfect sacrifice of his life and talents and work to the Father, which is his rational worship (Rom. 12. 1).

Whenever we end a prayer with the phrase 'through Jesus Christ our Lord,' we bear witness to the Christian's one and only way of drawing near with confidence to the throne of grace. When we say the collect for Trinity XII and use the words 'forgiving us those things whereof our conscience is afraid, and giving us those good things which we are not worthy to ask, but through the merits and mediation of Jesus Christ, thy Son, our Lord,' we spell out the same basic truth more fully. And when

M

in celebrating the Eucharist we make not only in word but in dramatic action the memorial of Christ's redemptive work and offer up the gifts of bread and wine for God to take and bless and give back to us as the channels of his life, we find Christ's once accomplished yet eternal sacrifice made present in our midst through the power of the Spirit. It is entirely right therefore that we should include in the great eucharistic (or consecration) prayer the clauses that ask God 'mercifully to accept this our sacrifice of praise and thanksgiving' and continue that by the merits of that redemptive work we and all God's Church through faith 'may obtain remission of our sins, and all other benefits of his passion.' In the words of the Moravian Liturgy of 1959 and of one of the Eucharistic liturgies in the *Book of Common Order* of the Church of Scotland, which is included also in the Congregationalist *Book of Services and Prayers* in England, we are in this great service 'pleading Christ's eternal sacrifice.' We are doing so, not in any sense of adding to what Christ has done nor of suggesting that God's favour has continually to be won,[1] but in order to show forth in the great sacrament of Remembrance the one ground on which we who have been baptized into Christ can freely draw near to the Father.

I believe that this comes close to what Fr. A. G. Hebert was saying in his now classic statement about the Eucharistic sacrifice which was quoted with approval at the Anglican Congress in Minneapolis in 1954 and endorsed by the Lambeth Conference Committee of 1958.

'The Eucharistic sacrifice, that storm-centre of controversy, is finding in our day a truly evangelical expression from the "catholic" side, when it is insisted that the sacrificial action is not any sort of re-immolation of Christ, nor a sacrifice additional to his one sacrifice, but a participation in it. The true celebrant is Christ the High Priest, and the Christian people are assembled as members of his body to present before God his sacrifice, and to be themselves offered up in sacrifice through their union with him.'

[1] 'It was generally agreed that it [sc. the phrase "pleading his eternal sacrifice"] need not carry a connotation of propitiating the Father and that it does not compromise the centrality and unrepeatability of the sacrifice of Christ, which is eternal at least in the sense that it is . . . the everlastingly efficacious foundation of all sacramental communion between God and man' (*The Anglican-Presbyterian Conversations*, p. 29).

The statement goes on to declare that such a definition 'involves a repudiation of certain medieval developments'; e.g. the habitual celebration of the Eucharist without the Communion of the people; the notion that the offering is the concern of the priest alone rather than of the assembled church; the idea that in the Eucharist we offer a sacrifice to propitiate God.

'We offer it only because he has offered the one sacrifice, once for all, in which we need to participate.'

Personally I am quite happy with such language, for I would find myself in agreement with the statement that 'the Eucharistic sacrifice is a sacramental representation of the sacrifice already complete, and is not a fresh sacrifice,' which David Edwards rightly claims in *A Conversation about the Holy Communion* would now receive general agreement 'in the Catholic movement, Roman or Anglican.'[1] Indeed, the other participants in that Conversation, Anglican and Free Church alike, found themselves in substantial sympathy on this matter.

Nevertheless, we must recognize that, with whatever qualifications we surround them, phrases such as 'presenting before God Christ's sacrifice,' 'offering the sacrifice of Christ' and still more 'offering Christ,' start a whole chain of alarm bells ringing in many Protestant breasts. In part, this is due to the basic approach to worship, which we have seen reason above to reject. But in part, it is due to the fear that, however safeguarded, such terminology detracts from the uniqueness and finality of Christ's atoning work and suggests that what avails to meet our needs is our action rather than his sacrifice.[2] For this reason I believe it is wiser, as

[1] *Op. cit.*, p. 57. For an exposition of this doctrine in the light of recent Roman Catholic thinking, see E. L. Mascall, *Corpus Christi*, Ch. IV.

[2] The Evangelical opposition to the phrase in the Revised Eucharistic Liturgy, 'we offer unto thee this bread and this cup' arises from this fear. Churchpeople of other views must recognize that, while these words originally referred to the oblation of the elements *for consecration*, ever since the words of institution come to be regarded in the West as 'the moment of consecration', these words have come to imply an oblation of the elements *as already consecrated* to be the Body and Blood of Christ. It was because of the difficulty this phrase was likely to cause Evangelicals that I suggested some years ago in an article in the *Church Quarterly Review* the phrase 'we make here with these thy gifts our thankoffering unto thee,' which comes close to combining the two alternatives now approved by the Convocations.

well as less ambiguous, to emphasize the language of W. Bright's well-loved hymn:

> Look, Father, look on his anointed face
> And only look on us as found in him.

We should thus be making demonstrably clear that at the very heart of our understanding of the Eucharistic sacrifice is not an assertion of so-called Pelagianism, but its repudiation. We are making clear in word and sacramental action that all is of God through Christ. It is his eternal sacrifice which alone is the ground of our freedom of access to the Father, the basis of our continuing forgiveness, the assurance of our salvation at the last day, and so the cause of our unceasing thankfulness in the Spirit. *Soli deo gratia*—praise to God alone—this is as true of the Catholic tradition at its best as of the Calvinist.

The pleading of Christ's perfect sacrifice, however, has the final purpose that in Christ we may make the only sacrifice that in the last resort we have to make—ourselves. This is a note struck most clearly in St. Augustine. 'If you wish to discern the body of Christ, listen to the Apostle speaking to the faithful, "You are the body of Christ." If therefore *you* are the body of Christ and his members, it is the mystery of yourselves which is placed on the altar; it is the mystery of yourselves which you receive' (Sermon LVII). So the Roman Canon which goes back far behind the abuses of the Middle Ages prays for the acceptance of the earthly gifts at the heavenly altar, that the heavenly gift of God may descend to the altar on earth. The members of Christ's body offer themselves through the symbols of bread and wine so that, receiving back in Communion the sacred gifts now sacramentally identified with the body and blood of Christ they may themselves become ever more deeply the body of Christ. The Eucharist is the supreme means by which the Church makes not only the individual offerings of the lives of its members, but the offering of its whole corporate fellowship. As St. Augustine put it, echoing 1 Corinthians 10. 17, the Eucharist is 'the sacrament of unity,' so that 'we, being incorporated in his body and made his members, may be that which we receive.'

To this scriptural truth the offertory procession, as now developed in many churches, gives appropriate liturgical expression. It does so, however, only when it is made quite clear that the offertory is not an act of oblation in itself, but just the bringing forward of the gifts of bread and wine and the lives of the worshippers which they represent in order that they may be lifted up in the Eucharistic prayer and there united with Christ's perfect offering of himself to the Father. For this reason, among others, the prevailing trend in revisions of the Liturgy to bring the offertory, the *Sursum Corda* and the consecration prayer into an unbroken sequence is to be warmly welcomed. This is the pattern of the ancient liturgies, which to its credit the Scottish Liturgy first renewed in the Anglican Communion and which other liturgies are now adopting.[1]

3

The Pauline-Augustinian emphasis on the oblation of the faithful which culminates in the act of communion leads naturally on to the second great meaning of the Eucharist. It is *the sacrament in which the once crucified and now risen Christ is present to impart to us all the unsearchable benefits of his sacrifice, the family meal in which he feeds us with his very life; binds us ever closer to himself and to one another in the unity of the one body; gives us a foretaste of the Messianic banquet and sends us out as members of his body to his service in the everyday world.*

Christ our eternal High Priest is present in this sacrament as the true celebrant and as the host who invites us to his feast. He is present as the Bread of Life and the True Vine to give us the food and drink that endures to eternal life. In the Eucharist we find the supreme fulfilment of Christ's promise to be in the midst where two or three are gathered together in his name. Like the two

---

[1] Cf. e.g. C.S.I. Liturgy, Liturgy for Africa and the Draft Order of Holy Communion, Second Series, in the Church of England.

disciples at the supper table at Emmaus we find Christ made known to us in the breaking of the bread.

So we come to consider the gift given to us in communion and the relation of Christ's presence to that gift. Of the gift there can be little question, for here Roman Catholics, Eastern Orthodox, Lutherans, Calvinists and Anglicans are all agreed.[1] It is the gift of Christ's body and blood, the gift of his very life, once sacrificed for us and now imparted to us. This is the united testimony of the Gospel accounts of the Last Supper, of St. Paul (1 Cor. chs. 10 and 11) and of St. John (chs. 6 and 15).

All Christians would also agree that the gift is not to be thought of in a sort of semi-magical isolation. The act of communion takes place within the context of the whole Eucharistic rite, of which the ministry of the word forms part and in which in word and action the whole drama of redemption is set forth and made present in our midst. (In cases where, as I believe rightly, the sacrament is reserved for the sick and others unavoidably prevented from being in church, such communicants are encouraged, unless in *extremis*, to read the scripture lections, etc., at home.) Moreover, there would be equal agreement that, whatever *ex opere operato* means, it certainly does not imply that the act of communion by itself, without regard to the spiritual state of the communicant, automatically guarantees spiritual benefit. Only where there is sincerity and faith in receiving the gift will the communicant be profited. Otherwise, as St. Paul says, 'he eats and drinks judgement upon himself,' and the apostle is not afraid to speak of this judgement in terms of weakness, illness and even death (1 Cor. 11. 27–30).

It is when we come to the relation between the outward and visible sign of the bread and wine and the inward and spiritual gift of the body and blood of Christ after consecration that we find ourselves face to face with controversies that have rent the Church down the centuries. In the early centuries the language

[1] For Anglican statements cf. Article XXVIII, para. 1 and the statement in the Catechism, 'The body and blood of Christ . . . are verily and indeed taken and received by the faithful in the Lord's Supper.'

used is unreflective, sometimes realist and sometimes (in the same writer) what has been called 'realist-symbolist.'[1] Justin Martyr, for instance, writes 'as through the word of God Jesus Christ our Saviour was incarnate and took flesh and blood for our salvation, so also we have been taught that the food over which thanks have been given through the prayer of the Word (or 'word of prayer') which is from him, by which food our blood and flesh are nourished by assimilation, is the flesh and blood of that Jesus who became incarnate.'[2] But if language of this kind can be widely used in the first three centuries, so also are phrases such as 'figura,' *representat*, 'likeness' and 'symbol.' These words are sometimes used in connection with the Eucharistic offering, for the bread and wine, as lifted up in the consecration prayer, not only represent God's gifts in nature and the lives of the worshippers who offer them, but also bear already in anticipation something of the significance they will receive when blessed and given back by God to the faithful. But such words are used in a wider context, and emphasis is laid on the spiritual nature of communion.[3] It is not until Cyril of Jerusalem in the East that we find the words 'change' and 'convert' used of the elements and parallels drawn with the miracle of Cana in Galilee, and it was only gradually that the liturgies came to reflect such ideas. Roman usage, as always, was conservative and the Roman Canon still preserves the older way of thinking when it speaks of 'the holy bread of eternal life and the cup of everlasting salvation.'

In the first centuries, then, the bread and wine were regarded as the focal point of unity between Christ and his Church in the one body, crucified, risen and glorified, and in the blood shed for many for the remission of sins. But there was certainly no thought of Christ localized in the elements as distinct from his presence in

---

[1] C. W. Dugmore, *The Mass and the English Reformers*. Scholars doubt, however, if Dugmore has made out his case for two distinct traditions, one reaching its climax in the doctrine of Transubstantiation and the other finding its classic exposition in the teaching of Reformers such as Ridley and Cranmer.

[2] Ap. 1, 66.

[3] Cf. St. Augustine, 'The body and blood of Christ will be life to each one, if what is visibly received in the sacrament is spiritually eaten and spiritually drunk in very truth' (*Sermons* 131. 1).

the power of the Spirit in his Church, and no idea of the annihilation of the bread and wine. Two tendencies, as Gore pointed out, led Christian thinking in the latter direction. First there was the influence of monophysitism—'the tendency to absorb and annihilate the human in the divine,' which Catholic Christianity stoutly resisted in regard to the Person of Christ but made no attempt to apply to the doctrine of the Real Presence. Secondly, there was the 'almost brutally superstitious disposition in a very dark period of the west.'[1] 'The Teutonic peoples' says Brilioth, 'wanted an active God, and for them the natural expression of God's activity was miracle.'[2]

The result was seen in the condemnation of Berengar in the eleventh century and in the 'gross and horrible doctrine,' as Gore describes it, to which Berengar had to give his assent in the recantation that was forced upon him.[3] Transubstantiation in a materialistic and localized form was the order of the day, and it was held in a crudely superstitious manner by the masses. The doctrine, as officially formulated in 1215, certainly opened the door to a more spiritual understanding of the sacrament, though it did nothing to condemn current crudities; and the hymns written by St. Thomas Aquinas, as also his own exposition of the doctrine, breathe a more wholesome spirit and devotion. Today the scholastic distinction of substance and accidents which he employed is no longer tenable, and the denial that the elements in all their properties continue to exist does indeed 'overthrow the nature of a sacrament.' Yet we can certainly be thankful that he was able to assert the doctrine of the real and essential presence of Christ's glorified body in the sacrament in a way that preserved the spiritual nature of that presence and that avoided the dangers of localization.[4] John Henry Newman was true to the best teaching of St. Thomas when he wrote in 1877, 'Our Lord . . . neither descends from heaven upon our altars, nor is moved when

---

[1] *The Body of Christ*, pp. 113 and 116.
[2] *Eucharistic Faith and Practice, Evangelical and Catholic*, p. 85.   [3] *Op. cit.*, p. 117.
[4] 'So far as concerns place, Christ in himself according to his own being is not moved' (S.T. 76. 7); 'The body of Christ is not locally in the sacrament of the altar' (Sent. 4. 44.2).

carried in procession. The visible species change their position, but he does not move. He is in the Holy Eucharist after the manner of a spirit . . . his presence is substantial, spirit-wise, sacramental; an absolute mystery, not against reason, however, but against imagination, and must be received by faith.'[1]

The Reformers, however, were faced not with such spiritual understandings of the Real Presence, but with the crude materialistic interpretations common among the masses. They were faced too with a situation in which the Mass was commonly regarded by the populace as a near-magical religious ceremony, designed either for achieving benefits for the living and departed in return for money down or for producing the weekly miracle of transubstantiation, the response to which was the adoration of the host and not communion. Reaction was inevitable, and it took the two main forms associated with the Lutheran and Calvinist traditions respectively.

Luther rejected transubstantiation as one of the three bondages in which the Eucharist was currently held, for he rightly believed that, as with the two natures in Christ, so in the sacrament the substance of the bread and wine remain, as well as the real body and blood of Christ. He frequently used the illustration of iron and fire wholly fused together in glowing red-hot iron. On the other hand, he rejected Zwingli's stark transcendentalism which made so sharp a distinction between God and man that it denied altogether the sacramental principle. Christ is everywhere present, said Luther, in his indivisible divine-human nature, but he wills that his body and blood should be sacramentally received in the bread and wine over which Christ's words have been spoken. 'What a childish silly idea they have of heaven,' he said, 'making for Christ a place up in heaven, like a stork's nest up in a tree!'[2]

Calvin believed with Luther as against Zwingli that 'we are quickened by a real participation of him (Christ), which he describes by the words eating and drinking so that no one should think that the life which we receive from him is received merely

[1] *Via Media*, ii. 220.   [2] *Sermons*, XXVI, 39.

by thought.'[1] But Calvin rejected Luther's doctrine of Ubiquity. To define Christ's glorified body as something independent of time and space was to make it in fact just another name for a spirit. Christ's body is locally in heaven, and it is through the virtue of Christ which is not locally limited that he conveys to us all the benefits of his passion.

The chief Anglican Reformers and the Caroline Divines in general followed the Calvinist rather than the Lutheran tradition in their doctrine of Christ's presence. Indeed, for a time (in the 1552 Prayer Book) it seemed as though the Church of England was going to be swamped by a Zwinglian-type doctrine, but mercifully that liturgy only lasted six months.[2] When the first Elizabethan Prayer Book was issued, the Ornaments Rubric was back, the 1549 Words of Administration were placed before the 1552 ones and the Black Rubric had gone.[3] The alterations to Articles XXV and XXVIII were also significant. By these changes room was found in the Church for those who held to the doctrine of the Real Presence in something like the traditional form, though not of course to transubstantiation. So there have been traditionally and particularly since the days of the Oxford Movement two schools of thought in the Anglican Church. One school of thought holds to the doctrine of the Real Presence, i.e. that by virtue of consecration and before communion Christ brings the bread and wine into close association with his body and blood and makes them the channels of his divine life. The

[1] *Inst.* IV. 17. 5.

[2] E. C. Ratcliff describes the 1552 Rite as a remarkably skilful expression of what by that time had become Cranmer's conception of the Lord's Supper, namely that it 'consists in the eating of bread and drinking of wine in thankful remembrance of Christ's death' (Lambeth Lecture, *The Liturgical Work of Cranmer*). A. G. Dickens says that, while he incurred official responsibility for the book, Cranmer was nevertheless 'under heavy pressure from the Hooper-Knox-à Lasco group' (*The English Reformation*, p. 249).

[3] The fact remains, however, that from that day to this the Church of England has had as its 'incomparable liturgy' a rite originally designed to express a 'near-Zwinglian' theology botched to include ideas that the 1552 revision was designed to exclude. It must be a cause of great regret that in the short-lived hope that the Restoration Church could include supporters of the Commonwealth as well as Royalists the opportunity was not taken in 1662 to authorise a revision along the lines of the Scottish Liturgy of 1637, which many of us would regard as by far the most satisfactory Anglican liturgy of the 1549–1662 period.

other school of thought, which is commonly called Reception-
ism, holds that Christ gives his body and blood, his very life, to
the faithful communicants in the act of receiving the sacred
elements, so that the presence of Christ is to be found, not in the
bread and wine, but in the hearts of those who have worthily
received the sacrament. (The Catechism indeed speaks of two
parallel processes taking place, one on the spiritual and one on the
physical level.[1]) The Doctrine Report recognized both doctrines
as having a place within the limits of Anglican loyalty.[2]

What are we to say of all this in the modern age? First, at a
time when everyone has been protesting that we do not believe
in a God who is literally 'out there,' we must recognize that the
doctrine taught by Calvin, Cranmer and the Black Rubric that
Christ's body is locally in heaven and not here is no longer valid.[3]
Luther's emphasis on the omnipresence of Christ in his divine-
human nature is a truer insight. Secondly, we can no longer think
of a body as just so much matter. Even our physical bodies
renew a number of their cells over the years. A body can
only be defined as the organ of expression of the personality
of which it is part. Christ's physical body was perfectly suited to
the life of the Incarnate Christ. Christ's risen and glorified body
is his equally perfect organ of expression in a sphere to which
time and space are wholly subject. Calvin's criticism of Luther
falls to the ground at this point also. Thirdly, we can no longer
think in terms of parallel processes taking place in the act of
communion, one on the spiritual and the other on the physical
level. We are psycho-somatic unities and the whole sacramental
principle is designed to meet our needs as body-soul entities.
This is well expressed in the words of administration 'preserve
thy body and soul unto everlasting life.' And the Revised

[1] Cf. the answer in the Catechism to the question about the benefits of Holy Communion, 'The strengthening and refreshing of our souls by the body and blood of Christ,
as our bodies are by the bread and wine.'
[2] Pp. 168–171.
[3] J. H. Newman expressed the same view as Calvin in the passage from which the
quotation above is taken.

Catechism has provided an alternative answer to the 1662 Catechism's question, precisely to avoid this dichotomy.[1]

For myself I believe that with all its obvious limitations one of the best illustrations we can use today is that of a transistor radio. The wave-lengths of the atmosphere are filled with the programmes being broadcast from different stations. Switch on a transistor set and the programme is focused for the immediate listeners. Carry the radio from one room to another and the programme is not moved, only the focus through which it is audible. Put it in a room of deaf people and they will hear nothing. Put it in a room of people not paying attention and they will merely hear odd scraps. Only those who listen attentively will receive the full impact of the programme.

So Christ is universally present, but he has provided this supreme meeting place for the members of his Church in the sacrament of his body and blood. Carry the consecrated elements from the altar to the line of communicants at the altar rails and you have not moved Christ, only the focal point through which he gives himself to us in all his life-giving power. Administer the sacrament to those without faith, or to the careless and indifferent, and they will eat and drink judgement to themselves. Administer it to those whose faith may be weak, but who yet are sincere, and they will indeed receive the spiritual food of the most precious body and blood of Christ and be assured thereby of God's favour and goodness towards them. They will know themselves to be very members incorporate in the mystical body of his Son, for they will be united across their individualities with Christ and with each other, through partaking of the one loaf (1 Cor. 10. 17). And they will know too that they are heirs through hope of God's everlasting kingdom, for they will have received a foretaste of that heavenly banquet which Christ will share with them in the Kingdom of God.

---

[1] 'The benefits we receive are the strengthening of our union with Christ and his Church, the forgiveness of our sins, and the nourishing of ourselves for eternal life.' I can speak of this from personal knowledge as one of the members of the Revised Catechism Commission specially concerned with the redrafting of the section on the sacraments.

Every Eucharist is thus the thankful commemoration of Christ's once completed and ever-availing sacrifice, the family meal of the living Christ with his people, and a milestone on the way to that glorious consummation when sacraments shall cease and we shall see Christ face to face. It is a challenge to us to live the eucharistic life in God's service in his world, knowing that we must one day give an account of our stewardship before the judgement seat of Christ. And as we hope and trust that by the power of Christ granted to us in this sacrament we may receive in that day the commendation 'well done, good and faithful servant,' so each act of communion becomes the ground of our confident prayer:

> O Christ, whom now beneath a veil we see,
> May what we thirst for soon our portion be,
> To gaze on thee unveiled, and see thy face,
> The vision of thy glory and thy grace.

THE MINISTRY OF GOD'S PEOPLE

A ministry acknowledged by every part of the Church as possessing not only the inward call of the Spirit, but also the commission of Christ and the authority of the whole body. . . . May we not reasonably claim that the Episcopate is the one means of providing such a ministry?

The fourth term of the Quadrilateral as incorporated in the 'Appeal to all Christian People' of Lambeth 1920. The wording of the original Chicago-Lambeth Quadrilateral of 1886/88 had: 'The Historic Episcopate, locally adapted in the methods of its administrations to the varying needs of nations and peoples called of God into the unity of his Church.'

INTRODUCTION

THE Lambeth Quadrilateral nowhere displays the outlook of the period in which it was written more clearly than in its inclusion of the ordained ministry among the four basic elements of a united Church, without reference to the ministry of the whole Church, in the context of which the ordained ministry can alone be rightly understood. The first draft of Vatican II's Dogmatic Constitution on the Church marked some advance on what was fairly normal half a century ago in that it included a section on the ministry of the laity, but it did so only after speaking of the calling and responsibilities of bishops, priests and deacons. The laity were brought in as a sort of appendage. The spirit of Vatican II was shown in the rough handling which this draft received, and as a result the final form is markedly different. In this, as in any official Anglican document that might be produced in the contemporary climate of thought, the priestly and minis-terial character of the people of God as a whole is first emphasized, and only in this setting is the specific vocation of the ordained ministry expounded.

The rediscovery of the laity and the working out of a theology of the *laos*, the people of God, have been part of the recovery of the doctrine of the Church as the body of Christ. 1 Peter's application to the corporate fellowship of Christians of the images applied in the Old Testament to the people of Israel has come home to us again, as we have grasped that all of us, clergy and laity together, are called to be 'a chosen race, a royal priest-hood, a holy nation, God's own people' (1 Pet. 2. 9); all of us together, as we share in the Eucharistic liturgy on earth, rejoice with the worshipping host of heaven that Christ has ransomed us for God 'from every tribe and tongue and people and nation,' and has made us 'a kingdom and priests to our God' (Rev. 5. 9 and 10). St. Paul's working out of the analogy of the body with its many members in 1 Corinthians 12 makes clear that Christians

N

have many varieties of service to perform for the perfect functioning of the body of Christ. Ephesians 4 works out the analogy
further. What eyes, ears, hands and feet are to the earthly body,
so apostles, prophets, evangelists, pastors and teachers are 'to
equip God's people for work in his service, to the building up of
the body of Christ' (v. 12 NEB). The New Testament portrays the
Church for us in organic terms, a living organism inspired and
directed by the Spirit of Christ who can act through all the
members of the body, and not in terms of a tightly-knit institution
in which a sharp distinction is to be drawn between the hierarchy
and the theologians, the *ecclesia docens*, on the one hand and the
inferior clergy and the laity, the *ecclesia discens*, on the other. It
is the Church as a whole which is the instrument of Christ's
action in the world and which derives its priestly character of
prayer for and service of the world from the high priesthood of
Christ its Lord and Saviour.

Recovered insights into overlooked aspects of the teaching of
scripture seldom arise from detached Bible study carried on in
academic seclusion. It is because such insights speak to men's
condition that they win a response in the life of the Church. So
with the recovery of the doctrine of the *laos*, the people of God.
In the Dark Ages, when the membership of the Church was
flooded with illiterate and still semi-pagan baptized members and
when parish priests were often only a little ahead of their flocks,
the monasteries fulfilled a significant role as islands of faith and
devotion and culture in a half-barbarian sea. It was natural in
such a context to speak of going 'into religion' when a man or
a woman entered a monastic order, and the still surviving distinction of 'religious' and 'secular' priests bears witness to this dichotomy. In the high Middle Ages Christendom came as near
realization as it ever has done, but the fact remains that the vast
mass of lay folk were unable to read or write. The very word
'clerk' referred to someone who was at least in minor orders and,
as we all know, it was the clergy who provided the civil service,
with bishops acting as high State officials and ambassadors and
the inferior clergy filling the lesser posts. From this historical

situation in Western Europe developed the clericalization of the Church, which has become an ingrained part of our inheritance, both Catholic and Protestant. The traditional use of the phrase 'going into the Church' in the sense of 'seeking ordination' is significant; it had been forgotten that we 'go into the Church' at baptism and that the Church consists of the whole company of the baptized.

Today the spread of education has meant that leaders in the professions and business and other walks of life are not merely educated on a level with the clergy, as was mostly the case in nineteenth-century England, but are often academically and in other ways better equipped. It is the scientists, the technologists, the social planners, the health and housing directors, who form 'the counsellors' of our modern society, and who can often speak with an insight and understanding that the clergy lacks. True, these technical skills do not often include a training in theology, but increasingly we are learning that theology must be worked out in dialogue with society. There is no longer a place for the clergy to say 'I'm telling you' and for the laity to follow the example of the Light Brigade 'their's not to reason why.' The genuinely lay theology, for which the Bishop of Woolwich has pleaded,[1] requires the interaction of trained theologians and persons involved in the complex structures of modern society.

Clergy and laity together share responsibility for all sides of the Church's worship and witness, its parish life and its constitutional assemblies[2], and that involves new outlooks on the part of both. For it is fatally easy for the priest to develop an *amour propre*, which makes him unwilling to surrender the predominant position that has been his in the past, and for layfolk to continue thrusting that role upon him, even when the priest himself seeks

[1] *The New Reformation, passim.*

[2] As one who in discussions in the Church Assembly nearly ten years ago spoke in favour of a National Synod I was very glad to see such a warm welcome given to the report *Goverment by Synod* by the Assembly in November 1966. Just as (in my experience) the effectiveness of Canterbury Convocation noticeably increased after the Upper and Lower Houses began sitting together, so I have no doubt that many of the present difficulties will be avoided when the House of Laity is joined with the other two Houses in the discussion of doctrine and worship, as well as all other business, from the start.

to fulfil his ministry in a genuine spirit of partnership. As Hans-Ruedi Weber of the Ecumenical Institute at Bossey has put it. 'The laity are not the helpers of the clergy so that the clergy can do their job: but the clergy are helpers of the whole people of God so that the laity can be the Church.'[1]

It is one of the most difficult things in the world for our limited human minds to keep things in balance, however, and some among the *avant garde* are so concerned to emphasize the Church's duty to be 'involved' in the world through the laity that they would like to see the distinction between clergy and laity blurred to the point of abolition altogether. For them the Society of Friends with its sense of the equality of all in the Spirit makes a particular appeal, and so would the structure of the Plymouth Brethren, if their theology were acceptable. Among others of a more traditional Protestant bent we hear again the cry of 'the priesthood of all believers,' not in what is surely the Biblical sense that all baptized members of the Church share in its character as a royal priesthood, but in the falsely individualistic sense of 'every man his own clergyman.'[2] Against such tendencies it is necessary to insist that the ordained ministry is theologically an integral part of the total life of the body of Christ with its roots firmly planted in the New Testament and that in practice the Church cannot do without some of its members being committed to the full-time service of the ministry of the word and the sacraments. With all that we owe to the Quakers for their witness to the Inner Light and for their record of disinterested service not least in time of war, the fact remains that the Society of Friends is never likely to be more than a select company of people, a sort of religious order with a particular tradition within the total life of the *Una Sancta*. Some Brethren at least (as they have told me) believe that they lose much by not having a full-time ministry,

---

[1] Cf. also G. Goyder, *People's Church*, passim.

[2] John Huxtable speaks of 'the curious use to which the phrase . . . is often put in Free Church circles where Dr. T. W. Manson once drily remarked, it more often means no priesthood of any believers instead of expressing in terms of actual, contemporary churchmanship the share which all Christ's people have in his obedience and ministry' (*Christian Unity: Some of the Issues*, pp. 85–86).

while those who shout loudest the old Reformation cry are for the most part found within Christian bodies which have an ordained ministry as a normal part of their life.

We must recognize also that in committing themselves to the goal of organic union as defined in the New Delhi statement of the Third Assembly of the World Council of Churches the member-Churches have accepted as one element in a united Church 'a ministry recognized by all,' and that every scheme for Church Union includes a ministry set apart for the preaching of the word and the administration of the sacraments and for pastoral care. The problems that have arisen and that have led to prolonged controversy and discussion do not concern whether there shall be an ordained ministry, but of what sort it should be and how separated ministries can be brought together in a united Church. And if sometimes we find ourselves getting impatient with the apparently endless negotiations, and tempted to say, 'What does it matter? God has used and blessed all kinds of ministries anyway. Let us get on with the work of the Gospel,' we shall do well to weigh carefully some words of John Huxtable: 'It is one thing to hope that the real values of all Church orders may be somehow combined into one which comprehends and transcends and so transforms them all; that is as different as possible from the view that it is a matter of small consequence which of them is used as long as the work of the Gospel is done, because *church order must be consonant with the Gospel*.'[1]

Those words which I have italicized succinctly express the basic principle. Biblical study has made clear that there is no clearly laid down blueprint in the New Testament for the ministry, neither the presbyterian as many thought in the sixteenth and seventeenth centuries, forgetting the overall pastoral oversight of the apostles in the first generation, nor the episcopalian as many Anglicans in the seventeenth and subsequent centuries emphasized, ignoring the lacunae in the evidence. What matters is that Church order shall be true to the Gospel. It must proclaim by its very character Jesus Christ as Saviour, Lord, High Priest and

[1] *Op. cit.*, p. 19.

Good Shepherd. It must have its place within the organic life of the Church, the body of Christ, with its life hid with Christ in God (its 'vertical' dimension) and its continuous history down the centuries (its 'horizontal' aspect). And it must serve the people of God in their enduring vocation 'to offer spiritual sacrifices acceptable to God through Jesus Christ' and 'to declare the wonderful deeds of him who called (them) out of darkness into his marvellous light' (1 Pet. 2. 5 and 9).

I. THE MINISTRY IN THE EARLY CHURCH

I

THE recounting of the study of the development of the Christian ministry in the New Testament period and the subsequent generations involves going over exceedingly well-trodden ground. Nevertheless, before we come on to the problems that confront us today, a summary statement setting out the conclusions that would, I believe, be accepted by the great majority of Biblical scholars is necessary.

1. First, then, the Christian ministry 'derives its essential nature directly from the person and work of Christ.'[1] God revealed his love for us by sending 'his only Son into the world, so that we might live through him' (1 Jn. 4. 9). The coming of Christ—his birth, life, death and resurrection, with all that flowed from it— is due to the initiative of the Father, who took action in the incarnate life of the Son to involve himself, uniquely and particularly, in the life of mankind and to bring deliverance and salvation to our fallen human race. So the Risen Christ, speaking to the company in the Upper Room (it is not clear whether a larger group is meant or only those who belonged to 'the Twelve' as representing the general body of believers), says 'as the Father has sent me, even so send I you' (Jn. 20. 21). The whole Church shares in Christ's apostolic mission to the world, and it is within that total ministry that some are called to a specific function within the life of the family of God.

2. We see the principle of some being called for a particular responsibility within the total life of God's people operating throughout the Gospels. Jesus chose twelve men out of the company of his disciples 'to be with him, and to be sent out to preach and have authority to cast out demons' (Mk. 3. 14). 'He who receives you' said Jesus 'receives me,' just as he who receives

---

[1] H. J. Carpenter, art. on Minister, Ministry, in A. Richardson (ed.), *A Theological Word Book of the Bible*, p. 146.

a prophet or a righteous man or gives a drink of cold water to a thirsty disciple obtains a reward (Mk. 10. 40–42). So the Twelve, those whom H. E. W. Turner has called 'the "right markers" of the New Israel, those upon whom the Church will, as it were "form up," '[1] were through the greater part of Jesus' ministry his constant companions. They shared in the task of administering the loaves and fishes at the feeding of the multitude and they saw Jesus stilling the storm on the lake. They were the group to whom was first granted some insight into the person of Christ, as revealed in Peter's confession (Mk. 8. 29), and they shared the meal in the Upper Room on the night in which Jesus was betrayed (Mk. 14. 17–25). In the great ordeal of that night they failed miserably, but by the resurrection of Jesus Christ from the dead they were born again to a living hope, and the early chapters of Acts show this group (with Judas replaced by Matthias) taking the lead in the fulfilment of the Church's apostolic task. They were in the early days 'the Apostles' *par excellence*.

3. Within the company of the Twelve there were degrees of closeness to Christ, degrees of responsibility in giving leadership to the Church's apostolic mission. At one end of the scale even the name of one of the Twelve seems to have been uncertainly remembered,[2] while at the other was the inner group of Peter, James and John, with Andrew hovering on the edge. It was this group of three whom Jesus took up the mount of Transfiguration and had closest to him in the Garden of Gethsemane. Foremost of all was Peter, who is shown 'warts and all' in the Gospel record. It was he who put into words the confession of faith of the Twelve at Caesarea Philippi, and who received both blessing and condemnation for what was in part a right insight and in part a woefully wrong understanding of Jesus' Messiahship. It was he who made such protestations of his loyalty to death and then failed dismally in the anteroom of Pilate's judgement hall. Nevertheless, there can be no doubt of Peter's position as *primus inter pares* in some at least of the traditions represented in the

---

[1] *Why Bishops?* p. 7.
[2] Mk. and Mt. have Thaddaeus, Lk. and Acts have Judas the son of James.

New Testament. The '*Tu es Petrus*' of St. Matthew 16. 18, which is such a basic text for the Papal Supremacy, at least bears witness to the pioneer example which Peter set of the Church being 'built upon the foundation of the apostles and prophets, Christ Jesus himself being the chief cornerstone' (Eph. 2. 20). The Matthaean tradition of Jesus giving the power of binding and loosing to Peter personally (16. 19) is significant, even though the parallel commission to the Twelve (18. 18) makes clear that Peter could exercise this power only in conjunction with them. Christ's prayer for Peter and his recommissioning of him show Jesus' concern to help Peter through the severe test to which he was to be subjected, for he was needed as a leader in rallying and guiding the company of Christ's disciples (Lk. 22. 32; Jn. 21. 15–18).

4. If Jesus Christ was 'the Sent One,' 'the apostle and High Priest of our confession' (Heb. 3. 1), so that the apostolic character of the Church and of the ordained ministry derives from him, it is also true that Jesus Christ fulfilled his mission in the spirit of the servant. When James and John asked if they could have the top places in Jesus' Kingdom when he reigned in glory, Jesus answered that all he had to offer was a share in his cup of suffering and in his baptism of death (Mk. 10. 38). They stood rebuked, but the remaining ten gave themselves away by their indignation, not because they knew better than the two brothers, but because they felt they had been 'beaten to the post.' So Jesus challenged them all, explaining the difference between earthly rulers and his purpose for the Twelve. Greatness belongs, he said, to the one who is ready to serve, 'for the son of man came not to be served but to serve, and to give his life as a ransom for many' (45). As the Anglican-Methodist Report recognizes,[1] *diakonia* is of the essence of the apostolic ministry, for it was the essential mark of Christ's ministry. Wherever and whenever it appears, it wins an honour and respect even from the unbelieving world that no amount of pageantry and pomp can command.

[1] P. 21. 'All Christian ministry is a sharing in Christ's service to God, the Church and the world.'

5. When we pass from the Gospels to the rest of the New Testament, we see the company of the Twelve augmented by Paul and Barnabas and apparently James, the brother of the Lord, and we read of others of whom we know nothing such as Andronicus and Junias, who are nevertheless described as 'men of note among the apostles' (Rom. 16. 7). 1 Corinthians 15. 1–8 suggests that the apostles represented a larger group than the Twelve, with the inner circle of Jesus' disciples taking a prior position of leadership. What the qualifications for apostleship were is not clear. (St. Paul's rhetorical question in 1 Cor. 9. 1 does not necessarily imply that only those who had 'seen Jesus our Lord' were eligible.) What is apparent is that the apostles' calling in the first place was to bear testimony, in many cases as eye-witnesses, to the facts of the Gospel. Some of them seem to have remained permanently in the mother-church of Jerusalem. But others like Peter and Paul and Barnabas carried the Gospel across the Mediterranean world. They were not of course the only proclaimers of the Gospel, for along with them were the prophets, and apparently in a somewhat subordinate capacity, the evangelists, like Philip who brought the Gospel to Samaria (Eph. 4. 11; Acts 8. 4–8). Many unknown Christians also carried the Gospel abroad in the course of their journeys like those who founded the Church at Rome before ever Peter or Paul reached the city. It is important to notice, however, that Acts records each new development and advance of which it speaks as receiving recognition and confirmation from the mother-church at Jerusalem.

6. Apostles, however, were not only proclaimers of the Word. Those who were founding-fathers of churches in the Eastern Mediterranean and beyond found themselves inevitably involved in the pastoral oversight of those churches. St. Paul's epistles are almost entirely concerned with this pastoral ministry of guidance, rebuke, exhortation and renewal, and it is clear that he kept in close touch with all the churches he had founded by correspondence, by the dispatch to them of emissaries and by personal visits.

If the churches were to survive as ordered Christian communities, however, a local ministry was also required, and the Acts' account of the choice and ordination of the Seven (ch. 6. 1–6) may well be a characteristic example of St. Luke's method of describing a first occasion as a paradigm of what later became standard practice. If so, we have here a typical picture of the devolution of apostolic responsibility to others, for Stephen and the others plainly had duties beyond the serving of tables, so that this passage should not be identified with ordination to the diaconate alone. However that may be, it is clear that it was St. Paul's practice to appoint elders in every church (Acts 14. 23), no doubt in many cases senior members of the congregation, heads of households in whose homes the local congregation met for worship. These Christian elders in all likelihood carried out the same kind of responsibilities as the elders who conducted business and exercised discipline in the Jewish synagogue, but the Christian *presbuteroi* also fulfilled a pastoral function in the congregation of which they were 'overseers' (*episcopoi*) (Acts 17. 28), as 'pastors and teachers' (Eph. 4. 11). The New Testament speaks of them as labouring in the word and in the teaching, visiting the sick and watching on behalf of the souls committed to their care. Inevitably they would be responsible for the oversight of the conduct of worship and for the due administration of the Eucharist. 'Responsibility to God for the welfare of the souls of the flock was inseparable from any exercise of ruling authority in the Church of Christ.'[1]

7. In one place in the authentic letters of St. Paul we find deacons linked with the *episcopoi* (Phil. 1. 1), who appear from this and other passages e.g. the farewell address at Ephesus, as well as the Pastorals, to be identical with the elders. (Perhaps *episcopoi* was used in Gentile churches and *presbuteroi* in Jewish ones.) But in addition to these set offices there were the many manifestations of the Spirit's working through such gifts as

[1] H. J. Carpenter, *op. cit.*, p. 150, where the N.T. references for the above statements are given.

speaking with tongues, interpretation of tongues, healings, working of miracles, and so forth (1 Cor. 12. 1–11). Church meetings for worship and fellowship provided ample scope in the early spontaneous days for the exercise of such gifts, but there was always present a twofold danger—the danger of rivalry and jealousy between the possessors of different gifts and the risk that the Church's worship would become a disordered chaos. Only the supremacy of love could triumph over the former and make possible the offering of the latter in decency and in order— (ch. 13 and 14. 40). Only as those who possessed gifts exercised them in the spirit of Christ the servant could their use be truly Christ-like. St. Paul set the key-note for all ministry in the Church of God, when he wrote 'What we preach is not ourselves, but Jesus Christ as Lord, with ourselves as your servants for Christ's sake' (2 Cor. 4. 5).

8. The main reason why there is no exact blueprint for an ordained ministry in the New Testament is that the first generation of Christians expected the Parousia in their own life-time. When the main body of the apostles were martyred or died naturally and the Church moved on to the sub-apostolic period, still more when Jerusalem was sacked in A.D. 70 and the members of the mother-church were scattered, Christians had to reckon with a new situation. Just as every movement has to face new problems when the founder-generation passes, so the Church had to consider the questions of faithfulness to the apostolic teaching, orderliness of worship and continuity of life. One result of this, as we have seen, was the collection of writings of apostolic authorship or with at least apostolic backing into the New Testament. In one sense it is true that the apostolic succession passed from the living witnesses to the written book—but only in one sense. For what we find is the emergence of an order of ministers, one of whose tasks was to preserve a living witness to the apostolic kerygma now enshrined in the New Testament and to preside over the Church's acts of worship in which Christians responded in praise to the message of the Gospel. It was in this context that mon-episcopacy came to be universally accepted.

Unfortunately the scantiness of the records makes it impossible to give any full account of the process whereby by the time of Irenaeus (A.D. 170) the threefold ministry of bishop, priest and deacon was almost everywhere established. Was one pattern followed in every place or did the process vary from church to church? Does the position represented in the Pastorals of an 'apostolic man' (G. Dix) or 'sub-apostle' (S. C. Neill) like Timothy and Titus settling for a period in a church show us the way by which in some churches mon-episcopacy developed? Does the practice which seems to have survived for a long time in Alexandria, whereby the presbyters corporately chose and consecrated the bishop, represent a practice that was once widespread? Is it possible that in some places a prophet settled and was given the prior position by the Church, so becoming the first bishop? The only honest answer to these questions is 'We do not know.'

9. What we can say is (a) that the position of James the brother of the Lord in the mother-church of Jerusalem provided an example for later days, (b) that the Pastorals do in fact show us a situation half-way between the apostolic oversight and later mon-episcopacy, (c) that, according to the evidence of Clement of Rome (A.D. 96) the apostles took definite steps to secure the continuance of the ministry (I Clem. XI ii and XI iv), (d) that the emergence of episcopacy was related to the presidency of the Eucharist, and (e) that in Syria and Asia Minor mon-episcopacy was established by A.D. 110, as the letters of Ignatius testify, and by the second half of the century it existed everywhere. Bishops were now regarded as 'successors to the apostles,' not because it was thought that they were indisputably linked with them historically through an unbroken chain of laying-on-of-hands, but because they fulfilled as nearly as possible the functions of the apostles in an earlier day. They were the living witnesses in their various sees to the truth of the Gospel, so that apostolic succession was to be found neither in the New Testament alone, nor in the episcopate alone, but in the two together, as the bishop 'guarded the deposit' and the Church constantly renewed its obedience to

the word of God.[1] The bishop too found himself committed to the same pastoral oversight as belonged to the apostles, and still today there would be few bishops who could not testify that it was after their consecration that the New Testament epistles struck home to them with a directness of meaning they had not had before. Here also the bishop is 'successor to the apostles.'

10. As there had been some in the apostolic company who took the lead, with Peter (in the Matthaean tradition at least) being the foremost 'foundation-stone,' so in the early Church we find the bishops of sees in important cities taking a natural precedence, which later was to develop into provincial and patriarchal structures. With the predominance of Rome, the eternal city, and with the destruction of Jerusalem and the scattering of the mother-church there, it was almost inevitable that a certain primacy of honour, a right to take the lead, should come to be recognized in the bishop there, particularly as both Peter and Paul were counted as its foundation-apostles. The Petrine texts were used to provide Scriptural support and encouragement for a position that developed primarily through the structure of the Roman Empire and the pressures of the Church's historical existence.

2

What then are the consequences to be drawn from this historical résumé?

1. We must abandon once and for all the claim that ordinations within the threefold historic ministry can be proved to go back in unbroken succession to the apostles. *The Apostolic Ministry* was the last major work to attempt to substantiate this claim and by common consent it failed. W. Telfer comes nearer the truth when he describes the tradition 'that the apostles had provided for the future of the Church by creating an order of monarchical

---

[1] Cf. Laud 'Most evident is it that the "succession" which the Fathers meant, is not tied to place or person but it is tied to the "verity of doctrine." . . . So that if the doctrine be no kin to Christ all the "succession" become strangers, what nearness soever they pretend' (*Conference with Fisher*, XXXIX, Works, vol. 2, p. 424).

bishops' as 'a historical myth' created by 'Latin churchmen.'[1] As we have seen, the threefold ministry is a gradual development and there are many gaps in our knowledge. No doubt the beginnings can be seen in the New Testament period, but it is significant that, in contrast to the wording of Canon C1 which repeats the language of the Preface to the Ordinal, the first version of the Revised Catechism presented to the Convocations described the three Orders of Ministers in Christ's Church as dating 'from ancient times' and not 'from the Apostles' time.' It is true that in deference to traditionalists who objected, the wording was subsequently changed, but it is significant that the wording of the Preface was not adopted. The historical reference was simply omitted.

2. With the recognition of the state of the evidence, the whole 'pipe-line' theory of the transmission of grace from Christ through the Apostles and the unbroken succession of subsequent episcopal consecrations collapses. You can only draw water from a tap if at every point along the line back to the waterworks the connection is sure, and if that is how grace is thought to reach us, then the only conclusion is that we have no guarantee that we are in any better state than those whose ministries are outside the historic succession. We may be able to pinpoint their 'break' to some particular date in the sixteenth, seventeenth or eighteenth centuries, but we cannot be sure that we have not got a similar one somewhere in the tunnel period of the late first and early second centuries.

To that argument from history must be added a theological one. Is this in any case the right way to think about the way the grace of God operates? God's grace is his love in action, his outgoing mercy and strength. It is something intensely personal and, while the Bible recognizes that God's gracious activity can be expressed through outward and visible means, it also makes clear that it is essentially part of his 'vertical' relationship with his Church, the eternal God meeting us in the here and now with his power and his love.

[1] W. Telfer, *The Office of a Bishop*, p. 118.

I believe these two things need to be said loudly and clearly from within the Anglican Communion, for these are the two elements which spring first to the minds of Free Churchmen and others, when they hear the phrase 'apostolic succession' used. These, they believe, are the essential ingredients of the concept and there has not yet been adequate Anglican repudiation of them.[1] Only when we make clear that in our thinking 'apostolic succession' does not imply either can we move forward to a more constructive understanding of the phrase.

3. Having thus cleared the decks, we can take a more positive approach. According to the Fourth Gospel, our Lord promised that the Holy Spirit, the other counsellor, would guide the Church into all truth (16. 13). The basic approach to the scriptures in this book is that they are to be understood dynamically, not statically. Within the New Testament itself, as within the Old, we see doctrine developing and practice being adapted for the sub-apostolic and subsequent generations. Here is tradition at its source, but the stream flows on and the question to be asked about any development is not, Can we quote chapter and verse for it? but, taking the scriptures as a whole, is this development consonant with it or not?

Just as we see the guidance of the Holy Spirit in the process by which the books of the New Testament came to be formed into a second Canon to be added to the one taken over from the old Israel, and in the developing pattern of Christian sacramental worship, so I believe we are right to see the divine guidance in the development by which the threefold ministry of bishop, presbyter and deacon became normative and accepted (apparently without opposition) throughout the entire Church. Thereby each church found its pattern of life and worship focused in a chief pastor,

---

[1] It is only fair to point out that in its cruder form this doctrine was rejected by Gregory Dix and A. G. Hebert (cf. *The Apostolic Ministry*, pp. 200 and 522). E. L. Mascall has emphasized the 'vertical' link (*Corpus Christi*, Ch. 1) and E. W. Kemp says, 'The commission to minister in the particular Order to which the man is being ordained . . . is, strictly speaking, the only thing that is transmitted by the Bishop' (*The Anglican-Methodist Conversations*, p. 38).

who had been elected by the faithful and consecrated by his peers and who ruled with the presbyters and the deacons in the corporate life of the Church in his diocese, whether it consisted (as at first) of the congregations in a single city or in the larger area of a district, as the countryside became Christianized. I believe too that without in any way committing ourselves to the doctrine of Papal infallibility we may recognize a certain primacy of honour in the Bishop of Rome as something which also developed under the guidance of the Spirit.

4. Anglicans may indeed be thankful that they belong to a part of Christ's Church which has preserved through all the trials and upheavals of the Reformation period the historic threefold ministry in unbroken succession. As we have seen, the Church has both a 'vertical' and a 'horizontal' dimension and, while we recognize that the outpouring of God's grace in ordination belongs to the 'vertical,' we do not for that reason minimize the value of historic continuity from the first creative age of the Church or underestimate the significance of the commission and authority bestowed through this historic medium. The impressive fact that the threefold ministry prevailed unquestioned through 1,300 years and is integral to the life of far and away the largest part of the Christian Church still today cannot be ignored. The historic ministry is by no means the only witness to the continuous life of the Church down the centuries, still less can it be regarded as the one element which alone defines whether a particular section of Christendom is or is not a true part of the Catholic Church, as though loyalty to the truth of the Gospel were a merely secondary matter. Nevertheless, it is *a* witness both to the Church's continuing life from the early formative days and, when rightly exercised, to the truth of the Gospel.

As such, we can indeed commend the historic threefold ministry to the Churches conventionally known as 'non-episcopal.' But we must be sure that we are commending a pattern of ministry that is true to the Gospel, must be ready to admit frankly the perversions and lopsidedness that have marred it in

o

the course of Christian history, and must show readiness to make the necessary changes in our own structure for the sake of the Gospel and the unity of the Church.

We proceed therefore to consider the orders of bishop, priest and deacon in turn.

II. BISHOPS AND THE EXERCISE OF EPISCOPE

'ALL *episcope* (oversight) in the Church belongs to Christ the one head of the Church, and it is by his gift and command that it is exercised within the body (Jn. 20. 19–23; 21. 15–17).' So says the Report of the Joint Commission on Church Union in Australia, and it goes on, 'it is given by Christ to his whole Church in such a way that the Church is launched from the beginning with persons exercising oversight in association with groups and the body as a whole' (Mt. 16. 19; 18. 18)[1] There can be no doubt that this expresses the conclusion of modern Biblical study, and it should lead us who are Anglicans to recognize two things more clearly than we always do. First, the fact that a church does not have bishops as we understand them does not mean that it lacks *episcope*. The Church of Scotland and the whole Presbyterian tradition would assert firmly that in their system of graded courts they exercise an oversight that in practice produces a degree of order not always apparent in the individualistic parish life of the Church of England. Methodism claims to have *episcope* in a corporate form and finds the word 'connexion' significant in this respect. And John Huxtable has recently protested that 'it is too widely and too easily assumed that only those churches which have bishops are or can be episcopal . . . without what *episcope* represents (*sc.* oversight, shepherding, pastoral authority) no order at all is possible.'[2] If, then, we go on to ask 'why in that case have you abandoned the historic episcopate in which that function has been through the centuries embodied?' the answer we shall receive is 'because at the critical time too many bishops were prelates rather than shepherds and because, even when they did value their duty of pastoral oversight, they thought of it as something they exercised in their order alone.' Humanly speaking, it would have been a great deal to expect for the bishops at the Restoration with their tradition of the divine right of kings and their bitter memories of the humiliations of the

---

[1] *The Church—Its Nature, Function and Ordering*, p. 45. [2] *Op. cit.*, p. 99.

Commonwealth not to have re-established monarchical episcopacy, but 300 years later we can listen more sympathetically to
the appeal of Richard Baxter in his plea for what in effect would
be a synodically based episcopacy. It is indeed the pattern of
episcopacy that prevails in almost all parts of the Anglican Communion outside England and that one hopes will soon be fully
established in the mother-church also.

It is, then, the office and work of a bishop, not thought of in
isolation but in organic relationship to the other orders of ministry
and to the whole Church of God, that we must try to set forth.
As we do so, we shall find that the significance of his office
derives from the meeting in the person and work of the bishop
of various diverse elements.

I

First, then, 'the Episcopate symbolizes and secures in an abiding
form the apostolic mission and authority within the Church;
historically the Episcopate became the organ of this mission and
authority.'[1] In the previous chapter I have tried to show how
this came about under, as we believe, the guidance of the Holy
Spirit. There have been times indeed when the episcopate, being
composed of fallible men, has failed in fulfilling this function. A
frank recognition of this unhappy fact in the *Anglican-Methodist
Majority Report* would have gone far to meet the legitimate
criticism of the Dissentients.[2] Yet it remains an integral part of
our understanding of what the bishop's office is intended to be.
Thus, when a bishop is consecrated, out of the three passages from
which the Gospel is appointed to be read, one is the apostolic
commission of the Risen Christ in St. Matthew ch. 28 and one
the commission in St. John ch. 20, which includes the apostolic
sending, the giving of the power to remit and retain sins and the
promise of the Spirit. These, we know, are commissions to the

---

[1] This and most of the subsequent statements of the office and work of a bishop are
quoted from *Doctrine in the Church of England*, pp. 122-123; they are quoted in the Anglican-Methodist *Interim Statement*, pp. 25–26, in the final *Report*, pp. 24–25 and in *The
Anglican-Presbyterian Conversations*, Report, pp. 23–24.

[2] *Op. cit.*, p. 58.

whole Church, but they have their particular relevance to those through whose guidance and leadership under Christ the Church fulfils them. The bishop is successor to the apostles, as he himself proclaims the Gospel and as he constantly sets before his diocese by teaching and example Christ's call to his Church to be an apostolic body, not inward-looking and ingrown, but open to the world which is God's world and ready to speak out and live out in it God's word of reconciliation in Christ.

Secondly, 'the bishop in his diocese represents the Good Shepherd; the idea of pastoral care is inherent in his office. Both clergy and laity look to him as chief pastor, and he represents in a special degree the paternal quality of pastoral care.' The Doctrine Report places this fourth in its listing of the elements that go to make up the bishop's office, but H. E. W. Turner is surely right in thinking it should 'appear much higher on the list.'[1] It is certainly central in the Order for the Consecration of a Bishop in Anglican Prayer Books. For not only do these provide the charge of St. Paul to the elders of Ephesus and the re-commissioning of Peter by the Risen Christ as recorded in St. John ch. 21 among the appointed lections, but at a most solemn moment after the laying on of hands the newly consecrated bishop hears words he is likely to find ringing in his ears throughout his ministry.

'Be to the flock of Christ a shepherd, not a wolf, feed them and devour them not. Hold up the weak, heal the sick, bind up the broken, bring again the outcasts, seek the lost. Be so merciful that you be not too remiss; so minister discipline that you forget not mercy; that when the chief shepherd shall appear you may receive the never failing crown of glory.'

One of the marks of the Good Shepherd is that he knows his sheep and his own know him. That does not mean that the bishop as chief pastor should be on the doorstep of every parish every month or be seen at every local function of more than trivial importance, though in some dioceses outside England which I know there are people who apparently hold that idea. A bishop

[1] *Op. cit.*, p. 44.

quite so ubiquitous would deprive his fellow-workers of any initiative. But he must be the known and trusted friend and counsellor, particularly of the clergy, to whom he stands in the same pastoral relationship as the parish priest does to the people of his parish. And that can only happen if he knows them personally, knows their homes and family life, their joys and sorrows, their hopes and discouragements. What all this might mean for the ordering of diocesan life we will consider later, but of one thing we can be sure—only a pattern of episcopacy which sets forth in its day by day expression in life the image of the bishop exercising his pastoral care as father in God will commend itself to those whose tradition of *episcope* has been different.

Closely associated with this office of the bishop as chief pastor under Christ the Good Shepherd of the flock is his liturgical character. The father presides at the family table, and it was in this context, as we have seen, that the office of the bishop developed. The whole relationship of bishop, presbyters, deacons and people was indeed set forth most characteristically in the celebration of the Eucharist in early days—the bishop behind the table at the centre facing the people, the presbyters on either side him, the deacons collecting the gifts brought up by the people and distributing them, after the bishop had 'eucharistized' them, in communion to the people. Even when daughter-churches had grown into separate parishes (to use modern terminology), the sense of unity with each other in the bishop's Eucharist was maintained in some places, e.g. Rome, by the taking of a piece of the consecrated bread from the central celebration and the placing of it in the cup at the other altars. The bishop was the focal point of the Church's priestly action in offering spiritual sacrifices acceptable to God through Jesus Christ.

In the dioceses of today the relationship cannot be so close, yet, as the Bishop of Bristol has put it, the bishop 'is pre-eminently the president of the Eucharist, standing in awe and trembling, please God, to "do" what Christ bade his Apostles to do in remembrance of him. . . . The bishop is never more truly seen in his proper light than when he presides, in cathedral or parish church, in Christ's name at Christ's table.'[1] Even when he does not celebrate personally, the Prayer Book reserves to him the pronouncing of the absolution and the blessing at the Eucharist. To the bishop too is reserved, exclusively in the Anglican and normally in the Roman Catholic tradition, the prayer and laying-on of hands in Confirmation. He alone lays hands on those being made deacons or deaconesses, is joined by the presbyterate in prayer and the laying on of hands in the ordaining of priests, and shares with the archbishop of the province and other bishops in the consecration of new members of the episcopal order. He institutes priests in his diocese to parishes saying, as he commissions them, 'Receive this cure, which is both mine and thine.' He similarly licenses lay readers and full-time women workers in his diocese.

The bishop has sometimes been thought to have a *jus liturgicum* enabling him to authorize all kinds of variations of the appointed forms of worship. Canonically this is highly doubtful, though in an age when the Church's forms of worship were frozen by the State connection the claim had a practical usefulness—and was indeed inevitable. Now that 'Lawful Authority' has been defined in the Church of England, the claim to this episcopal *jus* is not so cogent. Constitutional episcopacy requires that the bishop, as well as the other orders of ministry and the laity, should feel himself bound by the decisions of the Church's lawful assemblies. Only within that larger loyalty should he exercise an independent initiative—though within those limits he should certainly be encouraging liturgical and para-liturgical experiments for the rapidly changing conditions of many sections of modern society.[2] He has, of course, in all circumstances the responsibility of seeing that the worship of the congregations in his diocese is offered up 'decently and in order.'

[1] Glyn Simon (ed.), *Bishops*, p. 32.
[2] The use of the 1662 Confirmation Service alone, after the failure of the House of Laity to pass what was in effect the 1928 Revised Service by the required two-thirds majority in 1966, shows that this point has been well taken by the bishops of the Church of England.

The Doctrine Report speaks of two other functions of the Episcopate. One of these is 'to guard the Church against erroneous teaching.' 'In early times the continuous successions of bishops in tenure of the various sees were valued because they secured the purity of apostolic teaching as against (for example) the danger of the introduction of novel and erroneous teaching by means of writings or secret traditions falsely ascribed to Apostolic authors.' The appeal to the consensus of teaching of the great sees was certainly an effective answer to the claims of the Gnostics; and it was in this context that the meaning of 'apostolic succession' was first understood. The Doctrine Report recognizes that 'the need for this safeguard became less urgent when authoritative formulations of doctrine were drawn up and the Canon of Scripture was finally fixed'; it might have added also that the complexity of the bishop's office meant inevitably that much of the creative thinking about the Christian faith and its relation to the society of each particular age became the special concern of the theologians. Nevertheless, the Report adds, the guarding of the Church against false doctrine 'has remained a function of the Episcopate.' It is in accordance with that long standing tradition that in the Ordinals of the Anglican Communion one of the questions addressed to the consecrand is:

Are you ready, with all faithful diligence, to banish and drive away all erroneous and strange doctrine contrary to God's Word; and both privately and openly to call upon and encourage others to the same?
Answer: I am ready, the Lord being my helper.

Here, as previously, we have to confess that bishops, being fallible men, have not always been faithful to this aspect of their office. We can never forget that the corruptions of the medieval Church which Christians of all traditions now openly recognize and deplore grew up in a church which was episcopally governed under the supreme rule of the Papacy. It is not bishops *per se*, but bishops as faithful witnesses to the apostolic Gospel enshrined in the scriptures, who are guardians of Christian faith and doctrine.

In these days of theological questioning, when many feel they can only take soundings and that the setting of a course for the next stage of the Church's voyage cannot be undertaken for some while yet, the bishop in his diocese or the bishops together in council, whether as the House of Bishops of a National Synod or in a Lambeth Conference or a Vatican II, have no easy task. Conservatives criticize them bitterly if they fail to defend, not only the faith once for all delivered to the Saints, but also the time-honoured and hallowed phrases in which that faith was expressed in past generations. Radicals dismiss them scornfully, unless they are evidently backing the latest, most tentative and perhaps still only half-baked, contemporary theological reconstruction. Bishops need to have a firm grasp of what are the essentials without which the Christian faith would cease to be itself. They need to be alert to the climate of opinion in their day and sympathetic to those of the clergy and laity who feel called to expound the eternal Gospel and express their obedience to the living Christ in new ways. Above all, they must stand for the wholeness of the Catholic faith, helping those of one tradition who see some truths with great clarity to discern others which may be emphasized by another school of thought. In all these they need the help of theological and other advisers to whom they can turn individually and corporately. The *periti* played a most valuable part at the Vatican Council and it is welcome news that there will be for the first time non-episcopal assessors at a Lambeth Conference, when the bishops of the Anglican Communion meet in 1968.

So we are led on to the last function of the bishop. Because he is the focal point of the Church in his diocese, summing up in his person and office so many things which belong to the local church as a whole, he represents his diocese in the wider councils of the Church. Nothing was more significant at Vatican II than the way in which the bishops from Asia and Africa and Latin America, as well as those from the de-Christianized areas of Europe and N. America, challenged the presuppositions of the conservative elements in the Curia with insistent, down-to-earth demands for change and renewal that sprang from their understanding of the needs and aspirations of the Church in their various local situations. The voice of the *corpus Christianum*, so far as that is represented in the Roman Catholic Church, made itself listened to from all over the world, and that was entirely right. Similarly, the bishop represents the whole Catholic Church to his diocese. He brings to its possibly limited and over-localized outlook and life the breadth of understanding and experience represented in the wider Church. Thus the bishops of the Roman Catholic Church, now back in their dioceses after Vatican II, are implementing decisions taken about national episcopal conferences, liturgy in the vernacular, ecumenical co-operation, and the rest.

As we look forward to the Lambeth Conference of 1968 with its theme 'The Renewal of the Church,' we can hope that Anglican bishops from all over the world will bring before the Conference with equal vigour the needs and outlook of the Church in their many different areas and will later return with the pooled knowledge, the enrichment of personal meetings and the resolutions of the Conference as a guide for the part of the Church to which they belong.

On a smaller scale I can testify to the reality of this two-way communication through the person of the bishop in the Council of the Church of South-East Asia, where bishops who represent dioceses belonging to different provinces and national churches meet annually.[1] Through that meeting scattered and diverse dioceses in the same part of the world are brought out of an isolation that might otherwise narrow their vision, and as a result a sense of belonging to a larger community of fellow-Christians is in process of being created.

Some whose tradition places *episcope* in a corporate body, a presbytery, an assembly or a conference, accepting the above as a fair statement of the office of a bishop, may yet wonder whether it is good that these aspects of Church life should be focused in one person, however much the emphasis may be placed on the

---

[1] Joined by a clerical and a lay delegate from each diocese in alternate years.

bishop-in-presbytery, the bishop governing synodically, and so on. In answer, I would emphasize two points. First, a personal *episcope* answers to a need in men and women. For all our talk of 'man come of age,' we have an inner urge to look to the example and leadership of a person, whether in the field of government or education or even of 'pop' music. It is in a person that qualities come alive for us as they never do in corporate bodies. The pastoral, liturgical and doctrinal oversight of Christ's flock is essentially a personal activity; and not least does the care of the undershepherds fall under this heading. There is a 'crying need for a ministry to ministers, an oversight of overseers, as none know better than the clergy.'[1] It is not surprising that the Moderator of the General Assembly of the Church of Scotland, originally just a chairman for the annual meeting of that august body, should have become a sort of *persona* of the Kirk for his year of office, nor that other churches should have developed superintendents, district chairmen and moderators also.[2]

Secondly, personal *episcope*, when exercised with faithfulness and humility, exhibits, I believe, better than any corporate oversight can do the character and work of him who is the Good Shepherd. The Gospel is at heart good news of the restoration of a broken relationship between a personal God and those who have been created to be his children; the Christian life is life in fellowship with the Father through the Son in the power of the Holy Spirit. It is most fitting therefore that life in the Church which is the family of God should be a life of personal relationships, life lived under the guidance and care of one who is properly described as a 'father in God.' It is significant that the majority of the signatories of the Church Union document in Australia (all of them Congregationalists, Methodists or Presbyterians) should have felt led to say:

'The personal expression of *episcope* is essential to the life of the Church . . . our Churches have recognized this necessity on the congregational level, and forced by modern developments in society to see the importance of

---

[1] E. M. B. Green, *Called to Serve*, pp. 48–49.

[2] There are those who refer to the full-time clerical secretaries of the Free Churches in England as 'the Dissenting Primates'!

transcongregational levels of the Church's life, they would be justified also in providing personal as well as corporate *episcope* at that level. Because this form of office is acceptable in the New Testament, is widely attested in Church history including our Protestant tradition, is justified by the Church's needs in contemporary society, and also helps to symbolize the wider unity of the Church, we recommend its adoption at the time of union.'[1]

2

I conclude this chapter on the office and work of a bishop in the Church of God with two observations. The first is that, whereas the pattern of episcopal ministry described above can reasonably be exemplified in many Anglican dioceses overseas, it is extremely difficult, indeed almost impossible, in the very large dioceses of the Church of England or of the large cities of Canada, Australia or the United States. Something is wrong when the incumbent of an English parish, whose church is next door to the episcopal residence of the diocese, confesses, 'many people here don't even know the name of the bishop' or when a leading member of a non-Anglican church in one of the State capitals in Australia says, 'the Archbishop is so rushed off his feet that it is very difficult for us to get any idea of what having a father-in-God means'—and both things have been said to me. One solution of the problem may lie along the lines of an episcopal group ministry, as suggested by the Bishop of Woolwich,[2] and the dioceses of London and Oxford with their delegation of a good deal of authority to the suffragans in their separate areas go some way in this direction. The weakness, however, as many suffragan bishops, as well as parish priests and people in their areas, recognize, is that the diocesan bishop cannot in the nature of the case delegate ultimate authority. After all, the word mon-episcopacy means *one* head of the family, and I believe that E. M. B. Green is right when he speaks of the difficulty of commending episcopacy as we know it in England to our Free Church brethren.

[1] *Op. cit.*, p. 46. The minority did not oppose the adoption of personal episcopacy in principle, but believed that it should be the united Church which decided whether to adopt it or not.

[2] *Bishops*, pp. 125–138.

'The larger the diocese, the less justification there is for mon-episcopacy. Sole leadership of a million or more people cannot possibly be pastoral, and runs great danger of becoming prelatical. . . . The collegiate nature of Ignatian episcopacy is in sore need of being recovered in England. Twelve times in his epistles does he mention the three orders of ministry, and in ten of them they form an inseparable unity—the other two references are indecisive. We could not realize this today without far smaller bishoprics—the size perhaps of an archdeaconry, coupled with some form of synodical government.'[1]

It is often objected that the Church of England could not produce the required number of 'national leaders,' nor could it face the cost of new cathedrals or the burden of multiplied diocesan bureaucracies. Three things can be said in reply: (a) any such recovery of Ignatian episcopacy would need to be grouped under a senior bishop of the regional area (whether he were an archbishop or not) and only such senior bishops would need to be of 'national leader' calibre; (b) there must be very few arch-deaconries which do not have a central mother-church which could serve as the cathedral of the diocese as envisaged; (c) one regional office and staff should be able to serve all the dioceses of the region. Difficulties would not be insurmountable and the gains would be immense, for the bishop could then fulfil his calling as chief pastor in a way that is only too often frustratingly hard in present circumstances. He could know and be known by all the clergy and at least the leading layfolk, the churchwardens and others in the parishes or in industrial or other specialized ministries under his care.

The second observation arises from the fact of which we are becoming aware at the parish level, namely that in our techno-logical society men and women no longer live just in the one community of their place of residence. The steel works or factory provides the setting for another area of life and the football or cricket club the setting for still another. Group ministries in some areas, industrial missions in others, supplement the deeply rooted parochial system, which all open-minded observers recog-nize can no longer minister adequately to all the needs of a shifting

---

[1] *Op. cit.*, p. 49.

population. What we have not yet grasped is that similar pressures will call for episcopal oversight on a non-territorial as well as on a territorial basis.   Particular ministries may well require the pastoral care of a father-in-God as much as the traditional life of the parishes. The Roman Catholic Church has long recognized this, and bishops are appointed to titular sees for specialized work. The Australian Church Union report significantly says, 'the possibility should be kept open that the regions for which bishops are given responsibility could include, as well as the traditional geographical region, sociological regions, such as industry, education, health institutions, or oversight of areas of work now carried on by departments of the church.'[1] The U.S.P.G. (and one of its parent bodies, the S.P.G.) has a long tradition of General Secretaries in episcopal orders; and (if I may be forgiven a personal word) perhaps my own appointment to be General Secretary of the British Council of Churches is another example. 'You are being called,' said a wise priest whom I consulted before accepting the post, 'to exercise a pastoral *episcope* over the ecumenical movement in the British Isles and over those who are engaged in its work.' Flexibility and readiness for new approaches are as necessary at the episcopal, as at the clerical and lay levels of the Church's life in our changing society.

So we come back to the place of the bishop in the life of the whole Church, and I end this section with some words of the present Archbishop of Canterbury written thirty years ago:

'The growth of all Christians into the measure of the stature of the fullness of Christ means their growth with all the saints in the unity of the one body, and of this unity the Episcopate is the expression. It speaks of the incompleteness of every section of a divided Church, whether of those who possess the Episcopate or of those who do not. And those who possess it will tremble and never boast, for none can say that it is "theirs." It proclaims that there is one family of God before and behind them all, and that all die daily in the body of him who died and rose.'[2]

[1] *Op. cit.*, pp. 48–49. Leslie S. Hunter tells how a plan to second an English diocesan bishop for the full-time oversight of Training Men for the Ministry was frustrated by the Crown lawyers (*The English Church. A New Look*, p. 80).
[2] *The Gospel and the Catholic Church*, pp. 84–85.

III. PRESBYTERS (PRIESTS) AND THE PASTORAL OFFICE

THE gaps in our knowledge of how mon-episcopacy became universally established and our uncertainty about the pattern of development make it impossible for us either to regard those who serve as priests in the Church of God as just 'episcopal curates' or to think of bishops as merely 'presbyteral chairmen.' It is true, of course, that when the Ignatian type of episcopacy established itself, the bishop presided at the Eucharist in the congregation where he exercised *episcope* and that as new congregations developed in and around the city of his bishopric, he delegated his liturgical functions to the presbyters in the new centres of worship. But in some churches at any rate it appears to have been the presbyterate which appointed one of their numbers to be bishop in the first place; and in any case the presbyterate was established under the apostles before the emergence of mon-episcopacy. 'We must, therefore, avoid saying,' the Church Union negotiators in Australia comment, 'either that the bishop has all authority committed to him and delegates some to presbyters and deacons, or that presbyters (or some corporate expression of the Church's life) have all authority and delegate some to bishops. Each must be able to exercise the *episcope* committed to him by Christ, and each must exercise it responsibly within the wider *episcope* of the Body.'[1]

It is significant that, when a bishop ordains to the priesthood, he does not act alone. Not only does he act in the presence of the assembled Church, but also he has immediately associated with him those who represent the presbyteral order. They stand (or should stand) grouped on either side of him as he leads the Veni Creator and says the Ordination Prayer over the kneeling candidates, and they join with him in the laying on of hands. Those who are ordained to the priesthood are thus commissioned, authorized and empowered with the Spirit by the living Christ in

[1] *Op. cit.*, p. 49.

response to the prayers of the Church and through the outward and visible acts of those who represent both the episcopal and presbyteral orders of ministry. When, therefore, a bishop says to a priest on instituting him to a parish 'Receive this cure which is both mine and thine,' he is not saying 'act as my agent in a sphere of responsibility which is basically mine,' but 'share with me a sphere of responsibility which at different levels belongs to both of us.' It is when a bishop shows a rightful trust in his clergy and encourages their initiative that he will win from them a willing obedience 'in all things lawful and honest.'

The work of the parish priest or of the minister of a congregation has been so often described that there is no need to make more than a summary statement. As Christ's ministry can be spoken of in terms of his work as prophet, priest and shepherd-king, so the ministry of the parish priest can be defined as prophetic, priestly and pastoral. He is an ambassador of Christ, commissioned to make known the gospel of reconciliation, of deliverance from our estrangement from him who is the Ground of our Being into the glorious liberty of the children of God. He is called to help his people live out their vocation to mission and service in the area where they live and beyond, and not become an inward-looking religious club. He leads the worship of his people, speaking the words of praise and thanksgiving and intercession on their behalf, and in Christ's name and the name of his Church celebrates the sacraments. He orders that worship in such a way that his congregation are made aware of their participation in an activity that is offered to God on behalf of the world—the world that is already redeemed by Christ and yet so often unaware or careless of that deepest truth about itself. He is the pastor, with a ministry of caring to whole as well as sick, to those who are called the fortunate in life, as well as the unfortunate. Wherever a town or village is of the size or character to be a true community, the parish priest, as he throws himself into the life of that community and proves himself the friend and servant of all, can still be the *persona* of his parish and make an impact on its corporate life, as well as on the lives of individuals within it.

In many respects the vocation of the Anglican priest in his parish and of the Free Church minister in his congregation can be described in similar terms. But there are questions to be considered in the current situation. The *Report of the Anglican-Methodist Conversations*, for instance, has sparked off fresh theological discussion about the meaning of priesthood as applied to the presbyterate. At the practical level, the parish system has manifestly broken down in our great conurbations and not least in the inner-city areas where the Church of England is saddled with plant that is frequently a white elephant and always costly to maintain. Again, the sharp decline in the number of ordinands reflects not only the theological uncertainty of the times, but also doubts about the worthwhileness of full-time service in a Church in present circumstances. We must look at some of these questions in turn.

I

First, then—what do we mean by the words said by the bishop at the laying on of hands 'receive the Holy Ghost for the office and work of a priest in the Church of God, now committed unto thee by the imposition of our hands?' There are certain things on which all are agreed, and it is important to get them clear. In doing so, we can use much of the language of the Anglican-Methodist Report.[1]

1. 'It is our common belief that, in the New Covenant of the Lord Jesus Christ, he alone is priest in his own right. He has offered the one perfect and final sacrifice which atones for the sins of the world, he intercedes eternally for the world, he is the one mediator between God and man; through him alone God reconciles the world to himself.' As E. M. B. Green says, 'it is recognized on all sides now that Christ sums up in himself all that was symbolized by the sacrificing priesthood of the Old Testament. . . . It is now, thank God, universally recognized that Christ's priesthood is final and complete, and that his sacrifice of

---

[1] *Op. cit.*, pp. 23–24.

P

himself upon the cross for man's forgiveness can neither be added to nor repeated.'[1]

2. 'By sharing in his priestly ministry, the Church corporately is a royal priesthood, a holy nation. In and under Christ it offers God's pardon and grace to the world, intercedes with God for the world, and offers itself and its worship as a living sacrifice to God.' In this respect, as we have seen, the New Israel fulfils the calling of God to the Old Israel.[2] To quote E. M. B. Green again,[3] 'the priest (in the Old Testament) represented God to the people, when he declared to them God's will, and the people to God, when he interceded with him on their behalf . . . this two-way mediation of evangelism and prayer is the solemn, life-long calling of every Christian, and it is significant that these two activities are both spoken of as priestly ministries in the New Testament' (Rom. 15. 16; Rev. 8. 3 ff.). Here is the doctrine of the priesthood of all believers, which, rightly understood, was one of the great rediscoveries of the Reformation. So also the Anglican-Methodist Report speaks of the responsibility of every individual believer 'within the corporate priesthood of the whole Church' to worship, witness and serve, and of 'his own privilege of direct, personal access to God in Christ for pardon and grace.'

3. In the New Testament the term 'priest' is never applied in a particular sense to those who carried out the functions of apostles, prophets, pastors, teachers or presbyter-bishops. There are obvious reasons for this. In the apostolic age the word 'priest' was associated either with the offering of the Levitical sacrifices in the Temple at Jerusalem or with the rites of Gentile worship, the offerings to the gods and goddesses of Greece and Rome and to the darker gods of nature-worship that infiltrated into the Roman Empire from the East. But, as the Epistle to the Hebrews makes clear, the one perfect sacrifice of Christ has fulfilled and brought to an end the daily and yearly sacrifices offered in the Temple. The Levitical system is now superseded. And the whole Christian revelation of the one, living and true God stands in

---

[1] *Op. cit.*, pp. 76–77.   [2] See Section B, chap. III above.   [3] *Op. cit.*, p. 79.

sharp opposition to all forms of nature-worship, of deifying the instincts, whether expressed in the Canaanite and Oriental cults of the ancient world or in Hitler's worship of blood and soil and D. H. Lawrence's equal idolatry of sex in modern times. The Church itself is a priestly body, but in New Testament days those within it who were appointed to perform the functions of oversight, pastoral care and *diakonia* were not yet thought of as belonging to a 'professional' or a 'permanent' ministry. They were more like lay-elders in the Church of Scotland, office-holders in their own church who earned their living in profession or trade, but not *ex officio* office-bearers if they moved from one church-centre to another.

If we are prepared to recognize in the development of a 'professional' ministry the guidance of the Holy Spirit—and all the main historic churches of Christendom must surely acknowledge that guidance, seeing they all have such a ministry—then a new situation inevitably arises. It is likely that even from the beginning the 'priesthood of all believers' did 'not mean that every individual believer' had 'the *right* to perform every ministerial or priestly function,' but only those appointed by the apostles or others in authority within the Church. From the beginning there were varieties of service under the same Lord. But with the development of a 'professional' ministry the differences became more marked. Christ, it is now recognized, calls some to the full-time ministry of the word and sacraments and to the pastoral care of his people, the Church recognizes and tests that call and then presents the men thus approved to the bishops, i.e. to those with authority to ordain in the name of Christ and of his Church. This ordination is thought of as giving its recipients a 'stamp,' a 'character' that remains with them through life. 'Within the exercise of the corporate priesthood there fall to be performed certain actions, historically and generally regarded as priestly, which are in many cases, including the Church of England, reserved to those who have been specifically ordained, as ministers of the word and sacraments, to perform them.'

The authority to pronounce absolution is one example. In an earlier chapter we noted that the commission to forgive or retain sins in St. John ch. 20 was given either to the Twelve, representing the whole company of believers, or to that larger company directly. It is within that wider context that the Epistle of James can bid its readers 'confess your sins to one another, and pray for one another, that you may be healed' (5. 16). But the early Church found, as the Oxford Group Movement had to learn in its turn, that public confession of private sins has grave dangers of psychological exhibitionism on the one hand and of spiritual damage to the innocent on the other. Hence the rise of the practice of confession to God in the presence of one with the authority of Christ and his Church to receive such a confession and to be the instrument whereby Christ and his Church speaks the word of forgiveness. So the words said by the bishop over the candidate for the priesthood at his ordination include the St. John 20 commission to forgive and retain sins. So also the words provided for the priest to use in absolving a sick person in the Order for the Visitation of the Sick (and in fact used by priests in hearing all confessions) make the true nature of his authority clear (italics mine):

> Our Lord Jesus Christ, who hath left *power to his Church* to absolve all sinners who truly repent and believe in him, of his great mercy forgive thee thine offences: And by his *authority committed to me*, I absolve thee from all thy sins, In the name of the Father, and of the Son, and of the Holy Ghost. Amen.

The priest, it is plain, is acting as the ministerial agent of Christ in and through his body, the Church.

To assert this is in no sense to deny the reality of God's forgiveness received by a penitent sinner who kneels at his bedside alone or opens his heart to a lay friend who prays with him. Nevertheless, the Church has surely been right not to leave such matters of deep spiritual importance to individual initiative, but to recognize that within the total life of the body of Christ God has given power and authority to his ministers to declare and pronounce to his people, being penitent, the absolution and remission of their sins, both in the public worship of the Church and (where desired) in the privacy of sacramental confession.[1]

Similarly, the priest acts with the authority of Christ and his Church as he leads the worship of the congregation, speaking the words which are the Church's words and to which the people assent with their *Amen*. In this general offering of worship he is joined by others—a deacon, lay readers, servers, as well as by the whole congregation. But in the central acts of the two sacraments of the Gospel he has a particular responsibility. Though a deacon may baptize 'in the absence of the priest' and a lay person when 'extreme urgency shall compel,' the priest is the normal celebrant of the sacrament of Holy Baptism. Whatever part others take in the service, he says the prayer for the blessing of the water and baptizes the candidates. In the Eucharist the ministerial commission given to him is in the Catholic tradition still more strictly guarded. Others may read the lections and say some of the prayers, but he alone has the authority of Christ and his Church to take on the Church's behalf the gifts of bread and wine, to lift them up to God in the sacrifice of praise and thanksgiving to God and in the pleading of Christ's sacrifice once offered, and to say and do over them the words and actions of the Lord on the night in which he was betrayed. He distributes the Bread in the communion of the people, though he may be helped by a deacon or a specially licensed lay reader in the administration of the Cup.

It is important to emphasize the priest's representative character, in view of the wrong ideas of the Middle Ages which, coupled with a perverted doctrine of the sacrifice of the Mass, provoked the vigorous reaction of the Reformers and made the very words 'priest' and 'sacerdotal' stink in many Protestant nostrils. 'It is an abuse of the sacerdotal conception,' wrote R. C. Moberley 'if it is

---

[1] It is significant that the verse about confessing sins to one another (Jas. 5. 16) is dependent on the preceding sentences, in which the writer exhorts the sick person to call for the elders of the Church to pray for him and anoint him in the name of the Lord. The prayer of faith spoken by the elders will restore the sick man, 'and if he has committed sins, he will be forgiven' (14 and 15). The ministry of the presbyters to the sick is directed to wholeness of life, both spiritual and physical.

supposed that the priesthood exists to celebrate sacrifices or acts of worship in the place of the body of the people or as their substitute.' 'The ministers are the organs of the body, through which the body expresses itself in particular functions of detail.'[1] Similarly, the Anglican-Methodist Report says, 'the ministerial priest acts representatively and in conjunction with the laity's exercise of its priesthood.' Through the words spoken and the actions performed by him on its behalf, the congregation exercises its royal priesthood of worship and praise, of intercession for and witness to the world.

The Anglican-Methodist Report speaks of 'a measure of theological uncertainty or disagreement as to the intrinsic nature of the priesthood of ordained ministers and its relation to the priesthood of the laity or of the whole Church' and believes (or at least the signatories of the Majority Report do) that it 'is not incompatible with the establishment of communion between our two Churches or with fellowship in one Church.' In a matter of considerable difficulty in finding the right words to preserve the doctrinal balance correctly, such 'theological uncertainty or disagreement' is understandable. At the same time there is, I suggest, a fairly clear distinction to be drawn between a view of 'the intrinsic nature of the priesthood of ordained ministers' which results in thinking of them as constituted thereby 'holy men,' with some kind of *mana* attaching to them, and the view which thinks of them as exercising towards the people they are appointed to serve a priesthood similar in kind to that which the people as a whole are called to exercise towards the world. If, in E. M. B. Green's phrase, the 'two-way mediation of evangelism and prayer is the solemn, life-long calling of every Christian' in relation to the world, and if 'these two activities are both spoken of as priestly ministries in the New Testament,' then in a particular way this calling belongs to those ordained as priests in the Church of God in relation to their people. In their ministry of preaching and

[1] *Ministerial Priesthood*, pp. 95 and 68, quoted in A. T. Hanson, *The Pioneer Ministry*, p. 138.

teaching they 'declare to them God's will,' and in their inter-
cessions they seek to fulfil the vocation:

> To bear thy people in their heart,
> And love the souls whom thou dost love.

An interpretation of ministerial priesthood along such lines as
these should surely win the acceptance of most Anglicans and, as
A. T. Hanson suggests, of many Free Churchmen also.[1]

2

The working out of the prophetic, priestly and pastoral functions of the parish priest over the centuries has meant in practice
that he has been established in a position of leadership with the
people committed to his care passively accepting his ministrations
or at most undertaking the duties he has asked them to perform.
A number of phrases in the Prayer Book encourage this conception. The prayer for the Church Militant, for instance, intercedes
for God's people and 'specially this congregation here present'
that 'with meek heart and due reverence, they may hear, and
receive' God's holy word expounded by the 'bishops and curates,'
and so may serve him 'in holiness and righteousness all the days
of their life.' Similarly, the collect for St. Peter's Day prays,
'make, we beseech thee, all bishops and pastors diligently to
preach thy holy word, and the people obediently to follow the
same.' E. L. Mascall has commented that Article XIX defines the
Church as 'a congregation of faithful men' in which the only
functions referred to are the clerical ones of preaching the pure
word of God and duly ministering the sacraments according to
Christ's ordinance.[2] No doubt squires of the Sir Roger de Cover-
ley type and powerful females like Mr. Collins' patroness, Lady
Catherine de Burgh, were anything but obedient in following the
parson's injunctions, but the 'image' of the parish priest as the

---

[1] *Op. cit.*, p. 138, n. 2. Perhaps we should help people more, if we stopped using phrases
like 'asking the bishop to give us *his* blessing,' as though it were his private possession. He
is the appointed minister of the Gospel through whom the blessing of God, Father, Son
and Holy Spirit is given to the congregation.

[2] *The Recovery of Unity*, p. 7.

person in full authority, who alone can initiate and authorize anything, who performs all the 'spiritual' functions of evangelism and pastoral care, and who presides over every Bible class and every committee meeting is still strong, despite nearly half a century of the Enabling Act and the existence of parochial Church councils.

The recovery of a theology of the laity, the complexities of modern society and a rising standard of education, require, as we have seen, a change of perspective and a new relationship between clergy and laity. If the Church is indeed the body of Christ, with each member called to play a particular part in the healthy functioning of the whole body, then the old distinction between an active clergy and more or less passive laity goes. The aim and object of the parish priest's work is 'to equip God's people for work in his service, to the building up of the body of Christ' (Eph. 4. 12 N.E.B.). The old relationship has to give way to a new sense of partnership.[1]

We may take preaching as an example. J. G. Davies has quoted with approval some words of Lesslie Newbigin, in which he says that what is required in preaching

'is an understanding of the relation between what God has done—uniquely and finally—in Christ and what he is doing in the life of mankind as a whole, an understanding which will enable Christians to communicate the Gospel in words and patterns of living which are in accordance with what God is doing, and is calling men to do, in their secular life' (*The Relevance of Trinitarian Doctrine for To-Day's Mission*, p. 28).

But J. G. Davies asks whether this is any longer possible through the traditional sermon method.

'When life was a unity, when the horizon was that of a closely knit community, the parson could know his people and their problems, in work and leisure, and could speak to their situation. Today, because of the phenomenon of differentiation, he can no longer be familiar in depth with the living issues and the circumstances of work of the many social groups that compose modern society.'

---

[1] For a careful examination of the changing circumstances of our society and of the changes in the patterns of ordained ministry they necessitate, see *The Shape of the Ministry*, the Report of a Working Party of the British Council of Churches.

He goes on to speak of the need for team work in the preparation of a sermon 'so that through joint participation the concrete situation of the contemporary world, known to the laity from within, may be taken into account.'[1] Another method, used recently on B.B.C. 1, is to have a sermon preached in the normal way and then on a subsequent occasion to have a discussion session in which questions are raised and difficulties considered. Partnership in the ordering of worship, in the planning of parish strategy, in the business of studying together what it means to be a Christian in the complexities of the technological world of science, the professions and industry today—this is essential.

There are other changes which the clergy and the laity of the Church must face. Whatever the right assessment of the recommendations of the Paul Report, the facts revealed are disturbing enough. No one thinks the right policy is simply to divide the population of the country by the number of clergy and settle parish boundaries accordingly; many other factors need to be taken into consideration. But, admitting that, we must surely recognize the undue imbalance of manpower between diocese and diocese, the need in many areas for drastic rationalization of resources,[2] the call to experiment in appropriate situations; one such experiment is the ordaining of suitable men to the priesthood who continue in 'secular' employment, sometimes called 'voluntary clergy,' of which the dioceses of Hong Kong, and now Southwark, have been providing some notable examples. It is the slowness and cumbersomeness of the machinery, the powerful forces of conservatism and the refusal of many to face an uncertain future, that raises questions in the minds of a growing number as to whether the Church of England can ever catch up with the rapid changes in our society. It leads some parish priests to abandon the parochial ministry and not a few prospective ordinands to become disillusioned.

[1] *Worship and Mission*, pp. 134–135. H. Thielicke writes similarly of 'The Preacher as a Helpless Soloist' (*The Trouble with the Church*, pp. 25–28).

[2] There are no less than five parish churches within five minutes' walk of the British Council of Churches headquarters!

In case I seem to be writing of that which by virtue of recent service overseas I do not know, I quote the testimony of Alan Webster, the present Warden of Lincoln Theological College:

'I believe that the malaise which, judging from the letters I get, leads a few men to decide to leave the parochial ministry is in part stimulated by the administrative muddle in the church. . . . Great industrial concerns are often not only more efficient but more sensitive and humane than the church in the way they treat their staff. . . . In the industrial, inner areas of great cities there are breakdowns, nervous or physical, as well as loneliness, despair and loss of faith, which need not happen so frequently if men were not given such vast and ill-defined tasks. We live in a society where change is assumed . . . it is hard therefore for young men to understand why administrative reform is postponed, and they hold back from ordination, so draining the system of energy and increasing the strain.'[1]

From his knowledge of the strong steady work going on in many parishes where conditions are at least tolerable Alan Webster believes that 'dioceses can be renewed and recreated.' The place of residence, the family unit, the neighbourhood loyalties, these all need strengthening if the terrifying anonymity of our vast urban agglomerations is to be counteracted, and the parish church and its fellowship (perhaps in the setting of a group ministry) have a continuing part to play which we must never underestimate.

But the Church must be ready to encourage new forms of ministry, and parish priests must accept such developments with sympathy and understanding and with freedom from the suspicion and even resentment that some find hard to conceal. One notable experiment along these lines has been that of Industrial Mission, in which Sheffield over many years pioneered the way. What other new forms will be needed it is not easy to say with any precision, for the wind of the Spirit is moving and none of us can define as yet where he will lead. As Basil Moss said at the A.C.C.M. Conference in 1966,

'I have no formula for you. I think as little of the formula of blowing up all the shrines, as I do of the formula of letting everything carry on as it always has. . . . Rather I think a chaotic period of flexible experiment is beginning. On the one hand, many shrines (parish churches) will remain visible, and it will be the

[1] Fellowship of the Bishop's Hostel Paper, No. 136. Easter 1966.

vocation of some to make them work in a contemporary way, where conditions are favourable. On the other hand, many people are going to find the community of Christ which is the Church in new units, not shrine-based at all, but meeting irregularly in houses. . . . Shrine-centred or hearth-centred, the Church will, I believe, find its effective units in a multiplicity of *small groups* of people who find their commitment to Christ in their commitment to each other, and their commitment to a common concern in the world.'

And he makes an essential point which is being driven home to us by the realities of our situation and which is demonstrated in the ever-increasing number of local Councils of Churches.[1] 'We face among ourselves the dawn of the ecumenical age. Obedience and renewal can be attempted by the churches only in co-operation.'

If the loss of positions we have taken for granted, the removal of familiar landmarks and the development of new and perhaps (to some) not very attractive forms of Christian community, seem to threaten all we have held dear and to destroy the inheritance of our fathers, then perhaps we shall do well to turn back to what St. Paul says about the Christian ministry in 2 Corinthians 4. 1–16. We carry about in the body the dying of Jesus, so that the life of Jesus may also be manifest in our bodies. Death is at work in us, but life in those whose servants we are for Jesus' sake. As A. T. Hanson says, commenting on the passage:

'The ministers must live out Christ's dying life in the world in order that those to whom they minister may live. Thus we revert to the great pattern in its most profound form: Christ has died and lived again that we may live. Christ's ministers must therefore likewise die daily and live out the life of suffering and dying in this world, that life may work in the Corinthians'[2]

and in the people of London and Lucknow, Sydney and Singapore, Birmingham, Alabama, and Birmingham, England.

Whatever the arguments for or against the parson's freehold, the priest's ultimate security lies, not there, but in Christ crucified and risen, who is the Lord of Glory.

[1] Over 500 are affiliated to the British Council of Churches.
[2] *Op. cit.*, p. 75.

IV. DEACONS AND DEACONESSES

WHATEVER our interpretation of the apostolic laying on of hands upon the Seven, the New Testament makes clear that from the first days God called some to take the lead and others to be 'helpers' (1 Cor. 12. 28). E. M. B. Green, in the work already quoted,[1] gives a short account of New Testament and later evidence, and D. Nicholson provides a convenient summary of a Report covering the same ground which was accepted by the Provincial Synod of the Scottish Episcopal Church in 1963.[2] A pastoral ministry with special concern for poor believers who needed financial help seems the most satisfactory interpretation of that evidence. In the patristic period deacons were the immediate assistants of the bishops both in liturgical functions and in the business of the Church. This meant that sometimes a deacon succeeded to a bishopric direct without serving in the priesthood, but quite often the result was that a man served in the diaconate all his life. This is still in a few cases the practice in the Eastern Church and it was a frequent occurrence in the medieval Church of the West. Those who attended to the administration of the Church's life remained in deacon's orders, and the memory of the practice survives in the title 'archdeacon.' Today we are faced with the double anomaly that archdeacons are without exception in priest's orders, sometimes with the care of a parish, while a good deal of the diocesan administration, inspection and repair of churches, parsonages and so on, is in the hands of full-time lay diocesan secretaries and of qualified architects and surveyors.

We have, in fact, in the Roman Catholic and Anglican Communions lost any distinctive and separate order of permanent deacons, and the office is one in which men spend a preparatory

[1] *Called to Serve*, Ch. 5.
[2] *A Discovery of Deacons*, art. in St. Mary's, Graham St. Quarterly, Autumn 1966; cf. also World Council Studies, No. 2, *The Ministry of Deacons* for a fuller treatment of the subject.

year before being ordained to the priesthood. This is certainly not a full or complete way of using the order of deacons, but before considering possible developments it is, I believe, worth emphasizing that the present use has its values.

First, it is a common, and surely wise, practice in many professions that a man has a probationary period before being allowed to exercise his professional qualifications with full authority. The doctor has to serve a period as a house surgeon, the solicitor works in a junior capacity in an established legal firm, the commissioned officer in the armed forces serves in a subordinate rank for what is recognized as still an 'under training' period. In monastic orders a postulant is admitted to the novitiate and tested there, before taking life vows. It is surely wise that a candidate for the sacred ministry should also have such a time of probation. His superiors can see how he fares in the actual work of an ordained minister of the Gospel. He himself can test his sense of vocation against the day by day demands of that work and make doubly sure that this is the calling for which God intends him. And having faced such testing and found, as in most cases he will, that this is indeed God's purpose for his life, then at his ordination to the priesthood he can offer himself afresh with a deeper and more realistic dedication, because now it has woven into it the joys and strains, the demands and the achievements of the preceding twelve months.

More importantly, the present practice means that the man who is ordained priest or consecrated bishop carries into these higher orders the mark of the servant. He does not cease to be a deacon when he is admitted to the presbyterate or raised to the episcopate. He is 'a deacon for ever' and like his master he wears 'the form of a servant' (Phil. 2. 7). With St. Paul, as represented in the Pastoral Epistles, he can say, 'I thank . . . Christ Jesus our Lord, because he judged me faithful by appointing me to his service' (1 Tim. 1. 12). If I may quote a trivial personal example, there were several occasions in Singapore and Malaya when well-meaning churchpeople, seeing me helping with the cleaning up at the end of a parish reception, said in shocked tones, 'you mustn't do *that*. You're the *bishop*!' To which my regular reply was, 'yes, but I am still a deacon!' To turn from small to great, there have been times when the pomp and splendour of the Papal court, and of the Pope himself, have made a mockery of the Pope's proud claim to be 'Servus servorum Dei.' But when, as with Pope John XXIII or the present Pope, that title is lived out and exemplified in life, then the world pays attention. Whenever our Lord's words are being demonstrated, 'whoever would be great among you must be your servant, and whoever would be first among you must be slave of all' (Mk. 10. 44), then in a remarkable way an appeal strikes home to the human heart. Men and women are paradoxically drawn by a standard of values and a way of life that cuts right across all their human ambitions and pride.

Having said that, I must nevertheless affirm that it is not an adequate use of the order of the diaconate to treat it only as a stepping-stone to the priesthood. If we mean all we say about the historic threefold ministry, then we should surely be working for an order of permanent deacons. In the Reformation period Calvin, rightly or wrongly,[1] drew a distinction between ministerial or teaching elders and lay or ruling elders, and this distinction survives in Presbyterian polity today. The minister of the congregation has associated with him in the pastoral oversight of the parish and in the administration of the Holy Communion those who earn their living in 'secular' employment and do not normally go on to serve in the ordained ministry. In Congregational and Baptist churches laymen who are appointed to fulfil similar functions are called 'deacons.' Anglicans must recognize that in the sixteenth and seventeenth centuries a greater attempt to restore what was in effect the primitive diaconate was made outside the borders of the Church of England than within, even though sometimes the Reformed tradition put too much stress on administration and not enough on worship and service.

In subsequent centuries Methodists have had their local preachers from the days when they were still a society within the Church

---

[1] For the arguments for and against, see E. M. B. Green, *op. cit.*, p. 40.

of England, and in more modern times the Anglican Communion has developed an officially approved Order of Readers, licensed on a parochial or diocesan basis according to training and need, and permitted in appropriate circumstances to administer the Chalice at Holy Communion. Readers who have such permission, as well as a licence to conduct services and to preach, do all that a deacon may do, and so form a *de facto*, if not a *de jure*, permanent diaconate. And it must be added that without the voluntary services of this devoted body of laymen it would be quite impossible for the parish clergy, particularly in country districts where they may have several churches in their care, to arrange for the leading of the Church's worship by qualified people.

It is interesting to note what those from the Congregationalist, Methodist and Presbyterian churches who have worked out the scheme for Church Union in Australia propose in regard to the diaconate, for they surely point the way forward for Anglicans also, if we add to their categories a reconstituted order of Readers.

'We believe that the important insight represented by the Reformed office of ordained elders is that it takes into the oversight of the congregation representative laity who are involved in the vocations of the world, and symbolizes also the reaching out of the ministry of the Church into the secular occupations of everyday life. The time of union provides an opportunity for a creative re-interpretation and broadening of this valuable form of the ministry, so that members of the laity can be admitted to the diaconate. . . .

'Ordination of deacons implies a limited but genuine participation in the one order of the ministry of the word and sacraments; and therefore in preaching and teaching, liturgical and sacramental life, pastoral care and discipline.

'Within congregations deacons should be elected to share with and under the presbyter in the oversight of the congregation. Election should be by the communicant members of the congregation, and their appointment should be subject to the approval of the presbyter and the Council of the congregation.'

The signatories propose the merging of the institutions of lay elders in the Presbyterian Church, accredited local preachers in the Methodist Church and deacons in the Congregational Church into a reconstituted Diaconate and recommend that 'all appointed to the office of deacon shall be ordained by a bishop and presbyter with prayer and the laying on of hands.'[1]

The Sub-Warden of Lincoln, David Lunn, comes to a similar conclusion from a different angle.[2] He believes that the Church of England is being driven by circumstances to the use of an auxiliary ministry but in a thoroughly haphazard way. Those who have been properly trained for the full-time ministry 'feel justifiably sore when they see their calling increasingly thought of as an appropriate activity for a man's spare time or his declining years. We cannot expect people to respect and make use of a ministry that may be half-trained and casually selected—and there is no way of distinguishing "the genuine article."'

'The remedy,' he suggests, 'is simple: a whole time ministry of highly trained PRIESTS assisted by an auxiliary (or part-time) ministry of DEACONS, who have been given a training appropriate to the particular task that has become authoritatively theirs.' The end result is the same as is envisaged in the Australian Church Unity scheme—'a group of men of widely different training, and very varied daily experience, but united in the shared responsibility [sc. with the parish priest] for the ministry of word and sacrament.' The diaconate would thus become the link between the full-time ministry of the presbyterate and the work and witness of the laity in 'the world.' The permanent deacon would *both* be in Holy Orders *and* also involved professionally in 'secular' employment.

The Australian proposals refer to two other matters related to 'a creative re-interpretation and broadening' of the diaconate. One concerns the need for the Church to find expression in our modern technological societies in forms of common life based on associations other than those of people's place of residence. We have already seen the need for *episcope* on other than a territorial basis and for patterns of Church life supplementary to those of the parish. If this has its application to the episcopal and presbyteral orders, it has even more application to the diaconate as

[1] *Op. cit.*, p. 44.
[2] Fellowship of the Bishop's Hostel Paper No. 137, Michaelmas 1966.

envisaged above. So the Church Union Report includes the paragraph:

'Councils other than the Council of the Congregation shall also have power to elect and ordain deacons for the oversight of the special concerns for which they have responsibility.'[1]

The second matter concerns the future of the order of deaconesses. The Australian negotiators state boldly, 'deaconesses in the uniting Churches at the time of union also should be recognized as deacons in the Uniting Church and remain so for life.'[2] In that proposal they would presumably have the support of E. M. B. Green, who says, 'there is evidence to suggest that the primitive diaconate included women.'[3] Here also he provides a useful summary of the New Testament and subsequent evidence. 'It was not forgotten that dedicated women had followed Jesus about and "deaconed" for him' (Lk. 8. 3), and women such as Tryphaena, Tryphosa and Priscilla the wife of Aquila, clearly played a considerable part in the church life of the earliest days, as did such women as the two deaconesses whom Pliny examined under torture c. 112 A.D.[4] 'Through women's gossiping of the Gospel in the home, at the laundry, and to their friends, quite as much as through formal preaching by the man, the Christian message pervaded the ancient world.'[5]

The Anglican Communion has revived the order of deaconesses and declared that this is the one order open to women, but it has not been clear whether this order is distinct from the diaconate or not. That is a question which requires an authoritative answer.[6] Those who most strongly emphasize its distinctiveness and exclude it from the category of 'Holy Orders'

[1] *Op. cit.*, p. 44.   [2] *Op. cit.*, p. 44.   [3] *Op. cit.*, p. 55.   [4] *Ad. Traj.* 10. 96.
[5] E. M. B. Green, *op. cit.*, p. 56, n. 6.
[6] As the Archbishops' Commission points out in its Report *Women and Holy Orders*, the Lambeth Conference of 1930 went back on Lambeth 1920's declaration that 'in our judgement the ordination of a Deaconess confers on her Holy Orders.' The new Canon D1 recently promulgated in the Church of England followed Lambeth 1930 in stating 'The Order of Deaconesses is not one of the Holy Orders of the Church of England.' The Commission is thoroughly justified in saying that the present 'state of uncertainty ... both for the good name of the Church as well as to relieve the minds of deaconesses, should be once and for all removed,' and in asking for a definitive pronouncement from the next Lambeth Conference. (*Op. cit.*, pp. 36 and 37.)

Q

do so, it is not unfair to say, almost entirely because they are afraid that to do otherwise would be the thin end of the wedge leading to the ordination of women to the priesthood. That they would regard as a thoroughly uncatholic proceeding.

The Archbishops' Commission in its report *Women and Holy Orders* sets out the arguments for and against the ordination of women to the priesthood,. Significantly, they are agreed that the matter cannot be settled by a mechanical quoting of texts from Scripture. Personally, I find myself in agreement with what is called 'A Third View' (Ch. VII), namely that there is no theological bar, but that at present the difficulties outweigh the advantages. For that reason it is in my view urgent that women should be permitted as deaconesses to exercise a full-time ministry with authority to do everything that a deacon may do. I also have much sympathy with what Alan Richardson puts forward in his 'Suggestions for a Lay Ministry' (Appendix E), which approximate very much to what I have said above about a permanent diaconate. In this 'bridge-ministry' between the full-time priesthood and the life of the layman and laywoman in the world we should see the right opening for many women who are not called to full-time service as well as for many men.

Before concluding the chapter, we must consider two objections which are often raised to the proposal to have a permanent diaconate. The first is summed up in the phrase, 'the trouble about permanent deacons is that they don't stay permanent.' In present circumstances, it is too often the case that a man of perhaps limited ability or education is ordained a 'permanent deacon' and then after a few years begins to agitate for ordination to the priest-hood. Often the circumstances of the parish situation in which he serves provide an added argument, and the bishop finds himself under a pressure that is difficult to resist.

The answer surely is that we are not thinking of present circum-stances, but of a properly established permanent diaconate com-posed of those who earn their living in one of the professions, in business or in trade. If the Church of Scotland and the Presby-terian tradition generally have been able to maintain the practice of having two kinds of elders without difficulty, surely it should not be difficult for the Anglican Communion, or any united Church into which one or other part of it goes, to reproduce the pattern with two kinds of deacons, those in full-time service who in due course will be ordained priests and those in part-time 'lay' service who will serve as permanent deacons.

The other difficulty arises from the fact that a deacon has no authority to celebrate Holy Communion. In parishes with a number of centres or in para-parochial groups where he exercised a particular pastoral responsibility, it is objected, he would be of limited usefulness to the parish priest and would be frustrated at the most sensitive point of his ministry.

David Lunn says boldly in regard to this factor, 'For this two-tier ministry to be of any use, it would have to be possible to authorize deacons to celebrate Holy Communion. . . . Just as circumstances once forced the bishop to share his presidency of the Eucharist with the presbyterate, so now circumstances make it highly desirable that he should be prepared to share it with at least some of the diaconate.'

This is a radical proposal which many will regard as at least as 'uncatholic' as the admission of women to the priesthood. Apart from that, however, it would surely mean that in the eyes of ordinary people the very distinction which the 'two-tier' proposal is designed to make clear would be blurred afresh. The ordinary church member would see no distinction between priest and deacon in their sacramental responsibilities, and certainly would be unable to distinguish between a permanent deacon so authorized and a priest working at a 'secular' job, as envisaged e.g. in the Southwark ordination scheme.

Beyond that, the proposal surely obscures the very nature of the diaconate itself. It is fundamentally an auxiliary office, an order of helpers (1 Cor. 12. 28), and its subordinate and supplementary character needs to be maintained. In the developed life of large town parishes such permanent deacons would clearly be seen as those who *assist* the parish priest in the conduct of worship, in the administration of Holy Communion, in pastoral oversight and care of the needy. In the villages of a grouped rural parish or in a para-parochial group a permanent deacon would have a more direct responsibility for the people of his own congregation or grouping, but he would still come under the overall direction of the priest in charge. Part of the work of such a deacon would be the preparing of his people for the offering of eucharistic worship at the regular visits of the priest and joining with them in that offering. For the rest he could conduct other forms of worship, could administer the reserved sacrament to the sick (for there is no theological or liturgical objection to his administering in both kinds), and could preside at *agapes* or love-feasts, where such were held.

Perhaps in this whole matter of supplementary ministry, voluntary clergy and the like, we have to do some more thinking and experimenting before we can see whether the right solution lies in the ordination to the priesthood of men who continue in 'secular' employment or whether the answer lies in a permanent diaconate, as outlined above. Certainly the Anglican Communion would benefit from a pattern of pastoral oversight and ministry in which the priest functions not alone, but as the leader of a team of men and women exercising corporate *episcope* at the parochial or para-parochial level.

One final thing must be said. While there is a rightful place for the order of deacons in the threefold ministry, we must also recognize that *diakonia* must be a mark of the whole Church, and not least of the layman bearing his Christian witness in society. 'The true "deacons,"' the Director of the Society of the Sacred Mission has written, 'are the doctor, the teacher, the lawyer, the social workers, and all those others who in their work are bringing Christian influence to bear on others, Christians or not. . . . I feel very high respect for a layman who is a member of parliament or of a trade union, and who talks and acts not merely as a member of parliament or of a trade union, but also as a member of the Church. Probation officers and nurses are not usually in holy orders, but they are men and women who are doing what deacons were invented to do.'[1]

If an ordained permanent diaconate were to become, as suggested, a link between the life and ministry of the organized Church and its 'reaching out into the secular occupations of everyday life,' it would also serve as a reminder and example to all Christians 'involved in the vocations of the world' that they too are called to bear witness to Christ the servant.

[1] Fr. Gregory Wilkins, *SSM Magazine*, September 1966, p. 57.

V. EPISCOPAL AND NON-EPISCOPAL MINISTRIES

WE have now completed our examination of the threefold ministry, as we have received it in the Anglican Communion, noting
the theological significance of each order and also, I hope, considering squarely where our present practice falls short of the
ideal and in what ways reformation and renewal are necessary.
We are immediately faced with the fact that directly through
union schemes and conversations, as well as less directly through
our common membership of the World Council and the British
Council of Churches, we are in increasingly close touch with
churches which do not have the threefold historic ministry. What
are we to say of their ministries? Closely related to the answer
we give to that question are such matters as the meaning of
ordination, the way in which we see union being brought about
between episcopal and non-episcopal churches and the view we
hold of the rightness or wrongness of intercommunion across the
episcopal-non-episcopal division, as we move forwards towards
full unity. We must look at these important matters in turn.

1. *The Meaning of Ordination*

There are, I suggest, three elements in ordination to the
ministry of the Word and Sacraments. First, there is the inward
call of God. This may come to a man through some personal
spiritual experience, through the influence of a Christian community or congregation, through the advice and encouragement
of an understanding parish priest or through a sense of the needs
of men and women in our estranged and bewildered world.
Secondly, there is the maturing and testing of that sense of vocation by the Church through its constituted authorities. The
voice of the local church is heard through letters of reference;
ordination committees and selection conferences make their
assessments; university and theological colleges continue the
process of sifting and training; and finally the Bishop's examining

chaplains make their recommendations. A man comes to the laying on of hands, not only on the ground of his own inner sense of call, but on the ground that that call has been tested and found to be genuine and that in general qualifications and ability he has been found worthy by the Church.

Thirdly, there comes the actual ordination, the service of prayer with the laying on of hands by the Bishop (together with the presbyters, in the case of those being ordained to the priesthood). This is set in the context of the Eucharist and through it the candidate receives the commission and authority of Christ and his Church for the office and work to which he is being ordained and the grace of the Holy Spirit to empower him for that work.[1] He is admitted to an order within the total life of the Church of God in a commitment for life. He may renounce his orders or be disbarred from exercising his office for good and sufficient reason, but he cannot return to such lay status that, if later he wishes and is permitted to resume the exercise of his orders, he has to be ordained again.

I have expressed this in a way that accords with Anglican practice and that would be accepted, I believe, by the great majority of Anglicans.[2] In doing so, I must differentiate the understanding of ordination I have outlined from views held on either flank. On the one side, there is the view recently referred to by John Huxtable in his book *Christian Unity*. He recalls that 'in old-fashioned Congregationalism "recognition" was often used in connection with ordination and what we now call induction,' and adds that it 'points to an essential element in the Protestant understanding of ordination. To a large extent it is a recognition

---

[1] While the 1662 Ordinal contains the essentials of prayer with the laying on of hands, it must be admitted that liturgically it is far from perfect. The 1928 book improved the rites considerably (a) by including in the Ordination Prayer for Priests a clause which prays specifically for the candidates and (b) by providing an Ordination Prayer for Deacons which 1662 lacks altogether. It is much to be hoped that future revisions will abandon the Western medieval imperative forms and will follow the older tradition (revived in the C.S.I. Ordinal) whereby the laying on of hands is brought within the context of the Ordination Prayer itself.

[2] John Robinson in *Meeting, Membership and Ministry*, argues for the ending of the 'mediaeval idea of indelibility.'

of what God is believed to have done already. Indeed, it might almost be said that we ordain not to bestow gifts but because gifts have been bestowed.'[1] John Huxtable makes clear that this 'does not tell the whole story' and neither he nor the central Congregational tradition in which he stands would deny the significance of the Ordination Service itself as an occasion for the action of God. Yet it is true of some whose tradition is strongly independent both inside and outside Congregationalism that they would place almost all the emphasis on a man's inward call as the *locus* of God's making him a minister and would reduce the Ordination Service to a ratification by the Church of what God has already done. This seems to me to be open to the same objection as the view, considered in an earlier chapter, that regeneration is to be associated with a person's response in faith to the Gospel rather than with his Baptism.[2] If we accept the sacramental principle, then surely we must identify the actual ordination—the prayer with the laying on of hands—as the moment when the living Christ bestows his grace, commission and authority on the candidates, for ordination, though not a sacrament of the Gospel, is, as the Revised Catechism puts it, one of the 'other sacramental ministries of grace.' That is not, of course, to deny the working of the Spirit in the candidates and in all who have shared in the testing and fostering of their sense of vocation: it is to assert that here, as in Baptism and the Eucharist, Christ gives his gift through outward and visible means at a specific place and a particular moment in time. I would indeed share John Huxtable's hope that in our different traditions on this matter we are emphasizing different aspects of one great reality and not 'talking about two different realities.'

On the other flank, for reasons which I have tried to make clear in ch. I of this section, I do not believe the claim can be sustained that episcopal ordinations, as distinct from non-episcopal ones, are valid because 'the Apostles conferred this power and grace only to their successors the bishops and their successors, all of whom in turn at their consecration have the power

---

[1] P. 93.   [2] Cf. Section C, ch. I above, pp. 126-129.

conferred upon them. Thus, it is said, the Church secures and preserves its unity with the Apostolic times; indeed, this is how it remains Apostolic.'[1] For one thing, such a view presupposes an unbroken chain of episcopal consecrations back to the apostles, and, as we have seen, historical study does not support and certainly cannot prove such a claim. For another, in its cruder forms it makes the validity of the ministry entirely independent of the Church, with the logically absurd result, as O. C. Quick pointed out many years ago, 'that a man who has received ordination in some hole-and-corner fashion from a wandering bishop deprived of all office and jurisdiction, is fully and validly ordained, whereas one who has received the solemn authorization of one, say, of the great Presbyterian communions is not ordained at all.'[2]

The bishop acts, of course, not in his individual capacity, but as the appointed minister of Christ in his Church for the purpose of ordination.[3] And the reason why Anglicans value so highly the tradition of episcopal ordinations is that the bishop, embodying in his person and ministry so many aspects of the pastoral office and standing in an unbroken succession of consecrations from the first creative period of the Church's life till now, is in this act *a* witness (though not the only one) to the continuing historic existence and mission of the Church down the centuries. Here the truth is visibly set forth that the Christ who is imparting his gifts through prayer and the laying on of hands is the Christ who has been at work in his Church from the first day until now. Here we find the 'vertical' and 'horizontal' dimensions of the Church's life meeting.

2. Non-Episcopal Ministries

What, however, are we to say of those ministries which represent a break with the historic episcopal succession? In the light of what has been said above, they cannot just be dismissed

---

[1] J. Huxtable, *op.cit.* p. 95   [2] *The Christian Sacraments*, p. 143

[3] 'It is not believed that grace is given by the bishop as something that he possesses and can hand on, but that the Holy Spirit comes upon the ordinand in response to the prayer of the Church by the bishop who is authorized so to pray.' E. W. Kemp, *The Anglican-Methodist Conversations*, p. 38.

as having no ministerial status at all, and indeed the Lambeth Appeal of 1920 frankly recognizes that 'these ministries have been manifestly blessed and owned by the Holy Spirit as effective means of grace,' while the Memorandum of the Archbishops of Canterbury and York and eleven other bishops in 1923 speaks of them as 'real ministries of Christ's Word and Sacraments in the Universal Church.'[1] These statements, which would not have won Tractarian approval, do in fact concur with the standpoint of leading churchmen in the sixteenth and seventeenth centuries,[2] and today they would command widespread assent among us.

Two factors have brought about a change from the stiff attitude of the Oxford Movement. One is the greater readiness to appreciate the 'vertical' element in the Church's life. We recognize more fully than we did that in the great explosion of life in the sixteenth century, when the Reformers recovered for the Church so much that belonged to the essence of the Gospel, as also in the Methodist movement of the eighteenth century, the old wineskins of the historic Church could not contain the new wine of recovered spiritual vitality. Sometimes indeed the desire remained to preserve continuity with the historic Church, including its ministry, but those in authority made it impossible; sometimes the historic ministry seemed so bound up with falsity of doctrine and corruption of life that only a completely fresh start seemed tolerable; sometimes (as in the case of John Wesley) the historic Church was so fettered with the bonds of the Establishment that drastic action was seen as the only way to meet an emergency situation. So we have come to understand that the words of John the Baptist may well have an application in the sphere of the ministry, 'Do not begin to say to yourselves, "We have

---

[1] It should be noted that the 1923 Memorandum restricted this recognition to 'ministries which rest upon a long-established order, which have been conferred by some solemn and authoritative act complying Ordination to the ministry of the Universal Church and not merely commission to the ministry of a particular denomination, and which are regarded as involving a life-long vocation.' (Bell, *Documents of Christian Unity*, 1920-4, p. 158).

[2] Cf. N. Sykes, *The Church of England and Non-Episcopal Churches in the Sixteenth and Seventeenth Centuries.*

Abraham as our father"; for I tell you, God is able from these stones to raise up children to Abraham' (Lk. 3. 8).

The other factor, as the 1920 and 1923 statements quoted above make clear, is the evident mark of God's blessing upon non-episcopal ministries. These ministries, set within the great historic commissions that have resulted from the Reformation to which men have been ordained through prayer and the laying on of hands, have been manifestly used by God in the preaching of the Word and the administration of the Sacraments, and through them branches of Christ's Church have been nourished and sustained and the Gospel carried to the distant corners of the earth. Without the devotion and labour and self-sacrifice of many ordained into such ministries the world expansion of Christ's Church would not have taken place on anything like the scale it has. Where God has evidently been at work, we can only acknowledge the facts and give thanks for the clear signs of his blessing.

3. *The Unification of Ministries*

When the Anglican Communion or any part of it proposes to unite with one of the non-episcopal churches on the basis of a common acceptance of Scripture, Creeds and the two sacraments of the Gospel, then, on the basis of what has just been said, the question arises—how may their ministries be united? In the case of an individual minister joining the Anglican Communion the practice is for him to receive ordination according to the Anglican rite, and this is understandable while the two churches concerned are separate and the Preface to the Ordinal stands in the Prayer Book. When, however, the two churches are negotiating union, the position is different, for in such a case there is no intention of one church effecting a take-over bid, but of both churches bringing the fullness of their heritage to the enrichment of the common life of the proposed United Church.

There are, in fact, only two ways of solving the problem. One is the South India way. When the Church of South India came

into being, it was on the basis of acceptance of the historic episcopate. The Anglican bishops consecrated new bishops from the
non-Anglican traditions and it was agreed that all future ordinations should take place at episcopal hands. Meanwhile, all existing
clergy and ministers of the uniting churches were accepted as
equally presbyters in the Church of South India, a 'conscience
clause' being added so that any church which felt conscientiously
unable to accept as pastor a presbyter whose ordination it could
not accept as satisfactory was not required to do so.

That method was not too difficult to adopt in South India,
partly because outside the main cities the principle of comity
operated, so that one whole area was Anglican, another Methodist
and another Presbyterian or Congregationalist. A Christian
moving from one area to another had inevitably to move from
one ecclesiastical allegiance to that of another Church. And out
of the South India method, we must recognize, there has come
a widespread appreciation of the whole principle of episcopacy.
As an Indian presbyter of Congregationalist background put it,
'We do not look on our bishop as an administrator, or a tyrant,
or a master. We look on him as a father, and naturally we ask
for, and act on, the advice of our father in God.'[1] A number
of people advocate the adoption of the South India way
elsewhere, and not least in the union of the Church of England
and the Methodist Church in this country.

The fact has to be faced, however, that the Anglican Communion generally has shown no great readiness to follow the C.S.I.
example. The Church of England, and most other provinces,
were willing to enter into only restricted relationships with the
Church of South India at the beginning, and though the Church
of England established much closer links in 1955, it still remains
true that the two churches are not yet in full communion with
each other. The Churches of the Anglican Communion have
indeed got themselves into the somewhat anomalous position
that, on the basis of the Bonn agreement with the Old Catholics,

---

[1] Quoted in A. T. Hanson, *The Pioneer Ministry*, p. 169.

they will enter into full communion with churches whose doctrinal or liturgical tradition is considerably different, provided those churches have the historic episcopate, but will not enter into the same relations with churches which are closer doctrinally and liturgically, if their ministries are not entirely in the historic succession.

As a result, later reunion schemes have all followed the alternative method—that of a solemn unification of ministries from the start. Thus Ceylon, North India and Pakistan, Ghana and the Anglican-Methodist Report propose such a ceremony. Nigeria had intended at first to follow the South India method, but the recommendation of the Lambeth 1958 Resolution 32 led to the adoption of the same plan. All such schemes involve a mutual laying on of hands, a recognition of God's blessing of the person's ministry in the past and a prayer that God will bestow upon him whatever grace, commission and authority are needed for the work of a presbyter or deacon in the Church of God within the united Church.

Do Anglicans regard this as 're-ordination'? If so, the other participants inevitably interpret the act as a denial of their former ministry. If not, can those who receive the laying on of hands in such a ceremony be regarded as having been really admitted to the historic ministry with its links back to the primitive Church? The answer lies surely in the truth that ordination includes, as we have seen above, various elements. If one element is the giving of the Holy Spirit for the ministry of Word and Sacraments through prayer and the laying on of hands in the midst of the Church, then we cannot deny that those who have been so ordained have received that gift. If another element is the authority of the Church, then inevitably by its divisions, as O. C. Quick taught, all our ministries are defective, for none has the authority of the whole Church, visible and invisible. Through the unification ceremony at least a wider commission is given to the participants and the authority of a larger part of the whole Catholic Church imparted. Anglicans in this country, for instance, will enter into the Methodist heritage and Methodists into the Anglican one.

Part of the latter is the continuous link of ordinations back over the centuries to the early days of the Church. The 'vertical' and 'horizontal' dimensions in the Church's life will thus again converge. For the rest there is surely much to be said for 'reverent agnosticism' as regards 'what happens.' In such a ceremony we are attempting an entirely new thing in the context of seeking to fulfil Christ's purpose for the unity of the Body. What exactly we all need we are not sure and we are not agreed in such ideas as we have. So we lift the whole matter up to God who alone knows all and we pray that he will take the dividedness of our churches and make us one, that he will take our separated ministries and supply all that is needed for their fullness and authority in the united Church, so that hereafter there shall be no doubts or hesitancy among any of us.

In view of the very great problems which the adoption of the South India method would involve for the Church of England, and no doubt for most other parts of the Anglican Communion, this seems the most promising way forward, and we hope that those who are revising the form of words to be used at the mutual laying on of hands in the Anglican-Methodist plan for this country will be led to a solution satisfactory to the consciences of all.

4. Intercommunion

Inevitably in the process of growing together the question of receiving communion in each other's churches arises, and often becomes urgent. Lesslie Newbigin has spoken in the strongest terms of the danger of the ecumenical movement losing its sacramental awareness, because at its meetings the representatives of different churches cannot all receive together the one Bread and the one Cup at the most central point of Christian worship. Often too those who are brought close to each other in actual unity discussions find this deprivation almost intolerable. Equally there are others whose consciences would prevent them countenancing any open communion at this stage and who insist with equal sincerity that participation together at the Lord's table must await the coming into being of a united Church.[1]

So we are brought back to the familiar dichotomy—is sharing in the one Eucharist a sacramental expression of a unity which already exists by virtue of common membership of the one body, and therefore not to be encouraged so long as Christians remain divided? Or is it a means by which Christ may bring his separated followers into organic unity, and therefore to be used, if not indiscriminately, at least on certain specific occasions where Christians are working for the union of the divided parts of the Body of Christ?

For Anglicans the historic starting point is the last of the General Rubrics before the Order of Confirmation in the Prayer Book, which states 'there shall none be admitted to the Holy Communion, until such time as he be confirmed, or be ready and desirous to be confirmed.' Those who believe that intercommunion must wait till reunion has taken place lay great stress on this rubric, though it is interpreted by others as a purely domestic regulation. They can also point to Canon 27 of the Canons of 1604 which speaks of 'schismatics not to be admitted to the Communion.' They would use kindlier language, but would say that this principle remains the same and would point to the stand taken by William Sherlock and others of the Caroline period against the practice of occasional communion. The crown lawyers upheld this interpretation of the rubric, and it was to allow for greater freedom that Canon B15 (now withdrawn) was drafted.

On the other hand, Norman Sykes[2] and more recently G. E. Duffield[3] have amassed a good deal of evidence to show that in the classical period of post-Reformation Anglicanism the practice was widespread of receiving members of Continental churches, Lutheran and Reformed, to communion in this country. The

[1] For an account of four different approaches to this question see *Unity Begins at Home*, pp.17-20 and for a fuller treatment see O. S. Tomkins, *A Time for Unity*, ch. 5, where present World Council of Churches practice is described and Convocation regulations are discussed. See also J. G. Davies, *Intercommunion*, a booklet published by the British Council of Churches.

[2] *Op. cit.*   [3] *Admission to Holy Communion.*

practice was common too of receiving communion in Continental churches, though this seems to have become less frequent as time went on. In England the tradition of occasional communion in the established Church continued after the Restoration on Tillotson's principle that 'charity is above rubrics.' According to Norman Sykes, the practice was encouraged by some bishops in the hope that it would bring some dissenters back into the Church of England. More important, however, 'regarded as "a healing custom," it preserved the memory of lingering hopes of comprehension'[1] and though it disappeared when those hopes were disappointed, it was revived with the rise of the Methodist societies and their often ambiguous relationship to their parish churches, and has continued down to today.

A development in the recognition of the practice of receiving communicant members of other churches to the Lord's table in Anglican churches came in the Lambeth Conference 1930 Resolution 42 and in the consequent resolutions of the Upper Houses of Canterbury and York Convocations in 1933. By these resolutions a bishop was given freedom to allow non-Anglicans to receive communion in Anglican churches in certain circumstances e.g. when members of other churches were out of reach of the ministrations of their own church, when the people concerned shared in the common life of a school or college, or on particular ecumenical occasions when members of different churches were met together for the promotion of Christian unity. These rulings were not submitted for the concurrence of the Lower Houses but they have in fact served as guide-lines for the bishops, and indeed for the whole Church of England till now.

Overseas there has been much greater flexibility—and indeed without it the practice of comity would have been impossible. In South India, for instance, long before union, Methodists and others who moved into an Anglican area were freely received as communicant members. The corollary was also true, and Anglicans moving into e.g. a Methodist or Congregationalist area were encouraged to become communicant members there.

[1] *Op. cit.*, p. 42.

There was no other way of continuing to practise sacramental Christianity.[1]

With the growing relationships of the Churches to each other, their involvement in union schemes and the possibility that some churches in Britain may enter into a covenant before God to work and pray for unity by Easter 1980 or some other specific date, the pressures for intercommunion are today vastly stronger. The Open Letter of 32 theologians to the Archbishops of Canterbury and York in 1962 did not plead for a letting down of all the barriers and for acting as though the divisions of the Church did not exist. It did ask for the recognition of a considerably increased number of occasions on which intercommunion would be permitted, and it made a strong plea that such permission should be reciprocal i.e. that Anglicans should be free to receive communion on similar occasions in non-episcopal churches. In making this latter request they were not only expressing their own convictions, but recognizing what is an undoubted fact that ecumenically-minded Free Churchmen are not willing to go on indefinitely being guests at our altars, if Anglicans steadily continue to refuse to be guests at their celebrations.[2]

An Anglican Commission on the subject is sitting at the time of writing, and we must await its findings. It has no easy task, for strong convictions are held on this matter. For myself I believe that in the rapidly changing scene of today the Church of England must recognize a considerably larger number of occasions on which we can welcome communicants of other churches to our altars than the 1933 resolution did. If members of a school or college can communicate together, why not the members of a family where, say, the husband is a member of the Church of England and the wife a member of the Church of Scotland? There are also occasions where in a shared church or an ecumenical youth camp or in a close relationship between

---

[1] A. T. Hanson, op. cit., p. 160.

[2] The open letter was supported by the Bishop of Woolwich in *The Church of England and Inter-Communion:* Prism Pamphlet No. 2. A cogently argued plea for a wider measure of intercommunion has recently appeared in J. P. Hickinbotham, *The Open Table.*

R

two congregations we should be able to extend a welcome. There should certainly be no pressure to conform on those who feel difficulties about such an extension of hospitality, but there should be freedom for those who with equal conviction feel led in this direction.

What of the demand for reciprocity? This raises greater difficulties, yet are we not led by our whole understanding of non-episcopal ministries as 'manifestly blessed and owned by the Holy Spirit as effective means of grace' (to quote Lambeth 1920) to conclude that on the appropriate ecumenical occasion those who feel so led should be permitted to do so? John Cosin, afterwards Bishop of Durham, during his exile abroad in the time of the Commonwealth wrote that 'there is no prohibition of our church against' communicating in the French Reformed Church[1] and there has been a continous tradition of Anglican visitors receiving Holy Communion in the Church of Scotland or in Protestant churches on the Continent, though admittedly this has not been true of all Anglicans.

I am not pleading here for a completely indiscriminate practice of intercommunion, which only too often bypasses all those questions of ministry and order which must be answered if organic union is to come about. Most Anglicans would agree that, so far as normal practice in a divided church is concerned, members of a particular communion should communicate in churches of their own branch of Christendom, and that accordingly 'members of the Anglican Churches should receive the Holy Communion only from ministers of their own Church.'[2] But are we to close the door (as Lambeth 1930 did not) to those who would feel it right to receive communion *on particular occasions* at the hands of those not episcopally ordained? If so, how are we to rebut the charge brought against us by some of our non-episcopal brethren that we engage in a species of double-talk, using fine words about the Holy Spirit owning and blessing their ministries, but never

[1] Quoted in N. Sykes, *op. cit.*, p. 31.
[2] Quoted in Lambeth 1930, Resolution 42. This principle was much more explicitly spelt out in a Lambeth 1958 Committee Report, cf. *Report* 2. 44.

backing our words up by action? Moreover, we cannot forget the historic fact that in the long drawn out negotiations in South India it was only when the four Anglican bishops concerned received communion at the hands of non-episcopal participants in the negotiations that what seemed like final deadlock was broken and the conversations proceeded to final union. It is significant too that, in connection with co-operative interdenominational enterprises and with union negotiations, the provinces of West and Central Africa (the former including the strongly Anglo-Catholic diocese of Accra and the latter having had strong S.P.G. and U.M.C.A. influences in its history) should have been led to approve their members receiving communion at 'non-episcopal' celebrations on certain occasions. This new development has been described as a 'breakthrough' and it certainly suggests a shift in traditional Anglo-Catholic attitudes, which will reinforce the pressures for a more flexible and open policy than exists at present.

There is one final consideration which all of us, whatever our views, can keep in mind. It was suggested by Cardinal Bea at a memorable week-end for young people at the Taizé Community in September 1966. If we believe that the living Christ is at work by his Spirit in all our Eucharists, then we must believe that he is drawing us across our separated celebrations into union with himself and with one another. Thus, whether we are permitted or believe it right to receive communion in another church or whether that is not allowed by church order or contrary to our own conscience, the Eucharist remains, not just an expression of the unity already obtaining by common membership in one part of Christ's Church, but also an instrument by which the living Christ can draw us into that larger unity of the whole Church which is according to his will. If we offer every Eucharist and receive Holy Communion each time in that context of hope and prayer, then indeed we shall find in it a dynamic sacrament of unity.

VI. ONE CHURCH RENEWED FOR MISSION

THE title of this final chapter was the theme of the Nottingham Faith and Order Conference of 1964.[1] It brings together three essential elements of the Church's life which are inextricably interwoven and which cannot be fully exhibited in isolation. Christ prayed that his disciples might be one 'that the world may believe.' Schemes of church union, however theologically sound and ultimately successful, will avail nothing, if they mean the bringing together of church bodies from which the spiritual power and consciousness of mission have nearly departed. On the other hand, it could well be that the engagement of Christians on the frontiers of society in this new technological age will drive them willy nilly into an ecumenical relationship so close that if there is no united church to contain it, then it will find new forms of expression outside the institutional Church altogether. There can be no question of the churches first concentrating all their energies on becoming one, then at stage two seeking renewal and finally at stage three engaging in mission. Perhaps it would have been nearer the truth of the matter, if the Nottingham theme had been worded 'One Church Renewed *in* Mission.' For ease of thinking we must consider each of the three elements separately, but we must never forget that in doing so we are distinguishing between things that in life belong inescapably together.

1. *Unity*

Unity can be considered in a variety of contexts and at various levels of the Church's life. There is the unity of the spirit in the bond of peace in which one hopes all Christians are becoming increasingly conscious of a common loyalty to Jesus Christ that overrides all lesser differences. There is the unity in the one baptism, which makes us members together across the boundaries of our separate communions in the Body of Christ. Through

---

[1] For an account of the Conference, see the Report, *Unity Begins at Home.*

the ecumenical movement most of us outside Rome have come
to accept that unity *ex animo*; now since Vatican II many Roman
Catholic theologians are exploring what the one baptism means
for traditional types of teaching in their church which have
identified *tout court* the mystical body of Christ with the Roman
Catholic Church.

There is the unity of faith and liturgical heritage and ethos
which should exist within a particular communion. That is not
to say that members of a particular church should be so dominated
by their past inheritance that they are no longer open to the
pressures of God in the present or so regimented that the Holy
Spirit has no room for manoeuvre. It does raise questions,
however, for e.g. the Anglican Communion, and not least for
the Church of England, which has not only its recognized 'schools
of thought,' but its extremists ranging from those on the one
flank who probably find Cardinal Ottaviani a more congenial
figure than Cardinal Bea to those on the other whose standpoint
approximates to that of the undenominational Mission Hall.
This whole book is an attempt to help in the work of promoting
theological understanding which may lead us as Anglicans into
fuller unity among ourselves, as well as to greater openness to
others.

At another level the recovery of the New Testament picture of
the *laos*, the people of God, calls us to a new partnership of clergy
and laity in the common life of the Body of Christ. I have already
written about the ministry of all God's people, and as we come
to consider the mission of the Church in the world today, we
shall find that the laity are immediately involved.

Unity, however, is associated in our minds above all with the
organic union of the separated parts of the Body of Christ. We
recall the coming into being of the Church of South India, and
the many schemes in various parts of the world now in various
stages of development—N. India and Pakistan, Ceylon, Australia,
New Zealand, Nigeria, Ghana, Canada—as well as plans and
conversations in the British Isles. We think of the Anglican-
Methodist proposals, the Anglican-Presbyterian conversations

embracing England and Scotland, and the negotiations taking place between the Congregational and the Presbyterian Churches in England.[1]

Some of these schemes are nearing the moment of action. A decision on Stage 1 of the Anglican-Methodist proposals will be made by the two churches in 1968 or 1969, and decisions are likely to be implemented in the Congregational and Presbyterian Churches in England by 1970 or 1971. Further, those responsible for these negotiations, as well as those engaged in Anglican-Presbyterian conversations, are in touch with each other and have made clear their view that present negotiations are to be thought of as one step forward to a wider union of churches in Britain. If these plans are brought to a successful conclusion, then we may hope that, just as the birth of the Church of South India and its subsequent life have influenced churches in other lands, so union in various parts of the British Isles in the next two decades will bear fruit in other parts of the world also, and will prove a step along the road to the goal of an ultimate union in which the Roman Catholic and Orthodox Churches are included.

In that connection we are brought to consider the commitment which the great majority of the delegates from member-churches of the British Council of Churches at the Nottingham Conference of 1964 'dared to hope' their churches might enter into, namely to work and pray for the inauguration of union by a date not later than Easter Day 1980. This idea of commitment to a specific date has been criticized by some as an attempt to dictate to the Holy Spirit. In reply, those who voted for that commitment say that the Holy Spirit is calling us to union *now* —the delay in obeying his will is due only to our slowness of response and to the situation in our separated churches, in which at least a limited period of time is necessary for working out all the preparatory steps.[2] However that may be, I have no doubt

[1] For an up-to-date summary of union schemes in which Anglicans are involved, see D. M. Paton and R. C. M. Jeffery, *Christian Unity and the Anglican Communion*.
[2] Cf. N. Goodall's words at Nottingham, *op. cit.*, p. 45.

that a vague commitment in terms that give people an excuse for postponing any real decision to the Parousia is worse than useless.

The fact of which we all need to be more aware than we are is that the sands of time are running out. The various delays, postponements and frustrations which have affected the N. India and Pakistan and the Ceylon schemes, which halted the Nigerian scheme at the eleventh hour and which are holding back the day of union in Canada have a double effect. On the one hand, as time passes, the generation which heard the call of the Holy Spirit to work for the organic union of the Church—which was bred in the tradition of Edinburgh 1910, Tranquebar 1919, Lausanne 1927 and Edinburgh 1937, and which responded to the leadership of men like Bishop Brent and John R. Mott, William Temple and John Baillie, William Paton and George Bell—is passing, and in not a few places those remaining who stand in that tradition are wondering how many actual unions of churches they will live to see. On the other hand, the younger generation is feeling the pressure of the Holy Spirit in a different direction, a pressure to be involved in all the vital struggles of our time—war and peace, racial equality, freedom from hunger, and the like. Some who are most concerned about these things are beginning to despair of the institutional church, sunk (as it seems to them) in bourgeois complacency. Why spend all this time, they ask, in 'ecclesiastical joinery,' when the life has gone anyway?

There is a *kairos*, a right time when the Holy Spirit inspires a generation with a vision and a call to action, but the world moves on and the Holy Spirit calls another generation to a new vision and a different task. The nineteenth-century Church was obedient to the call of God to mission overseas, however inadequately and with whatever mistakes. Will the verdict of later Christians be that, when in the mid-twentieth century God called his followers to organic union, the Church across the world in far too many cases was disobedient to the heavenly vision? We are at a very late hour, but with perhaps just enough time left before the opportunity passes and a later generation has to start all over again.

2. *Renewal*

Certainly the union of separated parts of the Body of Christ will be a profitless exercise, unless the Christians concerned gain a fresh vision of Christ's purpose for his Church and for the world. Indeed, without such a vision no union is likely to come about, for union is not an end in itself, but part of a total obedience to Christ, which can make his Church a fitter instrument for his purpose in the world he has redeemed.

How may such renewal take place? By withdrawal from the world, by retreats, by increased time given to wrestling with the Scriptures so that the word of God may speak to us in our situations today, by extended times of prayer? Yes, indeed, there is a need for such times of withdrawal and for finding, as Christ did so often on the mountain-side, that in quietness and confidence is our strength as we attend upon the Lord without distraction.[1]

Yet how easily our religious exercises can become artificial and remote from the world! 'We have distorted the idea of holiness,' John Taylor has written, 'by focussing attention upon our own spiritual state. We have distorted the idea of prayer by concentrating upon intercession that is as anxious and activist as the rest of our service in the world. Small wonder if the streams of prayer dry up and holiness appears to be an alternative to social concern.'

If that danger exists on the one flank, an opposite danger can be present on the other. 'Among those who are trying to obey what we believe is God's call to responsible involvement in the arena of the world's life, far too many of us present not the image of God, but an image of self-assertive activity and rugged pugnacity, which may be bloody but unbowed, but is also inwardly

---

[1] Cf. A. M. Ramsey, *Sacred and Secular*, passim.

tired to the point of emptiness. . . . True holiness and real prayer mean an attention focused entirely upon Christ. It means loving him above all.' John Taylor continues

'It doesn't matter whether the Christ who fills our vision is the historical Jesus, or the living Saviour, or the Christ of the Body and the Blood, or the Logos and Lord of the universe, or the Master and meaning of history, or the Christ in my neighbour and in his poor. These are only aspects of his being. In whatever aspect he is most real to us what matters is that we adore him. For, loving him whom we think we know, we are drawn to that Lord Jesus who transcends our knowing. But all too often we have lost him amid our enthusiasms. What dominates our mind is not the figure of Jesus of Nazareth but our New Testament studies, not the living Saviour, but the doctrines of salvation, not Christ in the neighbour but the civil rights movement.

This is not a plea for pietism but for adoration. The Jesus of history, whensoever we discern him, is not a topic of debate but a Master and Brother to be loved and followed. Christ in his poor is neither a case nor a cause, but a mystery before whom we bow even while we serve. Whatever way of knowing him is valid for us—and it may be simply as the one whose 'give ye them to eat' sends us into the fight for a planned world economy—we must be in love with *him*, not with ourselves or our schemes. We must find time to let our minds dwell on him. The beauty of holiness in the midst of this revolutionary world belongs to those who set the Lord always before their eyes. *Venite adoremus!'*[1]

The General Secretary of the C.M.S. has spoken a word here of direct and urgent relevance to the life of the Church. No movement of renewal in the Church's history has begun except in terms of a fresh vision of Christ, of his relevance to men and women in their particular historical situation and of his call to his followers to be obedient in the power of his Spirit to the doing of his will at that time and in that place. It is only as enough members of his Church catch that fresh vision of Christ and respond to his imperative that we shall be able to shake ourselves free from inherited customs and traditional ways of working that are no longer relevant and reshape the Church's patterns of life and worship so that they may have meaning and significance in the society that is coming into being before our eyes.

[1] *C.M.S. News-Letter* No. 298 Nov. 1966.

S

3. Mission

So we come to the third term in the trinity—'One church renewed for (in) mission.' Mission, as we all know, means sending, and it has its origin in the outgoing love of God in his creative handiwork in the whole natural order. He is 'Maker of heaven and earth, and of all things visible and invisible.' 'Thou didst create all things, and by thy will they existed and were created,' the living creatures sing in the great vision of St. John the Divine of the worship of heaven (Rev. 4). Nevertheless, disorder and rebellion have disrupted the harmony in the created universe that God intended, and in man that mysterious power of evil has become conscious rebellion.

So God has taken action to restore the unity of the created order, and to reconcile the humanity that has become alienated from its true Ground of Being. It is significant that it was in the Captivity Epistles, when St. Paul's immediate outlook was restricted by the limitations of house-arrest, that his vision became most universal and far-reaching. 'God was in Christ' he had written some years before to the Church of Corinth 'reconciling the world to himself' (2 Cor. 5. 19). Now he writes that 'in Christ all the fulness of God was pleased to dwell, and through him to reconcile to himself all things, whether on earth or in heaven, making peace by the blood of his cross' (Col. 1. 19–20). Similarly, whether written by himself or by a disciple, the words of Ephesians 1. 9–10 sum up his thinking about God's purpose from all eternity to unite all things in Christ, things in heaven and things on earth. It is in that cosmic context that St. Paul sees the rationale of his ceaseless missionary labours and the imperative to mission that is inescapably laid upon the Church.

Mission then cannot be rightly understood if it is thought of as the rescue operation of a few chosen souls into the ark of the Church, so that they may be safe, whatever catastrophe falls on the rest of the world. That is to misunderstand even the stories of the Flood themselves, for Noah and his family were not saved for their sakes alone; they were the saving remnant

through whom God's eternal purpose was carried on. The
Church is never truly the Church if it is just an 'in' group,
calling men and women from the world into a cosy but cut-off
fellowship. It is truly the Church only when it is becoming
incarnated in all the areas of the world's life, like leaven in the
lump, when its lay members who are involved in the places of
decision and policy or are serving in the professions and industry
and in the social services of our welfare state are bringing to those
spheres of responsibility a Christian judgement and a Christian
concern. The Christian Church and its members are—or should
be—the first-fruits of God's renewal of creation in Christ, those
whose commonwealth is in heaven but who see in that fact no
excuse for escapism, but a call to participate in God's eternal
purpose to unite all things in Christ.

When Christians, then, work and study and pray continually
despite all set-backs for the peace of the world, for progress in
disarmament and for the limitation and control of nuclear
weapons, they are in the very process taking part in mission.
When, gathered together at the World Council of Churches,
from races and traditions belonging to all the political camps,
they work out a plan for an ending to the appalling struggle in
Vietnam and take steps to see that their voice is heard on both
sides of the iron and bamboo curtains, they are involved in
mission. When Christians see as great challenges of our time
the struggle for racial justice, in the United States or Rhodesia,
in Jakarta or Jerusalem, when they dedicate their lives to the
war on want and to the remedying of a situation in which half
the world is hungry, they are sharing in mission. So also Christians in our own country who work to establish housing trusts,
to provide a Samaritan service for the would-be suicides, the
alcoholics, the drug addicts and the other casualties of an
industrial civilization, are engaging in mission. All these things—
and much more—are part of the Church's involvement in God's
purpose in Christ to reconcile to himself all things, whether on
earth or in heaven. In the current jargon 'The world is the
agenda,' not in the sense that the world determines the nature of

the mission which the Church receives from its Lord, but in the sense that that mission has always to be carried out in a particular historical situation and that the particular circumstances will determine much in the way of priorities, methods and the like.

Christians too will find God at work in his world outside the Church and through the events and movements and commitment of men and women beyond the Church's frontiers will hear God speaking a word of warning and demand to themselves, to their inherited structures of Church organization and their accepted patterns of Christian living. We hear much today of 'Christian presence' in the non-Christian religions and in secular society. We are reminded that we do not take Christ into a situation, he is always there ahead of us. But he is there unrecognized, and it is for the Christian with the biblical clues to guide him to make Christ's presence known and to discern the word he would say in and through that situation to those who do not know him and those who are already his followers.

This requires the formation of a Christian mind among Church members, clergy and laity alike. H. Cunliffe-Jones has defined what having a Christian mind involves in these terms:

'(i) A Christian memory—able to possess and interpret past experience in Christ; (ii) A Christian imagination, by which a person is able to relate everything that happens to him to his life in Christ; (iii) A Christian judgement—able to see situations and persons without distortion as they really are, and to relate them to Christ.'[1]

For Christians who mean business, the formation of a Christian mind is a deep and prolonged matter; indeed it will require all our lives to be renewed in our minds, so that, as St. Paul expressed it, 'you may prove what is the will of God, what is good and acceptable and perfect' (Rom. 12. 2).[2] It means

---

[1] *Technology, Community and Church* p. 135, quoted by R. O. Latham, *Church for all Men*, p. 32.

[2] R. O. Latham makes a plea for the establishment of something like the Evangelical Academies of Germany in this country. These are places where for a few days those engaged in a particular occupation can meet with biblical theologians, sociologists and the like and seek the Christian way in the problems of that occupation. Perhaps William Temple College is the nearest equivalent in the English scene.

openness to Christ's call in different moments of history, willingness to face frankly the demands that may come to us for the abandonment of much impedimenta that our branch of Christ's Church may have picked up on its pilgrim way, readiness for change and renewal, so that the presence and power and compassion of Christ may be more effectively manifested in the world he has redeemed. It will certainly involve ecumenical co-operation on a new scale in the parish or the local congregation, as in our increasingly secularized society those who acknowledge the one Christ are drawn closer to each other.[1]

So the Christian Church, moving towards and in the not distant future (we pray) achieving by God's grace the fullness of unity, renewed in fresh obedience and sensitive to the guidance of the Spirit in the many and varied situations of its life across the world, will offer itself to Christ afresh to be his Body, so that through it Christ in all his living power may become the reconciling and unifying centre for all mankind and for all human life.

Does that mean that as we think in terms of God's cosmic purpose we forget the individual, that as we trace the footsteps of Christ in all religious creeds and in the political and social movements of our time, as well as in the world-wide expansion of the Christian Church, we no longer think in terms of bringing this man here and that woman there into the family of the Church? Some exponents of mission in this wider dimension have been, I think, in danger of drawing that negative conclusion. In my view, we must hold together both the cosmic and the particular, the life of God's world and the inner springs of life in Christ's Church. There are many gaps to be bridged and barriers to be overcome before in many cases men and women can hear the call of Christ to commitment and to membership of his Church. Yet sooner or later that call must be given and that demand made. For 'the most fundamental fact of a conversion to the Christian faith,' as a convert from Islam has said, 'is the contact of the soul with the disposition of Christ and the surrender

[1] Cf. A. H. Dammers *A.D. 1980* pp. 20-23 for examples of such co-operation.

of the soul to the exclusive worshipability of the loving, humble, suffering, serving and forgiving Lord Jesus.'[1]

Christ who is before all things and in whom all things hold together is also the head of the body, the church (Col. 1. 17–18). The Church is never to be identified with the kingdom of God, but it is that part of the human race which with all its conventionalism, fears and complacency has acknowledged the divine kingship, the saving and serving community which Christ seeks constantly to renew and through which he still wills to work in the carrying out of God's eternal purpose to unite all things in himself, things in heaven and things on earth.

May we who belong to one or other of the member-churches of the Anglican Communion offer ourselves afresh to our Lord, individually and corporately, so that he may make us with all our fellow-Christians one church renewed in mission, and to God be glory in the Church and in Christ Jesus to all generations, for ever and ever.   Amen.

---

[1] Dr. Rahbar, quoted in R. O. Latham, *God for All Men* p. 33.

INDEX OF AUTHORS AND DOCUMENTS

(quoted or referred to)